# A Wave of Hypercriticism

## The English Writings of W.C. van Manen

Willem Christiaan van Manen

With an Introduction and Afterword
by Robert M. Price

Tellectual
**Press**

tellectual.com

# Tellectual Press
tellectual.com
Valley, WA

Public Domain text by Willem Christiaan van Manen

Introduction and Afterword by Robert M. Price
are Copyright © 2013-14 by Tellectual LLC.

Print ISBN: 978-0-9851362-7-7
E-book ISBN: 978-0-9851362-8-4

*Tellectual Press™ is an imprint of Tellectual LLC.*

# Table of Contents

# Paul.................................................................99

Originally appeared in Encyclopedia Biblica, vol. III, ed.
Cheyne & Black (London, Adam and Charles Black 1902),
columns 3603-3606, 3620-38.

# The Epistle to Philemon..................143

Originally appeared in Encyclopedia Biblica, vol. III, ed.
  Cheyne & Black (London, Adam and Charles Black 1902),
  columns 3693-97.

# The Epistle to the Philippians..................153

Originally appeared in Encyclopedia Biblica, vol. III, ed.
  Cheyne & Black (London, Adam and Charles Black 1902),
  columns 3703-13.

# Epistle to the Romans...............................175

Originally appeared in Encyclopedia Biblica, vol. IV, ed.
Cheyne & Black (London, Adam and Charles Black 1902),
columns 4127-45.

# The Church of Rome...................213

Originally appeared in Encyclopedia Biblica, vol. IV, ed. Cheyne & Black (London, Adam and Charles Black 1902), columns 4145-57.

# Shepherd of Hermas..................241

Originally appeared in Encyclopedia Biblica, vol. IV, ed. Cheyne & Black (London, Adam and Charles Black 1902), columns 4456-58.

By Robert M Price

# Introduction

*A Wave of Hypercriticism is an instructive collection of basic essays by the doyen of Dutch radical Criticism. Can be read as a complement to* The Amazing Colossal Apostle. *A necessary book with an inspiring introduction.*

—Hermann Detering

## By Robert M. Price

Where along the line of historical development do we place Jesus, Paul—and William Christiaan van Manen? Was Jesus the founder of Christianity, as if he had created it out of whole cloth, or in a vacuum? Should the Apostle Paul be reckoned the "second founder of Christianity" as Wilhelm Wrede styled him? And is Van Manen to be considered the founder of the Dutch Radical School of criticism? None of these similar questions is simple.

Traditional Christianity, quick as it was to stress the position of Jesus as the fulfiller of the religion of Israel and Judah, and thus to reject the Marcionite doctrine of total and utter discontinuity between Christianity and Judaism, nonetheless often spoke as if the world had been an abyss of moral and spiritual darkness until Jesus came to light the path to heaven. Think of the weight scale at your doctor's office: The nurse weighs you in, carefully moving the abacus-like markers back and forth along upper and lower notched bars until the balance seems just right. Such was the anxious care of exegetes and theologians, and for more than one reason. In our day, the question of whether and to what extent we ought to deem Jesus the founder of Christianity comes up in at least two connections, depending on whether you are looking back at what preceded Jesus or what issued forth afterward, in his name.

Historical critics like Rudolf Bultmann wanted to delineate what was distinctive about Jesus. Where did he agree with the religious tradition he had inherited, and wherein lay his innovations (or revelations)? And where had the early Christians gone off in their own new directions, as Plato had from Socrates, interpreting Jesus and reinterpreting him, sometimes electing to neglect certain of his more radical proposals, as Lutherans left some of Martin Luther's suggestions, e.g., as to the canon of scripture, on the buffet table. Bultmann and his successors, notably Norman Perrin, famously employed what would come to be known as the Criterion of Dissimilarity.

This entailed bracketing any gospel sayings that looked a lot like contemporary Judaism or like subsequent Christianity. Though Jesus *may* have said any of these things, one had to assume he hadn't, as long as one's goal was to establish just what was unique or at least distinctive about Jesus. And this was quite plausible: Why had Jesus made such a splash if he merely agreed with contemporary Jewish teachers? The whole history of Christian theology illustrates the danger of assuming that Jesus would have signed onto what later generations of Christians taught on this or that point. Again, compare the situation of Martin Luther. In principle he was happy to admit that "apostolic tradition" *might* have preserved the extra-biblical teaching of Jesus' immediate followers, but could you be so sure?

Too much water had flowed under the bridge for that. So Luther decided one had to limit oneself to scripture. Bultmann and Perrin were thinking the same way. Like the liberal Protestants before them, these critics wanted to distinguish the historical Jesus from the corporate figurehead of the institutional Church. It wasn't that they were anti-Church; they just wanted a criterion with which to reform it.

In more recent days, the pendulum has swung the other way. Scholars with an admirable interest in Christian-Jewish harmony have decided to accentuate the continuity between Jesus and Judaism so as to bring the two faith communities closer together. Ultimately these interfaith Christians would seem to want to arrive at a Rabbi Jesus that Christians could share with Jews. Minimize the Jesus-early Church connection, maximize the Judaism-Jesus connection. And the same tendency is manifest in attempts to reformulate Paul and his teaching in such a way as to make him friendly toward Judaism and even, in important ways, a Jew rather than a Christian. He didn't teach salvation by faith alone, and Jews, revisionists assure us, didn't teach salvation by works.

But before Christians got so Ecumenically Correct, theologians debated the extent to which Paul should be considered a second Christian founder. To call him the Second Founder of Christianity was a function of the agenda to separate Jesus from subsequent Christianity: Paul could be identified as the point where Christianity veered off the track. A second Judas, really. He had, they said, severed the threads that should have connected Jesus and the Christian faith, abandoning the "religion of Jesus" for the "religion *about* Jesus." We are dealing with the Criterion of Dissimilarity again, though no one called it that yet.

Bultmann was close to taking this approach, since he relegated the historical Jesus to the status of a presupposition for New Testament theology but not one of its voices. Paul and the author of the Gospel of John seemed more important, as the apostles of existentialist Christianity. But he didn't picture Paul creating the religion of Jesus the savior *de novo* as others did. Bultmann knew it was not so simple as that.

He laid out in great detail the main features of Hellenistic Christianity, its beliefs and practices, as it existed before Paul. After all, it was already the Hellenized gospel of Stephen that upset the pre-Christian Paul so much. But once Paul converted to the faith he had so vehemently rejected, he placed his own stamp upon it. For Bultmann, Paul was like the traditional Christian Jesus in his relation to what had come before. Hellenistic Christianity was for Paul what Judaism was for Jesus: He did not abolish it but fulfilled it.

A.M. Hunter (*Paul and his Predecessors*) was inspired by Bultmann at this point, but he took a much more conservative approach, accentuating the continuity between Paul and the earlier Hellenists, minimizing Paul's supposed novelty. I believe the point of this subtle apologetic was to submerge Paul into the early Church, into the New Testament and Christianity generally. (This is what we might expect from one who wrote books like *The Unity of the New Testament*.)

Perhaps Bultmann's spotlighting Paul seemed to people like Hunter to be still too close to the liberal approach of C.H. Dodd, implying that Paul was a "religious genius" rather than one of several equally inspired and almost interchangeable voices in the biblical chorus. The same agenda, I think, underlay the tendency of conservatives (including the great critic Joachim Jeremias) to accept the (early Catholic) Pastoral Epistles as Pauline, and this not despite but because of these writings' dilution of the more radical Pauline teaching of the other epistles.

Where does W.C. van Manen fit into these deliberations? For one thing, his role among the Dutch Radical Critics was analogous to that of Paul as envisioned by Bultmann and Hunter: Van Manen did not start the movement; that honor belongs to Bruno Bauer, who played Kaspar Schwenkfeld to F.C. Baur's Martin Luther, a radical who pursued the insights of the pioneer further in the same direction, pushing the frontier back beyond what the trailblazer himself felt was safe. Van Manen began as a skeptic, eager to debunk and to refute the Dutch Radicals Abraham D. Loman and Allard Pierson. But the deeper he delved into the issues and the arguments, the more he began to see their point and, worse yet, to suspect they were right.

Even righter than they knew, for, before he was finished, Van Manen had set the Dutch Radical Criticism on a whole new footing. Like Paul, he emerged embracing "the faith he had once tried to destroy." But we need not try to measure Van Manen against his successors as we must with F.C. Baur, Martin Luther, Paul, and Jesus. For the Dutch Radical approach had few "takers." Its very many opponents never refuted it but only scoffed at it, gave it the cold shoulder, and went on with business as usual. Even Albert Schweitzer, who gave detailed attention to the school in a chapter of his book *Paul and his Interpreters*, immediately sloughed off the whole matter and returned to his own approach. His arguments, such as they were, seem remarkably hollow to me, where he offers any arguments at all.

The obvious antipathy of the mainstream orthodoxy toward the Dutch Radicalism seems to me plainly to have been theologically motivated. Even critical scholars who have gotten used to skepticism vis-à-vis Jesus and the gospels cannot bring themselves to entertain the possibility that *none* of the thirteen canonical epistles ascribed to Paul were really his work. And this has everything to do with their (perhaps vestigial) Protestant identity. Remember, for the Lutheran Bultmann, Jesus was not a voice of New Testament theology, but Paul was (in his seven authentic epistles, three more than F.C. Baur had left to Paul). For neo-evangelical Edward J. Carnell, the epistles "interpret" (control our reading of, take precedence over) the gospels, and Romans and Galatians "interpret" the epistles.

Even for liberal Protestants, like the Fellows of the Westar Institute's Paul Seminar, Paul matters so much that they must refashion him in their own image through an intricate process of Politically Correct bowdlerization. The reason they can afford to whittle away the gospel Jesus but not the epistolarian Paul is that, for Protestants, Paul, in his epistles, is the definitive formulator of Christianity, even if all this winds up meaning one uses "Paul" as a ventriloquist dummy for one's own views. One has at least to pretend to agree with the Great Apostle.

To be sure, Paul was not crucified for you, Jesus was. But it is Paul who tells you what Jesus' death meant. And if those epistles turn out not to be the work of a uniquely authoritative apostle, but rather an almost random collection of scraps from any number of ancient Paulinists of various stripes, then we are forced to recognize what we should have even when we thought Paul wrote most or all of them: They are merely collections of someone's religious opinions and cannot save us the trouble of thinking for ourselves.

But let us return to the "first founder, second founder" question, specifically the question of whether Paul created "the religion about Jesus" or only gave it its distinctive shape. It seems to me that Van Manen has, in his denial of all the epistles to Paul, provided a surprising parallel to the approaches of Bultmann and Hunter. They argued that the Paul of the epistles did not create Hellenistic Christianity but stood on the shoulders of the anonymous teachers and preachers who did. It did not spring full-blown from the Olympian brow of the Apostle to the Gentiles but had flowed like a river along a winding course till it reached the Pauline waterfall and surged with new and mighty force.

Well, Van Manen, for all his shocking strangeness, is saying something very similar. He, too, juxtaposes "Paul the author of the epistles" with the doctrine we read there. The Hellenized, mystical, anti-Judaic theology must have taken some time to form amid the evolutionary progress of early Christianity. A Torah-free, spiritualized successor faith to Judaism simply cannot have emerged overnight, on the day Saul was converted, or even during the short years of his missionary labors. Such faith-shaking developments are like Rome; they cannot have been built in a day.

The epistles in their extant, redacted forms are the only "Paul" we know. They represent the far end of a developmental process, analogous to the way Bultmann and Hunter pictured the historical Paul as inheriting an already established and evolving Hellenistic Christianity. Paul hadn't created the whole thing out of his head; he was not the second founder of Christianity but rather "only" the eventual definitive formulator of it. The same is true for the patchwork Paul of the epistles. These texts do not, and did not, generate Pauline Christianity but are instead the summation of it. They are—to borrow Loisy's metaphor—the oak, not the acorn.

You are in for an eye-opening experience as you read this first book collection of Van Manen's only English writings. He wrote voluminously in the Dutch language, but none of that has ever been translated, and it is not hard to guess why. But Van Manen did write several very extensive and detailed summary pieces for the *Encyclopaedia Biblica*, as well as an essay for *The Expository Times*. These are now readily accessible, thanks to the Herculean labor of Steven M. Stiles in converting them from eye-torturing print into digital versions.

In commending Van Manen's writings to you, I cannot help recalling (of all things!) the Pentecostal preaching of the Baptism of the Holy Spirit. Christian, you came to the point of tearful repentance and conversion to Christ, and you imagined you were done. Only the unconverted need feel the uneasy vulnerability you once felt when challenged to accept the

Christian gospel. You needn't feel uneasy under the gospel gun any longer, right?

Think again! The Pentecostal evangelist tells you that you are *still* on the defensive, because there is a further stage of conversion incumbent upon you! You need to confess your spiritual impotence, humble yourself, and invoke the Baptism of the Holy Ghost to gain the power to live the victorious Christian life. Here you are again at the mourner's bench!

Well, my friend, in the same way, you may already regard yourself as a Higher Critic in good standing. You have abandoned the theological Toy Land of fundamentalist literalism. You are confident in your sophistication. You have put away the childish things of traditionalism. But not so fast! Perhaps you are still committed through the inertia of faith and loyalty to tradition when it comes to certain matters of authenticity and authorship.

Dare you press on further? Will you be as open to shocking new perspectives as you once were, however reluctantly at first, when you first considered the Higher Criticism? "You know the assured results of criticism." "I have known these from my youth up." "You lack one thing. If you would be perfect, go and read Van Manen."

# Note to the Reader

This material was entered into digital form from print publications made over a hundred years ago. Some errors and omissions are inevitable, and the text is quite dense for modern readers, with long sentences and even longer paragraphs.

To improve readability without altering substance, many large paragraphs were split up into smaller consecutive ones. In addition, some of the more mundane details were relegated to footnotes, in many cases joining notes designated by Van Manen himself. Occasionally, listings have been clarified by being formatted into indented paragraphs, sometimes with bullet points added.

Greek letters presented a problem, as the English-language OCR could not interpret them. In a few cases, the proper Greek has been entered by hand.

Steven M. Stiles provided digital renditions of the text for all but the material under **III. Epistles** in "Old-Christian Literature," which was obtained from the public domain text reprinted at en.wikisource.org/wiki/Encyclopaedia_Biblica/ Old_Christian_Literature-Onions#III._EPISTLES. As the wikisource cite states, it is OCR text that "has been imported without a page scan and contains errors and page headers." Some effort was made to correct the most noticeable errors here, too, but some undoubtedly remain.

There are numerous instances throughout the collection where time simply did not permit investigation and correction of errors and gaps due to the conversion from print images into digital text. Those are indicated, where known, by a single x symbol ("×") for gaps and obvious transcription errors within a paragraph, and by a sequence of three ("×××") for gaps encompassing a full paragraph or more.

# A Wave of Hypercriticism

*People who thought they already knew the truth
found that they must go back again to the
beginning to hunt once more and see whether they
could reach the mark. Was it not enough that
criticism had left untouched only four authentic
epistles in the N.T.? Was it not sacrilege to ask these
four for their origin, as if everybody did not know
this perfectly?*

"The four Epistles of Paul, namely, to the Romans, to the
Corinthians, to the Galatians, have been the object of recent
attacks, though they had been generally considered
authentically Pauline. The Dutch theologians—Loman, Pierson,
Naber, Völter, van Manen, with the Swiss professor, Steck—
have impugned their Pauline authorship, especially that of the
Galatian epistle. But defenders have not been wanting, such as
Gloel, Lindemann, Schmiedel, Lipsius, Scholten, Godet,
Holsten, Hilgenfeld, and others. Doubtless the letters contain
difficult matters, arising out of a comparison of the Paul of Acts
with him of the Galatian epistle; but these are not removed by
relegating the four letters in question to A.D. 120-140, by
finding imaginary dependencies on the Gospels, or by
sacrificing their credibility to the historical truth of the Acts.
The tendency of the latter secures the authenticity of the
former . . .

"The arguments adduced against Paul's leading Epistles are for
the most part arbitrary and extravagant, showing inability to
estimate the true nature and value of evidence. As this wave of
hypercriticism is rejected by the best critics of Germany, and
will soon pass away, if indeed it has not already done so, it is
needless to describe it, or to show its futility. Whatever
permanency it may have is in the minds of ingenious seekers

after novelty; but it is devoid of interest for English theologians. The Pauline authorship cannot be shaken by shadowy or conjectural evidence."

So writes the Rev. Samuel Davidson, D.D., in his valuable work, *An Introduction to the Study of the New Testament: Critical, Exegetical, and Theological*, third edition, revised and improved, vol. i. p. 150-152 (London, 1894).

As one of the unhappy men who have been here exposed to public contempt, by a confessedly "learned and venerable author" (*Inquirer*, 25th August 1894), throughout the two worlds, it becomes me to protest against such a summary sentence.

# I.

The description of the so-called wave of hyper-criticism is not quite correct. It came less unexpectedly, or, at least, men were not quite so unprepared for it as one might infer from the words, "though they (the Epistles to the Romans, to the Corinthians, to the Galatians) had been generally considered authentically Pauline." Edward Evanson had already, in 1792, thrown doubts upon the authenticity of the Epistle to the Romans in *The Dissonance of the four generally received Evangelists, and the Evidence of their respective Authenticity*. Bruno Bauer, in 1850-52, had published his *Kritik der paulinischen Briefe* in three volumes, and in it assigned reasons why he could not, with F.C. Baur, the renowned head of the school of Tübingen, consider the Epistles to the Romans, Corinthians, and Galatians as the work of the Apostle Paul.

Besides many since, Semler doubted the original unity of Romans and 2 Corinthians. Even before this, the father of the newer biblical criticism, in his *De duplice appendice ep. Pauli ad Rom.* (1769), maintained that Romans 15-16 did not originally belong to the same book as Romans 1-14; although they also came from the hand of Paul. Heumann had remarked that our canonical Epistle to the Romans consists of two Epistles of the Apostle—chaps. 1-11 and 12-15—and two postscripts—16:1-24, and 16:25-27, which originally belonged to the epistle preserved to us in 1-11.

Ever since F.C. Baur, in his *Paul* (1845), tried to show that both chaps. 15 and 16 must be considered as a later addition to the Epistle to the Romans, and as not proceeding from the Apostle Paul, the acceptance of his opinion among German and non-German adherents of the Tübingen school became the fashion. Semler had sought, in his *Paraphrasis II Epistolae ad Cor.* (1776), to distinguish in 2 Corinthians four epistles, of which three were supposed to have been sent by Paul to the Corinthians, namely, (*a*) chaps. 1-8, to which originally belonged Romans 16 as appendix; (*b*) chaps 10-12:13 perhaps ending with 13:11-13; (*c*) chap. 12:14-13:13; and a fourth, chap. 9, to another community in Achaia.

Others had modified this opinion in some particulars, although adopting and defending its main point. After Hausrath (1870), many had accustomed themselves to call 2 Corinthians 10-13, the "Four chapters Epistle" (*Vierkapitelbrief*) of Paul to the Corinthians, and to consider them earlier than that which we find now in 2 Corinthians 1-9. Dr. Davidson also ranges himself, without reservation, on their side (*Introduction* 3, vol. i. 57-58, 63-64). There were many who for long had tried to escape the noticed objections to the obviously non-Pauline origin of certain communications, expressions, or words in the Epistles to the Romans, the Corinthians, and the Galatians, by accepting larger and smaller interpolations. We also find among these learned men Dr. Davidson, as to 2 Corinthians 6:14-7:1 (*Intr.* 3, vol. i. p. 63).

Although F.C. Baur had not doubted the original unity of 2 Corinthians, and apart from the attempts of some of those whose mental affinities agree with his to dispel entirely or partially his suspicions regarding Romans 15-16, yet even before the appearance of the recent opposers of the authenticity of the leading epistles (Romans, 1 and 2 Corinthians, Galatians), it would have been inexact to speak of "four Epistles . . . generally considered authentically Pauline." The history of criticism teaches rather that that contest had been prepared for, and necessarily had to come. As to Dr. Davidson's description of this "wave of hypercriticism," Dr. S.A. Naber is no theologian but a philologist, who has several times deserved thanks for his conjectures on the text of the New Testament. He has written, in collaboration with his late colleague, Dr. A. Pierson, *Verisimilia: laceram conditionem novi Testamenti exemplis illustrarunt et ad origine repetierunt*–A.P. et S.A.N.–(Amstelodami apud P.N. van Kampen et Fil.), 1886.

In this book it is supposed throughout that we do not possess authentic epistles from the Apostle Paul, and in it much is to be found to indicate that the Epistles to the Thessalonians, Galatians, Corinthians, and Romans have the character of a not happy compilation of the documents in hand, but the work cannot be called a regular essay on the question of the authenticity of Paul's Epistles to the Romans, Corinthians, and Galatians. The principal point was to explain clearly to the reader that not only the leading Pauline epistles, but also the other writings of the N.T. have come down to us in a very corrupt and deplorable text. There may be found in *Jahrb. für protest. Theol.* (Leipzig: J.A. Barth), 1887, pp. 395-431, an account of the contents as far as they relate to a supposed Paulus Episcopus as the author of New Testament "epistles of Paul."

Pierson had already stated, in his work, *The Sermon on the Mount, and other synoptical Fragments*, 1878, pp. 98-110,– shortly after Bruno Bauer had briefly repeated his old scruples in *Christus und die Cäsaren*, 1877, p. 372,–why the authenticity of Paul's Epistle to the Galatians was not an established dogma for him as for others. He was the first in Holland to declare himself of this opinion. Among his antagonists was the Amsterdam professor, Dr. A.D. Loman, who confessed afterwards that Pierson had made him waver in spite of his faulty and incomplete demonstration. He himself began, in a series of *Quaestiones paulinae*, published in the *Theologisch Tijdschrift* (Leiden: S.C. van Doesburgh), 1882, 1883, 1886, a justification of the conviction he then reached that the canonical Epistles to the Romans, Corinthians, and Galatians proceed, not from the Apostle Paul, any more than those that follow them in the N.T., but were written in the first half of the second century.

Although of great interest for the history of the question, and, in many respects, a scientific essay, this series is not complete, and is no regular, finished inquiry into the authenticity of the Epistles to the Romans, Corinthians, and Galatians. It gives, like prolegomena, general observations about the advance of the question and the necessity for renewed research. It contains, first, a chapter in which the *argumenta externa* for the Epistle to the Galatians are weighed in the balance and found wanting (1882-1883), and a second chapter in which the question of the authenticity of the whole collection of Pauline epistles is viewed in the light of the history of the canon (1886).[1]

Dr. Rudolf Steck, professor in Bern, was the first who wrote a sufficiently finished inquiry into the origin, not of the four, but

---

1. I may refer those who wish a fuller account of the contents, and cannot read Dutch but understand German, to my article on the *Quaestiones*, published in 1882-1883, "*Zur Literaturgeschichte der Kritik und Exegese des Neuen Testaments*," in *Jahrb. f. prot. Theol.*, 1883, pp. 593-605; or, for the whole, to *Der Galaterbrief im Feuer der neuesten Kritik*—von Lic. Dr. P.V. Schmidt (Leipzig: A. Neumann),1892, pp.23-232: an account so full that it is almost equal to a translation. It is the most important pages of this *Kritik* which Schürer and other competent antagonists of the so-called "wave of hypercriticism" have rejected with a positive *non tali auxilio*.

of one of the leading epistles—that to the Galatians. He had read, first, Loman's *Quaestiones*, and although not at all agreeing with it, he had been led by it to think. The firm belief in the authenticity of the leading epistles had been shaken, and gradually the conviction arose that it could not and should not be retained any longer.

In *Der Galaterbrief nach seiner Echtheit untersucht nebst kritischen Bemerkungen an den paulinischen Hauptbriefe*, (Berlin: G. Reamer), 1888, an account was given of Paul's conversion, and it was declared that the Epistle to the Galatians is not Paul's own, but the work of an unknown man living in the first half of the second century. This work deals first and principally with the so-called internal grounds, because Loman had anticipated it in speaking of the so-called external ones. Although important remarks are made with regard to the Epistles to the Romans and Corinthians, these cannot be regarded as an elaborated study, for which that was neither the time nor place.

The Amsterdam professor, D.J.E. Völter, a German by birth and education, can only be partly reckoned among the Dutch theologians who have opposed the authenticity of the leading Epistles. He wrote *"Ein Votum zur Frage nach der Echtheit, Integrität und Composition der vier paulinischen Hauptbriefe,"* published in the *Theologisch Tijdschrift*, 1889, pp. 265-325, and partly further elaborated in a separate work, *Die Komposition der paulinischen Hauptbriefe: I. der Römer. Und Galaterbrief* (Tübingen: J.J. Heckenhauer), 1890. The result of these studies seems to be that the Epistle to the Galatians is not authentic, but that to the Romans is a revision and development from the original shorter epistle, which Paul had really sent to the Christians in Rome, while both Epistles to the Corinthians have been compiled from three disjoined epistles of Paul, to which portions have been added by a third person. Völter wishes to be allowed to speak still about Paul's Epistles to the Romans and to the Corinthians.

He thinks that he knows the forms and contents of the original epistles, after the process of analysis, fairly well. It did not require Steck to convince me. In the course of other earlier studies, Pierson and Loman had opened my eyes, in spite of myself, although I tried to oppose their conclusions.

I had learned to read the leading epistles in a free and impartial spirit, without considering myself bound by the unchangeable dogma that they are the most authentic which we possess from Christian antiquity, and are Paul's own, written between the years 52 or 55 and 60. I had gradually reached the firm conviction that these epistles, as well as the others in the Pauline collection, are pseudepigrapha, of which the oldest portions certainly do not belong to an earlier date than the end of the first, if not the beginning of the second, century. To the preceding studies belonged an article entitled "Marcion's Epistle from Paul to the Galatians," published in the *Theologisch Tijdschrift*, 1887, pp. 382-404, 451-533.

This led to the surprising result that Marcion probably knew the epistle in an older form, although one not very different from that in which we read it in the N.T. The important bearing of this conclusion on the question of the authenticity was not expressed in words, but was felt immediately by our countryman, Kuenen, who, although he had struggled against Pierson-Naber (*Theol. Tijschr.*, 1886, pp. 491-536), and still was convinced of the purely Pauline origin of the leading epistles, exclaimed, after becoming acquainted with the contents, "But then it is impossible that the Epistle to the Galatians is Paul's own."

Indeed, if Marcion knew the epistle in an older—I do not say the original—form, which Christians in becoming Catholics changed here and there, in order to bring the writing more into agreement with their opinion, it is very likely that the work proceeded from the circle of those who were afterwards called "heretics," and that it belongs to the extensive literature which the "Catholics" pilfered from the "heretics" and made serviceable for themselves. How "heretics" could have got possession of an authentic epistle, written by Paul to the Galatians, known to no other Christians but themselves, is as enigmatical as the consequence is natural: that an epistle quite unknown to Catholic Christians must have had its origin from another circle, and that it was not written by him whose name it bears.

I have pointed out another result of preliminary research in the first volume of a little series of separate essays under the common title, *Paul* (Leiden: E.J. Brill). In *Paul I.: Acts of the Apostles* (1890) I have tried to answer the question, What do the Acts of the Apostles teach us about Paul and Paulinism, apart from the Epistles? While writing this I could not avoid a research into the origin of the Acts of the Apostles. This led to an acknowledgment that the relative unity of the work cannot be doubted, nor its composition from different originals, among which two rank first, which we can distinguish as *Periodoi* or *Praxeis Petrou* and *Periodoi Paulou*. In the latter is to be found the well-known "Travel-narrative," the much-talked-of "We source."

Now the way was open to answer the principal question. I had then to look at the Apostle in three different lights, according to what we find in the Acts of the real past, what is to be found in the *Periodoi Paulou*, and what Luke himself regarded as the truth. The conclusion might be summed up as follows (pp. 199-204):—Only in the oldest of the above-mentioned three lights in which the Apostle's life is viewed are we quite on historical ground. Here Paul appears to us as a "disciple" among the "disciples." There is yet no question about "Christians," of breaking with Judaism, of disregard of the law, or neglect of circumcision. The days of the Holy Ghost, which in these and other respects will teach the next generation to walk other ways, have not yet arrived.

No one knows that Holy Ghost. Nobody thinks himself guided by Him. The "disciples" are Jews through origin and conformation, that is to say, by their birth or by becoming proselytes, and remain so, whatever they may be besides in their own opinion or that of others. They profess a creed, and form a sect among the Jews, which, however this may distinguish, does not separate them from those who, with regard to manners and customs, law and prophets, temple and synagogue, are truly called Jews.

The centre of their particular deliberation is Jesus, whose "disciples" they consider themselves, with whose appearance they connect the fulfillment of certain Messianic expectations, and whom they, as it seems, acknowledge as the promised Messiah. The reminding each other of the things concerning Jesus, *ta peri tou Iesou,* and the preaching of these to others is what distinguishes them from the other Jews, and constrains them to lead a strictly moral life in mutual love.

Paul joined this community of brethren. He placed himself quite at the disposal of the "disciples" for the spreading of their principles. He travelled for this purpose through different countries, with varying success and varied experiences. The particulars of this period have come down to us only very incomplete, and mixed with strange elements from later biographies. We do not hear that he has ever written epistles of any importance, or that there ever arose between him and the other "disciples" any dispute as to belief and life, the opinion of the common confirmation, or its further effects.

A writer who lived later, and who could consult older originals —our Luke—seems to be acquainted with disputes of that kind, in which Paul's name was mentioned, but gives us plainly to understand that, at least in his opinion—and according to a true tradition (?)—they did not break out before Paul himself was withdrawn from the stage of his activities. He puts in his mouth, at his departure from the presbyters of the community in Ephesus, the prediction, "I know this, that *after my departing* shall grievous wolves enter in among you, not sparing the flock. Also of your own selves shall men arise, speaking perverse things—*diestrammena*—to draw away disciples after them" (Ac 20:29-30).

However this may be, we do not hear of any dispute, and we have no reason to suppose that it is hidden from our eyes on purpose, because we cannot even guess what it would have been about. Paul is congenial in mind with Peter and others, who, as well as he, although in another sphere, have devoted themselves to missionary labour on behalf of the common interests and wishes of the "disciples."

A long time elapses. The first generation, perhaps even more than one, have passed away. Among "disciples" away from Palestine, namely, in Antioch in Syria, an inclination to get rid of Judaism, and to break also in other respects with tradition, reveals itself. We may suppose that their communication with the heathen world and the admitting of former heathens into the communion of brethren caused and fed this inclination. The influence of the Greco-Roman civilization, and not least, the knowledge of the Scriptures and the philosophy transferred from Alexandria to Antioch, Ephesus, and other towns in Asia Minor exercise a positive influence on it.

However the particulars regarding the history of its birth may be explained, a reformation does arise among the "disciples." The "things concerning Jesus' are eclipsed, or rather men learn to judge more exactly about them. Religious truth is taken up more deeply and extensively, a new flight given to contemplation in the sphere of religion, matters relating to belief and life in nearly every point are revised and altered, and there is a resolute breaking away from Judaism. "The gospel of God's mercy" is born; the glad message which is brought to all without distinction that the Almighty God has sent His Son, the Christ, to save as many as possible by faith or by believing in him. To a particular revelation, communication, and leading of the Holy Ghost, they owe the new light thrown upon the past and the future of themselves and others, and on the true signification of Jesus, no other than God's Son, the Christ, at whose temporary appearance on earth they cannot stop. The "disciples," from being a Jewish sect, become "Christians" (Ac 11:26).

Those who follow this line combine with it the name of Paul. He becomes the hero, the patron of their sect. To him are transferred, to him are ascribed the thoughts and feelings born in others by the regenerated life and the endeavour of the "disciples" to become the first "Christians." He must testify, recommend, wish, perform in word and deed what they themselves esteem good and useful. In this way they came to describe his life. In so doing they may have used known traditions and written records. But they can hardly have derived anything without modifications, because they have before their eyes quite another, greater, sublimer image of Paul's life and work. His position must, besides, as now sketched, prove on the one hand that the doctrine connected with his name has its root in an honourable past, while it is not to be denied, on the other hand, that the doctrine which we now conveniently call Paulinism is really new.

From one source and the other we can explain the uncertainties in Paul's image as he appears before us in the Acts called after him, the *Periodoi Paulou*. In the meantime he stands there as a grand proof that Paulinism was born after Paul's death, that it immediately found much approbation, but also encountered opposition, and that in the old circle of the "disciples" a strong antagonism to the new doctrine was brought to life. Strange to say, there is no evidence at all of epistles written by this Pauline Paul.

Again several years elapse. The struggle has, in the judgment of men of influence, lost its importance and cannot be kept up.

Peter, the hero and patron of the "disciples," as Paul was of the "Christians," is delineated in Acts called after him *Periodoi Petrou*, after the model of Paul in the *Periodoi Paulou*. The opponents approach each other more and more. "Peter" appears in the character of "Paul," and the former seems to have been from the beginning of one mind and equal with the latter. There must, of course, be something altered in the picture of both lives to show this quite clearly.

Luke girds himself for this task. He makes one book out of the two, and combines the two lives, each completing and covering parts of the important whole: the oldest history of the Christian communities, their foundation and their extension over the world. To Peter he gives Pauline touches, to Paul words and tints through which he, more than in *Periodoi Paulou*, resembles Peter, and scarcely distinguishes him by anything remarkable from the other "disciples." Probably he knows Pauline epistles, but he does not mention them, and uses them sparingly.

His Paul bears a different character from the one in the epistles, and in the "Acts" assiduously consulted by him. He is the apostle who, next to Peter, can become the founder of the Catholic Church, the man in whom are combined the old and the new, the principles of the "disciples" and those of the "Christians," a respect for "the things concerning Jesus" and a love for "the gospel of God's mercy," a mode of life conformable with the hints and lessons given by men, and one under constant leading of the Holy Ghost, in a way, after all, it is true, unintelligible, but, notwithstanding, remarkable. Young Christianity has in him for those who delight in beholding its image, lost its history of development, and this is what ought to have been according to the wish and intention of the author of our Acts: one and the same as that of all sincere votaries, especially of men of name after whom parties and doctrines have illegally been named for some time.

In other words, the distinction of three images of Paul's life in our canonical Acts gives us a surprising glance at the oldest history of our religion. It teaches us that the old Catholic opinion, as well as that of the school of Tübingen must be considered untenable. There is a struggle between Peter and Paul, but not between the bearers of those names. They have lived and worked with others as "disciples of Jesus," while no dogmatical quarrels divided them. Not until after their death was Paulinism born, and with that, as with every improvement, an apple of discord was thrown among the people, who were called to live together as brothers.

Let us next examine the Epistles to see whether the result hitherto obtained is confirmed. The answer to this will be found in my *Paul II.: The Epistle to the Romans* (1891). The nature of this work, its unity, composition, origin, are there successively considered, and it is proved, I think, that we do not have here before us a real letter, but a literary one, an "epistle;" that is, a book in the form of a letter, as Deissmann proposes to distinguish between a *letter* and an *epistle*, in, as I regard it, the perfect first part of his *Prolegomena zu den biblischen Briefen und Episteln*, published in *Bibelstudien* (Marburg: N.G. Elwert), 1895.

I have tried to explain that that "Epistle" to the Romans is uncontestably one whole, although composed in the way of a synoptical gospel, with the help of older documents, essays, and possibly epistles, out of which much was taken over, perhaps sometimes *verbatim*. If the non-authenticity of the "Epistle" follows already from this, a further examination of the tradition brings its untenability to light for those who might have scruple touching the truth of the traces of additions and alterations pointed out, or those who were not entirely convinced thereby.

Attention is called to a series of probabilities relating to the dogmatical contents of the Epistle, the taking for granted the reader's knowledge of Paulinism, the tangible relation in more than one point with gnosis, the age of the community addressed, the using of a written Gospel and Acts, although it be rather the older *Periodoi Paulou* than Luke,–all of which show the origin of the Epistle to date from a later time than Paul (+ 64). Attempts made before and since to do away with objections and to confirm the authenticity, we weighed in the balance and found wanting.

Afterwards, it is declared that we may consider the Epistle as a remarkable witness to Paulinism, and an exhibition of the spiritual convictions connected with Paul's name, which we can call shortly and rightly a highly interesting reformation of the old Christianity, *i.e.*, the Christianity of the apostles and of those who immediately followed them. As proof of the whole contention, a series of facts are noted which come into full light if one admits the relatively late origin of Paulinism, or which harmonize perfectly with this supposition.[2]

## II.

That this wave of hypercriticism is rejected by the "best critics of Germany" is, as Dr. Davidson assures us, quite true. One could not expect anything else from the "right" wing. Men, so conservative as the German Gloel and the Frenchman Godet, who dare to defend the authenticity of the whole Pauline writings, who take it very much amiss that Dr. Davidson and

---

2. A fuller account of my book was given by Steck in German: *Protestantische Kirchenzeitung*, 1892, Nos. 34-35, as he had done in the previous year–1891, No. 34–with regard to *Paul I.: The Acts of the Apostles.* A third volume of these Pauline studies–*Paul III.: The Epistles to the Corinthians*–was published November 1896. It is reviewed and rejected by J.R. in the *Inquirer*, 27th February 1897; H.J. Holtzmann bestowed twelve lines on it in *Theol. Jahresb.* Xvi.144; Carl Clemen summarized the contents and criticized it in half a column of the *Theol. Literaturzeitung*, 1897, No. 21. A long review was given by Rudolf Steck, *Protest. Monatshefte*, i. 333-342. In this volume the Epistles to the Corinthians are treated in the same way as the Romans in *Paul II.*

those whose disposition is congenial with his, dare to express opinions adverse to the supposed Pauline origin of the Epistles to the Ephesians and Colossians, Timothy and Titus, will not easily look with an open eye upon scruples raised by us against the accepting of a pure Pauline origin, not to mention the authenticity, of the leading epistles. That the "left" wing, the school calling themselves by preference critics, should, with a single exception, express themselves very unfavourably about this "wave of hypercriticism," excites more amazement.

Gloel remarked rightly, in his controversy with Steck, *Die jungste Kritik des Galaterbriefs auf die Berechtigung gepruft* (Leipzig: Deichert), 1890, p. 24, that it would have been ever so much more consistent of them to take an opposite attitude, for the agreement between the leading epistles is no greater, and the difference between them no less, than the agreement and the difference between the leading epistles on the one side and most of the smaller Pauline epistles on the other.

But when one looks closely at the matter, the attitude adopted by the "best critics of Germany" is—I do not say justified, but at least partly explained. Their knowledge of the Dutch language is usually slight, and the way in which they read Dutch books very faulty. They passed Pierson's *Sermon on the Mount* and Loman's *Quaestiones Paulinae* almost without taking any notice of the contents. The *Verisimilia*, written in Latin by Pierson and Naber, unless some of their sharpness was to be taken off, were not in the least fitted to convince those who for many years had believed in the *non plus ultra* of the Tübingen criticism, or to bring them in the direction of the line of thought which F.C. Baur had begun but untimely broken off.

*Der Galaterbrief*, published by Rudolf Steck, was, for a great many people, a thunderbolt from the clear sky. One feels the mood to which this book led not a few people in the title of one of the first criticisms, *die Echtheit der paulinischen Hauptbriefe gegen Stecks Umsturzversuch vertheidigt von R.*

*Lindemann* (1889), which it called forth from those from whom one might have expected a calm and impartial examination of the contents.

One can imagine the terror which seized many at the painful thought that there might perhaps be some truth in this "wave of hypercriticism." This appears in the sad and ironically sounding sigh of Holsten with which he began his controversy with Steck in the *Protestantische Kirchenzeitung*, 1889, No. 15. "So then my Julius, the base whereon critical theology since Semler has by a difficult and laborious work, carried on for a hundred years, built up her view of the development of oldest Christianity, has been mere quicksand. A light footstep of two or three men—the sand shook, yielded, sank away, and the building collapsed." The fear of having "*ins Leere gelaufen*," as Hilgenfeld expressed it, when he spoke his whole mind in sad discomposure about his Bern colleague (*Zeitschrift für wiss. Theol.*, 1889, pp. 485-494), worked certainly in a perplexing way.

People who thought they already knew the truth found that they must go back again to the beginning to hunt once more and see whether they could reach the mark. Was it not enough that criticism had left untouched only four authentic epistles in the N.T.? Was it not sacrilege to ask these four for their origin, as if everybody did not know this perfectly? What shall the "right" wing say, whose judgment one has not to fear, but of whose existence one has to keep account, when it hears to what excesses that man, a professor in theology, has gone in the steps of Bruno Bauer and some Dutchman. "Righteous" indignation, reasonable trembling, ill-concealed conservatism, joined hands with lukewarmness and lack of desire for impartial research. Yet the fact cannot be denied that this wave of hypercriticism is rejected by the "best critics of Germany." But *rejected* does not mean *destroyed*. The scruples mentioned are not done away with, the arguments are not weakened.

Steck (*Prot. Kirchenztg.*, 1889, p. 864) had to charge Lindemann with not having reproduced his words exactly, yet all the same the wrongly reproduced words were enclosed within inverted commas as if they had been his. Holtzmann (*Theol. Jahresbericht*, ix. 116) reproached the same writer because his critique contained too much oratorical ornament to give sufficient room for a forcible refutation. He desiderated a well-weighed judgment of Steck's method and its application.

Holsten ("*Kritische Briefe über die neueste paulinische Hypothese,*" *Prot. Kirchenztg.*, 1889, Nos. 15-17, 20, 22, 26, which, in opposition to Steck, and according to the judgment of Holtzmann, 11. p. 117, "das Bedeutendste hat geliefert" in Germany) limited himself to some points. He held strongly that he (Holsten), and he only, had come thoroughly to understand the Epistle to the Galatians, after having tried previously in vain to understand it, although he had at times been convinced of the contrary. It was not difficult for Steck to refute the observations alleged in this way against him. He did so in *Prot. Kirchenztg.*, 1889, Nos. 339, 40, 42, 43. Although Hilgenfeld had been irritated he had not tried to refute his opponent.

Lipsius and Schmiedel did something more in the volumes of the *Hand-Commentar*, edited by them, published by Mohr of Freiburg, the former in his introduction to the *Epistle to the Galatians*; the latter in that to the *Epistles to the Corinthians*. But they did not come to a complete discussion of the question of the authenticity, not even to a regular treatment of the objections raised by Steck. Hardly any notice was taken of them in the exegesis of the epistles which followed.

In the first edition of his *Commentary on the Epistle to the Romans*, Lipsius could not, of course, take into account my study of that epistle published in the same year, 1891. In the second one, he mentions it in a single word, and speaks of me as one who "am Eingehendsten bisher die Echtheit des Briefes zu bestreiten unternommen hat." He mentions my name also occasionally in the commentary. But these references do not meet, far less refute, my remarks.[3]

When people want to see for themselves in another way *why* this wave of hypercriticism is rejected by the "best critics of Germany," they observe, for instance, how Holtzmann treats the question of the authenticity of the leading epistles in his *Lehrbuch der historisch-kritischen Einleitung in das N.T.*, 3 Aufl., 1892. He gives a couple of pages of general observations, which may be of use in proving the authenticity, and complains of our insufficient and capricious exegesis, but no effort is made to make it better known, not to speak of refuting it (pp. 206-208). Afterwards, speaking of the epistles separately, he writes sixteen lines concerning the authenticity of that to the Galatians, in which the principal objections are enumerated, but not criticized (p. 221).

Not a word about the authenticity of the Epistles to the Corinthians. Not a syllable about the authenticity of the Epistle to the Romans, notwithstanding that four pages (242-246) are bestowed upon former observations about chaps. 15-16, and every now and then two or more pages are devoted to the

---

3. "The best critics of Germany" know that I have written a book on the Epistle to the Romans. But up till now they have not thought it worth while to study seriously the contents. The ironical pitying-peevish tone in which Holtzmann (*Theol. Literaturztg.*, 1892, No. 9) describes it is characteristic, closing with this concise phrase, "Das grundubel einer solchen Kritik liegt darin, dass sie uber "der Verwantschaft mit der Gnosis" (S. 154 f.), die Verwantschaft mit der Synagoge nicht bemerkt, sonst wurde sie es mit der januskopfigen Theologie (S. 201) nicht so leicht nehmen." Elsewhere (*Theol. Jahresb.* xi. 119), the same learned man thinks to do justice enough to the contents by writing: "The radical school are still at work on the Epistles to the Romans and Galatians. As regards the former, van Manen constructs a shorter epistle (chaps. 1-8, 15:14-33), partly founded on a Pauline legacy, which has since been successively enlarged with chaps. 9-11, 12:1-15, 13, 16, so that, differing from Völter, chaps. 12 and 13 are removed from the earliest draft as far as possible." This is all. Besides, I do not know of a Pauline written legacy, on which others would have depended, of which I have not spoken.

objections from time to time raised against the remaining Pauline epistles.

To give a second example, Jülicher vents his wrath on our "*Hyperkritik*" on p. 17 of his *Einleitung in das N.T.*, "ganz kurtz" (very shortly), but does not take any account of the objections mentioned by us. With all the N.T. Epistles he refers to the authenticity, either to defend or to oppose it. Only in those to the Romans, Corinthians, and Galatians he considers this quite superfluous. We poor "modern sceptics" do not seem to be worth more than to be put in a corner with a few great words and to be referred to no more.

Dr. G. Kruger, professor in Giessen, of the same mind as Jülicher, describes, in his *Geschichte der altchristlichen Literatur*, 1895, p. 14, "this wave of hypercriticism" as a criticism which finds its pleasure in completely destroying, by unfounded phantasies, the little light which has been vouchsafed to aid our examination of the problems of primitive Christianity. He has told us lately how he has been partially converted from Ritschl to Schwegler. He had already read the latter's *nachapostolische Zeitälter*, but... "im Bann der Vorurteile" If one asks why these writings have been banned, the answer can once more be given in Kruger's words: "Wegen Vebreittung von–natürlich wissenchaftlichen–Irrlehren" (*Das Dogma*, p. 25).

It is a false doctrine of science which has fascinated "the best critics of Germany," so that hearing they do not hear, and seeing they do not see, and so become unfaithful to their principles respected everywhere else, and refuse to take serious account of objections, which they are bound to consider, once they have been felt and plainly brought into notice by theologians whom they used to honour as fellow-soldiers in the struggle for perfectly untrammeled scientific research. That false doctrine consists of the belief in the infallibility of our opinion of the history of the oldest

Christianity, which the great Baur has mostly brought to light, a light that can and must be tempered, but cannot be strengthened. To this opinion belongs, among other things, the dogma of the authenticity of the leading epistles which may not be doubted at any price, and which from the nature of the case does not need examination, much less proof.

## III.

Has Dr. Davidson walked in another and better path in the third edition of the *Introduction*? The latter is supposed to be revised and improved. We saw already how this honoured author would not leave unnoticed "this wave of hypercriticism." But in his separate treatment of the epistles scarcely anything is evident to this.

- In 1 Corinthians only these words: "The authenticity of the First Epistle to the Corinthians has not been called in question except by Bruno Bauer and the Dutch writers Pierson and Loman" (vol. i. p. 46).

- In 2 Corinthians: "The authenticity of the letter has not been questioned except by Bruno Bauer" (vol. i. p. 65).

- In Galatians: "The authenticity of the Epistle has been admitted by all except Bruno Bauer, who imagines that it was compiled from those of the Romans and Corinthians; followed by the Dutch scholars Pierson and Loman" (vol. i. p. 88).

- In Romans: "The authenticity of the Epistle has been called in question by Evanson and Bruno Bauer" (vol. i. p. 117).

The other names which might be taken account of remain unmentioned, even that of Steck in Galatians, and so of course mine in Romans. Our arguments are not enumerated, and consequently not examined or met. The same remark indeed applies to the arguments of the oft-mentioned Bruno Bauer, Pierson, Loman, Evanson.

In seventeen of the twenty-one N.T. epistles Dr. Davidson has spoken in more or less detail of the objections raised against their authenticity, as well as against Romans 15-16, and either approved or tried to refute them. He has not done this, however, with the Epistles to the Romans, Corinthians, and Galatians. Nevertheless he could not apparently assent to the opinion of many people, that all demonstration of the authenticity of these must be looked upon as superfluous. He devotes in each instance a paragraph to the question, and thereby shows how much he was in earnest in his judgment rejecting Baur's arbitrary acceptance of four epistles whose authenticity did not want research and on which that of the others depended. That adverse judgment was expressed in the words: "He (Baur) takes four Epistles, unquestionably authentic and forming a group by themselves, as the standard of measurement for groups of later and earlier origin" (vol. i. p. 20).

Of what does Dr. Davidson's demonstration of the authenticity of the leading epistles now consist in the pages bestowed upon it? He appeals almost exclusively to the old witnesses to prove the existence of the epistles. Beyond this no word in 1 Corinthians. In 2 Corinthians the assurance but no proof: "It (the authenticity) is confirmed by the contents of the First (canonical) Epistle." In Galatians no further explanation than: "The contents and style bear the apostle's stamp." In Romans the words without a peg to hang on: "The authenticity... is amply attested... by internal evidence" (p. 117), and "The internal character of the epistle and its historical allusions coincide with the external evidence in proving it an authentic production of the apostle. It bears the mark of his vigorous mind, the language and style being remarkably characteristic" (p. 119).

This last sounds very well, if we only knew now how we could become acquainted with the apostle's "vigorous mind," so long as we do not know whether the transmitted epistles, of which we are to discover the authenticity, are actually his. If Dr. Davidson knows it he has omitted to tell us it. A "remarkably characteristic language and style" may just as well have been the property of another as of the Apostle Paul. So long as we do not know whether we possess epistles from him we are not able to judge his language and style. Till we do know, it becomes us to be respectfully silent about the contents and style of a certain writing bearing "the apostle's stamp." Nothing is proved by reasoning in a circle except that who resorts to it does not want proofs himself, because he does not doubt and keeps to that he had accepted without asking on what ground the hypothesis rests.

Have we more certainty in the external evidence? One would think so, when one observes the admirable calmness with which Dr. Davidson makes his most ancient witnesses speak one by one in favour of the authenticity of the Epistles to the Corinthians, Galatians, and Romans (vol. i. pp. 46, 47, 65, 66, 88-90, 117-119).

Unfortunately the illusion disappears very soon when one hears the same learned man in the same work, speaking of the Second Epistle to the Thessalonians, which he does not attribute to Paul, declare: "External evidence attests the letter's authenticity" (vol. i. p. 251). At the conclusion of the examination of the oldest witnesses in favor of the Epistle of James, which he supposes to be written about the year 90, he writes: "Their evidence simply attests the existence of it when they wrote" (vol. i. p. 289). In the First Epistle of Peter, supposed to originate from Rome 113 A.D., we find: "The authenticity of the epistle is well attested by external testimonies both ancient and numerous" (vol. i. p. 538).

Writing on the Pastoral Epistles, which must have originated between 120 and 125, he says: "During that time (70-130 A.D.) they may have been written and accepted as Paul's without opposition, not only because the age was uncritical, but because they were thought useful and edifying letters with a Pauline stamp. The decision respecting their authenticity must turn upon internal evidence" (vol. ii. pp. 41, 42). After the examination of the witnesses for the Epistle to the Colossians, dated 125 A.D., we read: "As far as external evidence goes, the authenticity of the Epistle is unanimously attested in ancient times. But the fathers of the second and third centuries were more alive to traditional beliefs than to critical investigations" (vol. ii. pp. 241, 242). In introducing the witnesses for the authenticity of the Epistle of the Ephesians, which we must consider written in the year 130 A.D., he writes: "Antiquity is agreed in assigning the Epistle to Paul" (vol. ii. p. 272).

In other words, the external evidence of the most ancient witnesses is of great importance when we are convinced of the authenticity and do not want proofs, but it has no significance as soon as we have reason to doubt the exactness of the tradition, or ask earnestly for proofs. Then it must be acknowledged, the ancients were not critical; they accepted what they liked, without asking for the origin of the writings which they read for their edification; their evidence does not reach further than the declaration that the works mentioned or quoted existed when they were writing.

Would it not be more sensible, in speaking of the authenticity of the "Epistles" generally, to decline every appeal to the external evidence of the most ancient witnesses, to escape as critics the accusation of measuring with double measure or weighing with unequal weight?

At any rate, those who are outside cannot attribute value to an appeal to witnesses who are in turn approved and rejected, not on account of the kind and contents of their declarations, but because they are sometimes in accordance with what one expects and sometimes not. If, then, we observe that Dr. Davidson, in speaking of the authenticity of the leading epistles separately, did not take into account other people's scruples, or render these superfluous by adducing convincing proofs of the authenticity, we cannot offer as excuse for him that he was perhaps not acquainted with the doubts that had been cast upon the authenticity.

The above-quoted words, derived from vol. i. pp. 150-152 of his *Introduction*, prove the reverse of this. There, it is true, this learned man hides behind "the best critics of Germany." He says, however, seemingly independently, after having mentioned our names before: "The arguments adduced against Paul's leading epistles are for the most part arbitrary and extravagant, showing inability to estimate the true nature and value of evidence."

The accusation is not a trifling one. Has Dr. Davidson tried to show it justice? No. Has he made any earnest effort to make himself familiar with the contents of the writings which he unhesitatingly pillories as a "wave of hypercriticism" which "it is needless to describe, or to show its futility," "devoid of interest for English theologians"?

Having consulted both the volumes carefully, I find no evidence of it in his *Introduction*. A letter kindly sent to me enables me to add that he had not had my study on the Epistle to the Romans under his eyes. This last must also have been the case with two other learned men called to instruct the English-speaking public with regards to "this wave of hypercriticism"— Dr. W. Sanday and Rev. A.C. Headlam, the authors of *A Critical and Exegetical Commentary on the Epistle to the Romans* (Edinburgh: T.&T. Clark. 1895). They mention my book, *Paul II.: The Epistle to the Romans,* Leiden, 1891, as well as my magazine essays on Marcion's Epistle from Paul to the Galatians (p. lxxxvii, note), and seem to derive from it, in the text, this impression, as unjust as comical, "van Manen is distinguished . . . for basing his own theory of interpolations on a reconstruction of the Marcionite text, which he holds to be original." Just as if I had not opposed these theories of interpolations at least as strongly as Sanday and Headlam, and had not done something quite different, in seeking to explain the origin of the Epistle to the Romans, than starting a new theory of interpolations.

However, all that these learned authors say on the first three of the thirteen pages bestowed by them on a discussion of the integrity of the Epistle is an incomplete and faulty critical survey of what was written by Evanson, Bruno Bauer, Loman, Steck, Weisse, Pierson-Naber, Michelsen, Völter, and myself, either on the question of the authenticity or on the history and composition of the text of the canonical Epistle to the Romans.

Now, as all this had to be said within two pages, it is really not to be wondered at that the criticism is introduced with the sigh: "It has been somewhat tedious work enumerating these theories, which will seem probably to most readers hardly worth while repeating, so subjective and arbitrary is the whole criticism." One must pity the authors who had to compose these pages as much as the readers who had to make themselves acquainted with their contents. Three pages are devoted to the description and the treatment of the question of the authenticity, including the history of the criticism of the origin of the canonical text, against ten pages on the old question concerning chs. 15-16. And no further word about the authenticity of the Epistle in the whole work, in itself perfect in other respects. No word in the introduction, no word in the commentary. It is continually supposed, and without any vestige of proof accepted as certain, that the Pauline origin cannot and may not be doubted. All research relating to that is superfluous. Already the thought of it is "a somewhat tedious work."

Only complete ignorance on this point can make one speak of "an interesting account" by Dr. Sanday and Mr. Headlam "of the attempts recently made in Holland, as well as by one or two German scholars, to impugn the authenticity of the Epistle as a whole, or to show that it has been interpolated to a serious extent" (W.E. Addis, *Inquirer*, Nov. 16, 1895).[4]

In a note at the end of their rejection of the partly mentioned arguments alleged against the authenticity of the Epistle to the Romans, Sanday and Headlam add the following: "The English reader will find a very full account of this Dutch school of critics in Knowling, *The Witness of the Epistles*, pp. 133-243. A very careful compilation of the results arrived at is given by Dr. Carl Clemen, *Die Einheitlichkeit der paulinischen Briefe*. To both these works we must express our obligations, and to them we must refer any who wish for further information." Must we conclude from this that Knowling and Clemen have conducted them as guides through the lightly spoken of "Dutch school of critics"? How could they know, then, that the first of the two had given "a very full account," and the other "a very careful compilation of the results arrived"?

---

4. I suppose that the learned authors have not read, or even had in their hands, any or hardly any of the works of whose contents they speak (pp. lxxxvi, lxxxvii), except Evanson's *The Dissonance of the four generally received Evangelists*. Else it would, for instance, not have been possible for them to say of C.H. Weisse: "His example has been followed with greater indiscreetness by Pierson and Naber (1886), Michelsen (1886), Voelter (1889-90), van Manen (1891)." Not one of the men mentioned has defended the "style-criticism" of Weisse, and "professed to be able to distinguish by the evidence of style the genuine from the interpolated portions of the Epistle." Even Dr. E. Sulze, the most grateful pupil of the German professor, and the publisher of his *Beitrage*, 1867, did not defend it when he, in his criticism of Steck's Galaterbrief" (*Protest. Kirchenzeitung*, 1888, Nos. 41, 42), recommended the hypothesis that many objections to the authenticity of the leading epistles could be explained by accepting "Interpolationen und Erganzungen" (interpolations and supplements). An opinion to which Steck, appreciating Sulze's good intentions, objected with reason (*Protest. Kirchenztg.*, 1889, No. 6).

Knowling's work is not known to me. Clemen did not occupy himself with the question of the authenticity. Others had done that already sufficiently in his opinion. "Das war ja das nötigste, aber freilich auch das leichteste," p. 4. (That was the most necessary thing, but also the easiest.) The more difficult task for which he girded himself was to consist in considering all that belongs to the sphere of conjectural criticism, alleged interpolations, and supposed composition of Pauline epistles from larger and smaller fragments, essays, and older epistles. He performed his task with talent to a considerable extent, but not faultlessly.

One cannot leave unread the books used by him, if one does not want to receive many times an incomplete and faulty impression of what is said in them. For instance, he spoke constantly of a part of my criticism of Romans, namely, what I wrote about the composition of the Epistle, as if I wished to purge the canonical text from an endless number of interpolations. And this notwithstanding that he—unlike many others, especially German learned men—had understood my intention very well, judging from what he said about it (p. 73): "We are not able to point out what has been added at different times, and to say whether it came from the author himself, or from a source used by him."

At the same time, Sanday and Headlam in their *Commentary*, as well as Dr. Davidson in his *Introduction*, have professed to instruct their fellow-countrymen and those speaking the same language, and all these, trusting to the well known erudition of these illustrious men, consider themselves now acquainted with "the details of the study of the text, and the criticism of the various Dutch schemes of disintegrating the Epistle" to the Romans (M.W. Jacobus, *New World* (June, 1896), p. 372). This is further proved by their being able to perorate in this fashion: "Such theories"—as those developed by us concerning the authenticity of Romans—"deserve attention only on psychological grounds; they serve to remind us that learning may go hand in hand with the wildest extravagance of opinion, that the blindest prejudice may be united with an utter absence of dogmatic belief" (W.E. Addis, *Inquirer*, Nov. 16, 1895). They rest, without a single word of protest, on what their grey-headed, and indeed most reverend and learned, Dr. Samuel Davidson said: "This wave of hypercriticism...is devoid of interest for English theologians" (*Inquirer*, August 25, 1894).

## IV.

It is not my business loudly to assert a contrary opinion to that of Dr. Davidson, but I may utter a warning against misunderstanding based on faulty instruction. This "wave of hypercriticism" has not for its aim "attacks" on guiltless epistles, or to "condemn" them. It does not stand opposed to the Pauline leading epistles, but has in view nothing more or less than learning to understand those valuable memoirs of Christian antiquity better than has been the case up till now, in order to make the rich contents fertile for our knowledge of the oldest Christianity, its character, development, and history.

Those who are considered to belong to this "wave of hypercriticism" are no "ingenious seekers after novelty." They are too busy with the fulfillment of their functions and varied scientific research for this kind of work. Although they do not consider themselves ingenious, they are not simple enough to seek for "*imaginary* dependencies on the Gospels," nor do they wish to remove by any artifice whatsoever the "credibility" of certain writings. They do ask occasionally whether other writings might be found to depend on the Gospels, and how it is with their supposed "credibility." Their standpoint is that of a perfectly free, and as far as possible impartial, research, which cannot be bound by any tradition, either dogmatic or scientific. If they err, they will be glad to be instructed, but with arguments, not with great words, or with appeals to critics who have been unable to make themselves acquainted with their studies up till now, because as far as they read them they did so "im Bann der Vorurteile."

They hold that criticism can and must scrutinize everything, even what some people who may belong to the "best critics" in a certain circle consider the most critical, that is, superior to any criticism, and about which a strict *noli me tangere* ought to be taken into consideration. They do not know any reason why, in the research into the origin of the 13 or 14 Pauline epistles, an exception should be made in favour of the four to the Romans, Corinthians, and Galatians. They consider it their duty to ask these writings as well for their credentials.

With all respect for Baur and the great merits of the Tübingen school called after him, they cannot see any guarantee for the justness of their way of considering the matter, nor any reason for exempting the leading epistles from research as to their birth, in the fact that they are faithfully accepted by these men. They judge that if in inquiries about authenticity in other instances no positive value is allowed to external evidence, it cannot be done here either. The so called old witnesses generally prove only that the works under examination were extant when these witnesses wrote.

The very utmost that can be added in their favour is that they considered that the works originated from the persons under whose names they mention them. But this is no guarantee for the justness of that opinion, as is generally acknowledged by the "best critics" as soon as they come to deal with writings whose authenticity seems suspicious to them. The ancient witnesses were not critical in the sense which we give to that word. When the contents pleased them, the epistle or the book was welcomed by them, irrespective of its author. They did not make any inquiry as to its authenticity.

It is even a question whether they did not often know that they had to do with pseudepigrapha while they were busying themselves with the creation of the new pseudepigrapha. Besides, they lived, as a rule, too long after the time in which the supposed apostolical authors must have worked for us to found anything of importance on their conviction, if they had one, as to the authenticity of the intended writings.

We do not know the exact period at which the oldest witnesses for the Pauline leading epistles, Clemens Romanus, Basilides, and others lived. But they belong, at any rate, to the second century. Generally, we adopt the opinion that Paul died in A.D. 64. The witnesses are bearers of a tradition connected, rightly or not, with a particular writing. That tradition must be looked into independently, its truth examined as exactly as possible.

As often as the question is about the authenticity or non-authenticity of any writings, the essential part of criticism has to do with the internal grounds. Internal evidence must decide. However, once more to confine ourselves to the Pauline leading epistles, this does not compel us to see an identity of language and style, dogmatic and religious contents with the supposed Pauline language and style, the description given by ourselves of his religion, persuasions, and thoughts. As long as we do not know whether we possess authentic epistles from Paul or not, we cannot form a judgment about this and that. Until that time, perfect silence is indispensably necessary.

When one sets oneself to free and impartial research as to the authenticity of the Pauline leading epistles, there is no greater self-deception than making oneself in all simplicity believe that one hears Paul speaking, recognizes his language, his image, recalls his spirit, and with rich oratorical turns declares further things of that kind because—because one had learned previously to form an idea of Paul, of his religious physiognomy, of his appearance in writings, of his customs and manners, way of speaking and thinking, etc., with the help of those epistles whose authenticity was not then doubted. This is the great fault of Baur and his school, for which already he has been so often reproached alike by orthodox and liberal theologians, and also by Dr. Davidson (vol. i., p. 20), but of which, all the same, the "best critics" have made themselves continuously guilty on this side of the ocean as well as the other.

Internal evidence does not come from outside. It does not communicate itself to us except by earnest and thorough examination of the writing or writings in question. Whoever wants to become acquainted with the Pauline leading epistles in order to put himself and others in the way of a possible answer to the question as to their origin, ought to read and study them according to form and contents without cherishing beforehand a decided opinion as to their origin. Either begin by accepting the authenticity or not, but always leave room for the opposite opinion. The exegesis of one who does not do this is not free but bound, bound to tradition, bound to fiction. The one proper basis, the only truthful internal evidence fails him. These are the principles on which this "wave of hypercriticism" should be conducted. If there are unconscious mistakes, let one point them out.

But one need not get angry. The indignation of a learned man proves nothing except his momentary inability to refute his scientific opponent.

## V.

This wave of hypercriticism, Dr. Davidson assures us, "will soon pass away, if indeed it has not already done so."

This last can be contradicted safely. He who says it shows himself not well up in the particulars on which his assertion rests. Up till now not one of those who are considered as belonging to this "wave" has, as far as I know, proved faithless. They go on, keeping high the banner under which they strive, proclaiming their conviction and defending it when necessary.

Will that be of any avail, or will this "wave" not soon pass away altogether, notwithstanding their zeal every possible way? Who can tell? Prophesying is dangerous work, especially when the question turns on things which one does not know at all or only in a very faulty manner. It is safest to leave the result to time and the power of truth. *"Tandem bona causa triumphat."* *"Magna est veritas et praevalebit."* All can depend upon that.

Those of this "wave" are of good courage. They copy with gladness their Paul, while they are looked upon as written down to death: *Hos apothneskontes kai idou dzomen* (2 Co 6:9).

*"Nubicula est, transibit"* was the motto of the great Dutch theologian, Gisbertus Voetius, in heart and soul orthodox, with which he, like an earnest, pious man, does not only try to comfort himself for the sorrows of earth and the disappointments of life, but also tried to console himself and others as often as any apparition of something new in the ecclesiastic or scientific world troubled them. *"Nubicula est, transibit"* a great many before and after him have cried, in the same and similar words, with regard to several "waves," which have soon afterwards got the ascendency over them or have sometimes carried them away with their irresistible speed. Such prophets have never been able to obstruct the course of scientific research.

*"Nubiculas est, transibit"* "the best critics of Germany" declared when Baur and his companions appeared, and, with their new contemplation of the old Christian past, seemed to ridicule science, its best representatives and most firmly established results. "A wave of hypercriticism devoid of interest for English theologians," added the Davidsons of those days. Their namesakes, now already for a long time grown grey in the service of science, have come forward as the best interpreters of the Tübingen school for the thoughtful party of theologians of Great Britain and America. Why should it be

otherwise with the "wave of hypercriticism" now spoken of, whose task it is to continue the work commenced by Baur and to scrutinize once more the grounds on which the foundation of our knowledge of the oldest Christianity rests?

Notwithstanding much disappointment coming from many a circle where the contrary might be expected, signs which give courage are not wanting. To recall a single instance: H.J. Holtzmann, in one of his *Lehrbuch der hist.-krit. Einl. In das N.T.*, published in 1885, said this wave of hypercriticism was already hidden away in the grave of history. He bestowed only these words upon it: "Die von Evanson, B. Bauer, und A.D. Loman unternommenen Angriffe gehören der Geschichte der Kritik an" (p. 224). It could not be more decisively and sparingly touched upon.

But stop; in the third edition, published in 1892, the words quoted are altered. The objections raised against the authenticity of the leading epistles are no longer relegated to the "history of criticism." "The attacks undertaken by Evanson (1792) and Bauer, later A.D. Loman, A. Pierson, S.A. Naber, and W.C. van Manen, afterwards also by Steck and Völter," are discussed in some detail, albeit incompletely and indecisively (pp. 206-208). We even find (pp. 183-186) a new paragraph bestowed upon the description of "the radical criticism," by which, in distinction from the "critical school," ours is meant.

Others do not forbear to express their sorrow over the discord which has arisen in the international camp of liberal scholars in consequence of our views on the origin of the Pauline leading epistles, although we, as they remark, are all standing on the same scientific ground, and start with the same critical principles. If they could only resolve now, led by this conviction, to make themselves better acquainted with our main contentions, and with the books which we have written, laying aside the "Bann der Vorurteile," they would certainly, though not at once or perhaps ever in all points, give us their approval.

At first they might perhaps even continue to protest with powerful arguments, but at length, I have no doubt, they would acknowledge that we have seen rightly on the main point. They would soon help us to remove the mistakes made by us in elaborating our new ideas, to fill the gaps remaining after our research, to erect as firmly as possible the building of our knowledge of the oldest Christianity according to this modified plan on true grounds. Peace would be restored between friends congenial in mind, and this wave of hypercriticism brought a notable stage farther on its way towards blessing the literary, theological, and scientific research peculiar to our days, with the precious talent of distinguishing between truth and error entrusted to it, to the advantage of all.

# Old-Christian Literature

*The history of the origin and collection of the books of the NT has long ago enabled us to see that they arose one by one in the ordinary genuinely human manner, and only gradually were gathered together. Not at a single stroke, nor by any special divine or human providence, nor yet in virtue of exceptional talents or, if you will, supernatural gifts denied to other Old-Christian writers or collectors, was this task achieved.*

# Contents

## VI. TEXT BOOKS (45)

Literature (46)

# Survey of Literature

## 1. Idea of Old-Christian Literature

By Old-Christian Literature[5] is here intended the extant remains of Christian literature so far as these are connected with the elucidation, defence, or advocacy of the Christian religion, down to about the year 180 A.D. Since no other description of Christian writings has come down to us from within the period defined, we may also say that the designation covers the whole body of extant Christian literature, sacred or secular, canonical or uncanonical, whether pages, books, or collections of books.

It is usual to isolate the NT and to regard the twenty-seven books united under the title as a group standing by itself and not belonging to the Old-Christian literature properly so-called; and in accordance with this a distinction is commonly made between the two studies, which are regarded as mutually independent: "Introduction to the NT" and "Patristics"—the latter denoting the scientific investigation of such writings of the early Christian period as were not received into the Canon, and the first, whether as "Historical Critical Introduction to the NT," or as "History of the Literature" or "of the Books" "of the NT," or simply as "History of the NT" denoting the study, in the aggregate or in detail, of the works which make up the NT, whether this study be limited to the questions relating to their contents and origin, or extended to those relating to their text and its history, translation, interpretation, appreciation, etc.

---

5. The phrase Old-Christian for *altchristlich, oudchristelijk*, on the analogy of "Old-Catholic," is preferred as a technical term, less ambiguous than the more idiomatic "Early Christian" or the not sufficiently colourless "Primitive Christian."

The distinction, however, is not a just one, and its maintenance as recently exhibited by Theodor Zahn in his article "Einleitung in das NT" in *Real-Encyklopädie für protestantische Theologie und Kirche (PRE)* (3), 5:270-4 (cp *"Kanon des NT\1"* ib. 9 769-73) cannot be recommended. However powerful the practical considerations which can be urged in its support— such as the current usage of language, the peculiar importance of the NT for the faith and conduct of Christians, the place it occupies in dogma, in religious instruction, in university lectures and courses of study, the established practice of handbooks,—it is none the less without scientific justification.

It does not, in point of fact, rest upon any real difference in the character or origin of the writings concerned, but only upon the assumption of their differing values as sacred or non-sacred books, as if the NT contained the records of a special revelation—in the last result the only argument of Theodor Zahn—whilst none of the other literary productions of ancient Christianity can lay claim to any such title. The justice of the separation may be granted when the question is looked at from the dogmatic point of view; but it is none the less purely dogmatic, and on that very account inadmissible in a scientific research.

Moreover, the history of the origin and collection of the books of the NT has long ago enabled us to see that they arose one by one in the ordinary genuinely human manner, and only gradually were gathered together. Not at a single stroke, nor by any special divine or human providence, nor yet in virtue of exceptional talents or, if you will, supernatural gifts denied to other Old-Christian writers or collectors, was this task achieved.

It was done by men moved after the same manner as ourselves, men who were the children of their own time and, be it said with all reverence for the priceless work they accomplished, were gifted in very various degrees,—writers, speaking generally, of similar quality and similar endowment with those to whom we are indebted for the other literary productions of ancient Christianity; collectors who, governed by various views regarding the interest of Christian society as they had learned to understand it, brought together a group of gospels, two groups of epistles—the Pauline and the Catholic—neither of which, however, ever had fixed limits. To these were added, though not immediately or even unanimously, Acts of the Apostles and a Revelation of John; also, for a time, in one quarter or another, other writings which in the end failed to gain admission into the Canon. See Zahn, *PRE* (3), 9:768-796; Van Manen, *Handl. voor de Oudchr. Lett.* 119-123.

The same history enables us to see that the books of the NT were originally coincident with what subsequently came to be described as Old-Christian literature. They form part of it, an essential and highly interesting and important, nay, the most important part. The old distinction between canonical and non-canonical books as regards this literature must be abandoned; NT Introduction and Patristics must no longer be separate studies, they must be amalgamated in that of Old-Christian literature.

## 2. Gradual Recognition

In principle this has been recognised at various times during the course of the nineteenth century, and especially within the last decades, under the influence of a growing interest in the examples of Old-Christian literature which had not attained canonicity, however little the persons by whom the recognition was made may seem to have been aware of the full significance of their words. Authors of Introductions to the NT were often obliged to discuss more or less fully, besides the books received into the NT, other Gospels, Epistles, Acts, Apocalypses, which had arisen in similar circles.

Some of these scholars, such as Eichhorn, actually called their subject a history of Old-Christian literature. Hilgenfeld collected a *Novum Testamentum extra canonem receptum* 1866, 1884 (2), containing Epistles of Clement, Barnabas, the Shepherd of Hermas, fragments of gospels and other books.

The philologist Blass in writing his *Grammatik des NTlischen Griechisch* (1896, ET, by Thackeray, 1898) deemed it no longer fitting to confine his attention to the text of the canonical books of the NT, but took account also of the Epistles of Barnabas and Clement, the Homilies of Clement, the Shepherd of Hermas, the fragments of the Gospel and Apocalypse of Peter.

Harnack avowed on the first page of the first volume of his *Gesch. d. altchristlichen Litteratur* (1893)—although for practical reasons he passed over the NT in giving his account of the tradition of that literature, and in his writing on Chronology (*Chronologic der altchristlichen Litteratur*, 1897), dealt with it but in a stepmotherly way—"to the primitive literature of Christianity belong above all the twenty-seven writings which constitute the NT." G. Krüger in his *Gesch. d. altchristl. Litteratur*, 1895, would doubtless have devoted more than a few pages merely to the books of the NT, had not Jülicher been contributing to the same series his *Einleitung in d, NT.*

Holland, meanwhile, had been more thoroughgoing. As early as 1870-1871 an edition of the Apostolic Fathers, translated with introductions and notes, had been published by A. C. Duker and W. C. van Manen, under the general title *Oud-Chrisielijke Letterkunde*. Rauwenhoff in his sketch of a theological encyclopaedia (*Theologisch Tijdschrift* [*Th.T.*], 1878, p. 170) had substituted for NT Introduction and Patristics, "Original documents relating to the founding of Christianity." The same two branches of study ceased any longer to be officially recognised when the Bill relating to the Higher Education was passed in 1876.

The Act speaks only of Old-Christian literature—an expression including both branches, as was set forth and vindicated by the present writer in his inaugural address (*De Leerstoelder Oud-Christelijke Letterkunde*, 1885). J. M. S. Baljon, ten years later, expressed himself in substantial agreement with this view in his inaugural address at Utrecht (*De Oud-Christelijke Letterkunde*, 1895). The same author in issuing a Dutch edition of Cremer's *Biblisch-theologisches Worterbuch der NTlichen Gräcität* made so many additions as to make it in reality a first essay towards a *Lexicon of Old-Christian Literature* (*Woordenboek hoofdzakelyk van de Oud-Christelijke Letterkunde*, 1897-1899). Krüger declared himself convinced by the arguments of Van Manen, and wrote under this influence *Das Dogma vom Neuen Testament*, 1896.

At Leyden, since 1885, Hermeneutics and Textual Criticism have been taught, not as formerly with exclusive reference to the NT, but with reference to the whole body of Old-Christian literature. There also was published the first edition of a manual of Old-Christian literature, by Van Manen (1900), in which the old distinction between canonical and uncanonical writings was disregarded, and the material that had formerly been divided into these two was brought under a single category.

## 3. Extent

As regards the delimitation of this material no unanimity has as yet been reached. In common parlance the expression Old-Christian literature is used so widely as to be supposed to include all literary remains of Christian antiquity that can be regarded as, say, more than a thousand years old. Thus, for example, R. A. Lipsius entitled his great work *Die Apokryphen Apostelgeschichten uud Apostellegenden*, 1883-90, in which texts dating from the second, third, fourth, down to the ninth century, and sometimes even of a yet later date, are dealt with, a contribution to the history of Old-Christian literature ("ein Beitrag zur altchristlichen Literatur-geschichte").

Harnack placed upon the title-page of his largely planned *Geschichte der altchristlichen Litteratur down to Eusebius* (ACL), and in his preface (I. 1893, pp. viii, x) explained the words as meaning that he does not desire to include the Council of Nicea in the scope of his work although taking account of the writings of Eusebius. Moreover, he leaves out of consideration all that relates to the Manichaeans, a portion of the Testimonia of Origen and Eusebius, fragments of Julius Africanus, Origen, Eusebius, some things relating to Clement of Alexandria, Hippolytus, Cyprian. Krüger confined his *History of Old-Christian Literature*, 1895, to "the first three centuries."

For the last sixteen years the arbitrary character of any such limitation has been continually protested against in Leyden. It is liable to alteration at any moment and has nothing to justify it. Consistency of language is, moreover, greatly to be desired. If the subject of Old-Christian literature be accepted as equivalent to that of NT Introduction *plus* Patristics, the expression can no longer suitably be employed to denote what might more properly be described as "Old-ecclesiastical," or, in a wider sense, "later Old-Christian literature"—the latter being divided into "Old-ecclesiastical" and "Heretical."

The literary remains of most of the church fathers and their contemporaries—the category of church fathers including, according to Roman Catholic reckoning, writers down to the thirteenth century, while in Protestant circles it is limited to the first six centuries—fall outside the limits of Old-Christian literature. This embraces the NT and all that, speaking generally, pertains to it, as dating from the same or the immediately adjacent period, and breathing on the whole the same spirit—a spirit, that is to say, the same, apart from all difference that arises from mutual divergences in the personality, tendency, aim, environment of the writers.

The question to be asked is as to what they have in common with one another as distinguished from those who lived at a later period. What spontaneously and immediately presents itself as thus characteristic and distinctive is their attitude towards the NT canon. Irenaeus, Clement of Alexandria, Tertullian, and those who followed them hold towards this literature an attitude quite different from that of the Old-Christian writers who preceded. They not only, like some of the latter, show acquaintance with some, or many, of the "books" that now have a place in the collection called the NT; they also appear to recognise these, all of them or some of them, as authoritative for faith and practice—in a word, as holy writ.

Here we have a touchstone for discriminating what is "Old-Christian" from what is not. In this respect there is, as a rule, a marked difference between the Christian literature of an earlier date and that of the later date just indicated; let us say, before and after the year 180 A.D., the date of the principal work of Irenaeus, *Against Heresies*; according to iii. 83 written in the time of Eleutherus, 173 or 175-188 or 190 A.D. Here we find a criterion for "Old-Christian" which does not lie in the whim or fancy of the historian, but in the nature of the case, being supplied by the material itself with which he has to deal. We shall do well, therefore, to adhere to it even should we occasionally find that it is difficult to draw the line with equal precision at all points because in point of fact, strictly speaking, it does not always exist.

## 4. Subdivisions

Harnack and Krüger follow a classification of the subject-matter which cannot be adopted here partly because they extend their scheme so as to come down to Eusebius or to the end of the third century, partly because in point of fact they take no account, or almost no account, of the twenty-seven books of the NT. Nor is it advisable to follow them in their distinction between "original" (*Urlitteratur*), Gnostic, and churchly literature, with further subdivisions under each of these classes, in view of the fact that before 180 A.D. it is hardly possible to speak of "churchly literature" at all, that the line between "original" and "Gnostic" writings is difficult to draw, and that the further subdivisions—not the same in Harnack and Krüger—bear witness more clearly to the embarrassment of their authors than to any real endeavour to subdivide the writings in question as far as possible according to their contents.

Harnack, for example, begins with epistles of Paul that had not been received into the canon, and with gospels, including apocrypha, certainly dating from the so-called post-apostolic age; the "Preaching and other non-canonical works of Peter, the Acts and the Preaching of Paul, the Apocalypse of Peter, further epistles of Paul, epistles of Clement, the Shepherd of Hermas, the Epistle of Barnabas . . . Papias, Polycarp . . . Ignatius, the *Didache* . . . apologies of Quadratus, Aristides, Justin . . .; and apocryphal Acts of Leucius, . . . Thomas, John," etc. This is what Harnack calls the Christian "original literature" (*Urlitteratur*), which is followed by the Gnostic, whilst in the third division he deals with "Christian writings from Asia Minor, Gaul, and Greece," dating from the second half of the second century, including epistles of Themiso and the churches of Lyons and Vienna, apologies of Melito and Athenagoras.

Kruger divides "Original Christian" (*Urchristliche*) literature into Epistles, Apocalypses, Histories (Gospels and Acts), Didactic Writings, but discusses (to mention one or two examples) the Gospels of Valentinus and Marcion under Gnostic, the apologies of Quadratus, Aristides, and Justin under churchly, literature.

It is better to classify the writings according to their different literary forms, and in doing so to adhere as far as possible to tradition and thus avoid anticipating any estimate we may have to form regarding the Old-Christian writers at a later stage of our investigations.

## 5. Survey

Guided by these principles, we propose to adopt the following classification of Old-Christian literature: Gospels, Acts, Epistles, Revelations, Apologies, Didactic Writings. In the present article it will not be possible to do more than give a brief survey of the contents of these six classes.

# I. GOSPELS

In Old-Christian literature, the Gospels first demand our attention. Besides the usual word gospels (*euaggelia*) we find such designations as gospel-writing (*graphe euagellion*), Sayings of the Lord (*logia kyriaka*), Records (*diegeseis*), Memoirs of the Apostles (*apomnemoneumata ton apostolon*), Traditions (*paradoseis*), The Acts of Jesus (*ai ton Iesou praxeis*), The Book of Days (i) (*biblos ton emeron*). These writings all relate to the life and work of Jesus Christ. They have a twofold character, historical and doctrinal-practical. They are not mere memoirs, drawn up by disciples or friends, for the purpose of preserving in the memory of contemporaries and posterity the recollection of what Jesus of Nazareth was, aimed at, did, said, experienced; they are more: they are handbooks in which each writer in his own way sought to make known Jesus Christ, the Lord, the Son of God, in all that he was for the world. History here is employed in the service of religious instruction.

## 6. Gospels: The Oldest Gospel

As for their origin, the Gospels, on close comparison, point us back to (i.) an "oldest" written gospel (*to euaggelion*) which unfortunately does not exist for us except in so far as we can recover any traces of it preserved in later recensions. Perhaps it began somewhat as follows: "In the fifteenth year of the reign of Tiberias Caesar, Pontius Pilate being governor of Judaea . . . in the high-priesthood of Annas and Caiaphas, . . . there came down to Capernaum, a city of Galilee; cp Lk. 3:1-2; 4:31), Jesus Christ the Son of God;" and then proceeded to sketch, somewhat in the following order, his appearance at Capernaum, his casting out of devils, the proclamation of the kingdom of God, the transfiguration, the final journey to Jerusalem, his passion, death, and resurrection. Nothing was said as yet of his origin, birth, early life, meeting with John, baptism in the Jordan, temptation in the wilderness, nor much of consequence regarding his mission as a religious teacher and preacher in Galilee.

This work, presumably written in Greek, may be conjectured to have arisen in the post-apostolic age in circles which sought to combine their more developed Christology (a free speculation of what would then have been called the "left wing") with (ii.) the still older apostolic tradition—not yet reduced to writing— partly historical, partly not, regarding Jesus of Nazareth as the Messiah who had once appeared and whose return was to be expected. As over against the friends of this older tradition, who were able to point to it, those whom we have described (i.) as belonging to the left wing felt the need of a clear setting forth of what had been done and suffered by the Son of God in his manifestation in the world.

## 7. Recensions

The "gospel" thus produced (the first to be written, but, as we have seen, not the oldest form of what had been the oral tradition concerning the life, passion, and death of Jesus the Messiah) was soon supplemented and "improved" in various ways with the help and guidance of this older tradition. The book appeared in new recensions, new forms. Among others there was, probably, an Aramaic recension, which still survives in a whole group of extant (partly fragmentary) gospels: those of the Hebrews, of the Twelve Apostles and of the Ebionites, of Peter, of the Egyptians, of Matthias, and those of the synoptists, which were received into the canon (Matthew, Mark, Luke.). In any case there lie behind the text of the three synoptists one or more written gospels of which the respective authors made use, each in his own way, in the composition of his work.

Among the later recasts of the original written gospel ought also to be classed that used by Marcion. It bore no distinctive name, and was afterwards maintained by Marcion's opponents to be a mutilated form of Luke, although it would be more correct to say that it took its place alongside of that gospel as an independent redaction of the common source. This common source, along with its two derivatives, Marcion and Luke, may then be regarded as constituting a distinct group, the Pauline, as distinguished from the synoptic in the narrower sense of the word–i.e., the Old- or Jewish-Christian, immediately underlying our canonical Matthew and Mark, which have received Pauline touches (see Van Manen, *Handl.* chap, i., 31).

A third current in the development of the written gospel along the Old- or Jewish-Christian and the Pauline or Gentile-Christian lines, is the Gnostic, including the gospels of which we know practically nothing but the names of Cerinthus, Carpocrates, Basilides, Apelles, Valentinus, as also the later Gospels of Thomas, Philip, Eve, Judas Iscariot, the Gospel of Perfection (Consummation?) (*Euaggelion Teleioseos*), the "proper" (*idia*) gospels of the Severians, and others, now lost, which also dated probably from the second century. A main source for our knowledge of the type of writing here referred to is, notwithstanding its Catholic colouring, our canonical Fourth Gospel.

As belonging to the same branch of Old-Christian literature ought also to be enumerated the extra-canonical Words of Jesus, most recently collected with praiseworthy diligence by

A. Resch (*Agrapha*, 1889; *Aussercanonische Paralleltexte zu den Evangelien*, 5 parts, 1893-97; *Die Logia Jesu*, 1898). Cp J. H. Ropes (*Sprüche Jesu*, 1896), who criticises and classifies them into seventy-three Agrapha without any, eleven of perhaps some, and fourteen of distinct, importance.

Also the so-called *logia iesou* found in 1897 on a papyrus leaf among the ruins of Oxyrhynchus; the Fayum fragment; in so far as one can venture to hold its existence (which is not probable, or at least is not certain), the Words of the Lord, collected by Matthew and commented on by Papias; and the Diatessaron of Tatian (Zahn, *PRE* (3) 5:653-661; van Manen, *Handl.* chap. i. 44).

## 8. Apocryphal Gospels

Apocryphal gospels, even of a comparatively early date, such as those of James, Thomas, Nicodemus, in which narratives are given of the nativity and childhood, passion and death of Jesus; also concerning his father Joseph, his mother Mary, his descent into hell; or about Pilate, fall beyond the limits of time here assigned, although they occasionally contain noteworthy reminiscences. Strictly speaking, they can at best be regarded only as appendices.

# II. ACTS

## 9. Character

The next class of writings to be considered is the group of "Acts" (*praxeis*, *Acta*), Circuits (*periodoi*, *Itinera*), Preaching (*kerygma*), Martyrdom (*martyrion*), Passion (*Passio*), Consummation (*Consummatio*). These writings relate to the life and career of apostles and other prominent persons. They have, as a rule, a twofold character; they are narratives, but also works of edification,—sometimes didactic and apologetic as well. The oldest of them have disappeared, either wholly or in part.

The earliest of their kind, chiefly relating to the life of Paul, most probably had, like the oldest written gospel (§ 6, i.), its origin within a circle of Christians of a progressive or (if the epithet is preferred) "Pauline" type, who did not hold themselves bound exclusively by (apostolic) tradition. This conclusion is suggested by the consideration that the friends of tradition feel no need of "lives" as long as the opposite party do not feel it; by what is known as to the course of the development of the written gospel; by the conclusions of criticism regarding the canonical book of Acts, and by the circumstance that Circuits (*periodoi*) of Gnostic origin lie at the foundation of Catholic Apocryphal Acts (*praxeis*). The remnants of the work which we may call the Acts of Paul are to be traced in Acts 1:24 [D] 4:36-37, 6:1-15, 7:51-8:3, 9:1-30, 11:19-30, 13-28; but they have there undergone a change of form. In any case, one or more previous writings now lost underlie the canonical book of Acts (see van Manen, *Paulus* I.; *De Hand*, der app. , 1890; *Handl.* chap. ii. 2-7).

## 10. Fragments

Of the following works little more than the title is known.

- An Acts of Apostles (*praxeis apostolon*), according to Epiphanius (30:16), was used by the Ebionites. Probably a counterpart (and therefore not a polemic) to the Acts afterwards received into the canon; a recast of the same material but in another spirit—the anti-Pauline.

- An "Ascents of James" (*Anabathmou Jakobon*), according to Epiphanius (*loc. cit.*), contained blasphemies against Paul and utterances of James against the temple and the sacrifices and the fire upon the altar.

• An "Ascents of Paul" (*Anabatikon Paulon*), according to Epiphanius (38:2), was in use among the Gnostics (cp 2 Cor. 12:2-4).

• An "Acts of Paul" (*Paulon praxeis*), mentioned by Origen and others, perhaps closely related to the Acts of Paul mentioned already (§ 9, end) as having been employed in the preparation of canonical Acts, unless we are to regard it as the kernel of the (Apocryphal) Acts of Peter and Paul.

• The Preaching of Paul (*Pauli Praedicatio*), mentioned by Cyprian, is perhaps to be identified with the Acts (*praxeis*) just mentioned.


## 11. Preaching of Peter

Clement of Alexandria makes us somewhat better acquainted with a work called The Preaching of Peter (*Petrou kerygma*). It represents a liberal view of the preaching of the gospel, as designed for both Jews and Gentiles, in which "Paul" is presented neither in a favourable nor in an unfavourable light, and no other apostolate than that of the twelve is thought of. It seems to have proceeded from someone who was not a Jew by birth, and who most probably was a Greek, somewhere about 120-125 (see E. von Dobschütz, *Das Kerygma Petri*, 1893; Loman, *Th.T*, 1886, pp. 71-78, 333-6; Harnack, *ACL* 1, 1893, pp 25-28; 2, 1897, pp. 472-4).


## 12. Apocryphal Acts

Apocryphal Acts first appeared separately in considerable numbers, and afterwards came into collections. A group of Gnostic "Circuits of the Apostles" (*periodoi ton apostolon*), embracing Acts of Peter, John, Andrew, Thomas, and Paul, is attributed to Leucius Charinus; in a revised form and expanded into Catholic Acts of the Apostles (*praxeis ton apostolon*), to Abdias.

The study of this copious literature (Apocryphal Acts) discloses that it arose in Gnostic circles and that much of it was taken over by the Catholics after it had been duly revised (see R. A. Lipsius, *Apokr. Ap.-gesch.* 1883-1890; R.A. Lipsius and M. Bonnet, *Acta apostolorum apocrypha*, II, 1891, 2i, 1898).

The oldest of these Acts, probably old enough to fall within the period covered by the present article, although scholars are not agreed as to this, are now lost unless in so far as they survive in later editions and redactions. Such were, it is conjectured, "Circuits of Peter" and "Circuits of Paul" (*Periodoi Petrou* and *Periodoi Paulou*), absorbed into the extant Catholic "Acts of Peter and Paul" (*Praxeis Petrou kai Paulou*); "Circuits of John" (*Periodoi Ioannou*), which partially still survive in Catholic and later Gnostic recensions; the Acts of Paul and Thecla, preserved in a later redaction, unless we are to hold— what does not seem very probable—that this work was already used by Tertullian before 190 A.D., or take it, with C. Schmidt (1897), for a section of the "Acts of Paul" (*Praxeis Paulou*) (see Harnack, *ACL* 1:136-8 2:1 493-505; *Bibl. World*, 1901, pp. 185-190).

### *Martyrdoms*

Related to the category of Acts and in part belonging to it are the Books of Martyrs (*Martyria, Acta, Passiones, Virtutes*) of which Eusebius made a collection, now lost (*ton archaion martyrion sunagogen, suggramma, katalogos*); some of them fall within or just beyond our period. They are:

## 13. Paul, Peter

i. Accounts, known in various recensions, of the Martyrdom of Peter and Paul, which are supposed to have originally stood at the end of the oldest Acts of Paul and Peter (cp Harnack, *ACL* 1:130-134).

## 14. Polycarp

ii. A "Martyrdom of the holy Polycarp" *(Marturion tou agiou Polukarpou)*, in the form of a letter from the church of God at Smyrna, sent at its own request to the church of Philomelium and also, unsolicited, to all other churches belonging to the holy Catholic Church, within a year of the martyrdom of Bishop Polycarp, circa 155, for the purpose of setting forth the circumstances connected with it.[6]

The work is, whether we regard form or contents, not a letter, nor even an account of Polycarp's death, and certainly not written soon after that event; it is a decorated narrative of the saint's martyrdom framed after the pattern of the story of Jesus' passion as given in the gospels, and expanded into a writing in glorification of the true martyrdom and at the same time in depreciation of the self-sought, superfluous martyrdom commended by the Montanists. The legendary character of the contents, which is not to be set aside by the assumption of interpolations, as also the tendency of the whole, brings it to a date some decades later than that of the death of Polycarp *(circa* 155 A.D.), yet still within the second century, rather than in the middle of the third century, or even later, as some would have it.

---

6. The Greek text has reached us in five MSS.; in an abridged form in Eusebius *(HE* 4:15), and in an Old Latin translation; it appears in various editions of the Apostolic Fathers, the latest and best being those of Zahn, 1896, and Lightfoot, 1889 (2), cp Funk, 1901. The genuineness and historicity have been rightly questioned, either denied or disputed, by Steitz, *Jahrbücher für deutsche Theologie (JDT,* 1861), Schürer, *(Zeitschrift für die historische Theologie [ZHT],* 1870), Duker and van Manen *(Oud-Ckr. Lett.* 2, 164, 1871), Keim *(Celsus,* 1873, p. 145, and *Urchr.* 1878), Lipsius, *(ZHT,* i8 74),Gebhardt *(ZHT,* 1875), Holtzmann, *Zeitschrift für wissenschaftliche Theologie (ZWT,* 1877), Jean Reville *(De anno Pol.,* 1881), Rovers *(Th.T,* 1881, pp. 451-7),–and upon insufficient grounds maintained by Hilgenfeld *(ZWT,* 1861, 1874), Zahn (1876), Renan *(L' Eglise Chr.* 452), Lightfoot (1889 (2), Krüger (1895), Harnack (ii. 1, 1897, p. 341).

## 15. Pionius, Justin, etc.

iii. A writing concerning Pionius (*Pionios*), who, we learn, suffered martyrdom at Smyrna shortly after Polycarp, is mentioned by Eusebius, *Ecclesiastical History* (*HE*) 4:15, 4:47), and is extant in a transcript at Venice (Krüger, *ACL*, 106).

iv. Memoirs of martyrs: Carpus and Papylus and a woman Agathonice (*hypomnemata memartyrekoton Karpon kai Papylon kai gynaikos Agathonikes*), mentioned by Eusebius (*HE* 4:15), edited by Harnack, who holds it to have been written in the reign of Marcus Aurelius (*Texte und Untersuchungen zur Geschichte der altchristlichen Literatur* [*TU*] iii. 3-4, 433-466).

v. "Martyrdom of the holy martyrs Justinus, Chariton . . . who were martyred at Rome" (*Maptupiov tov agiov marturion Ioustinou Charitonos Charitous EuelpistouIerakos Pionos kai Aiberianou marturesanto en Rome*), published with a Latin translation by Otto in *Justini Opera* (3), 2, pp. 266-279, 1879. It is thought to have been written shortly after the condemnation of Justin and his converts, which was between the years 163 and 167 A.D.

## 16. Vienna and Lyons

vi. A particularly noteworthy account of the sufferings of the Christians during the persecution they were subjected to about the seventeenth year of the reign of Antoninus Verus—i.e., according to the preface of Eusebius (*HE* 5), Marcus Aurelius (177-178 A.D.). This writing, partly preserved in Eusebius (*l.c. 1*-4), has the form of a letter, written by the Christians at Vienne and Lyons to their fellow-believers in Asia and Phrygia (*oi en Bienne kai Lougdouno tes Gallias paroikountes doulois Christou tois kata Asian kai Phrugian... adelphois*). It is, however, no letter giving details regarding the persecutions endured, but a "writing" (*graphe*), a composition (*suggramma*) written, as Eusebius says, in other than a purely historical interest (*ouk*).

The writer's desire is to instruct and to edify; to judge by the portions taken over by Eusebius, he does not seek merely to inform his readers as to what the Christians in Gaul have endured, but also to make them see and feel how these Christians suffered, with wonderful fortitude yet without seeking martyrdom and without any trace of contempt or harshness towards those who had failed to stand the test; notwithstanding their greatness, not wise in their own eyes, but ready to allow themselves to be instructed, models of the true martyrship as also of sober Catholic Christian-mindedness in the whole conduct of life.

The purpose is manifest: to promote such a manner of thinking and of living; to warn against the Montanistic views and doctrines prevalent in Asia and Phrygia and tending to spread from these centres to Rome and elsewhere. This is the author's reason for making use of his fresh recollections—historical even if here and there adorned with touches of art—of the sufferings of the Christians of Vienne and Lyons, and especially those of Lyons. He speaks as if in the very person of these two churches, yet frequently betrays that he is really outside them, we are not told where and can only guess Lyons or Rome. It is certain that he was not, as is often conjectured, Irenaeus, whose style cannot be discerned here, although he may have lived at the same period; to judge by the relationship between this work, particularly as regards its tendency, and the Martyrdom of Polycarp, it was probably written towards the end of the second century, possibly, however, somewhat later (see P. A. Klap, *Theol. Stud.*, Utrecht, 1900, pp. 423-435).

## 17. Scili; Apollonius

vii. The sufferings of the martyrs at Scili in Numidia in 180 A.D., written and published in various forms, the latest in a (probably original) Latin text (*TS* 1:2:105-121 [1891]; Harnack, *ACL* 2:1:316; Kruger, *ACL*, 105, 5)

viii. A martyrdom (*marturion*) of Apollonius, who was put to death at Rome about 180-185 A.D. Lately published, so far as extant, by E. T. Klette, *TU* xv. 291-131.

# III. EPISTLES

## 18. Meaning of the Word

The greater proportion of the literary productions of the period of Christian history with which we are now dealing consists, in outward appearance, of letters; and many of these, though by no means all of them, are still regarded as having really been such—actual letters sent at first to definite persons and originally written with such persons in view—and as having penetrated to wider circles and become common property only at a later time. Continued examination, however, has led to the conclusion, first with regard to some of these, then with regard to a great number, and finally, in the opinion of the present writer and others (see below, 19), with regard to the whole of them, that they neither are nor ever were "letters" in any proper sense.

They were, from the first, neither more nor less than treatises for instruction and edification, bearing witness to the character, aims, experiences, adventures, of persons, opinions, tendencies, in the form of letters written to one or more recipients, usually in a tone of authority, by men of name. These authors are thought of as still alive although they really belong to an earlier generation. Such letters there fore seemed to be, even in the circle of their first recipients, as voices from the past.

Yet they bear unmistakable marks of having been written in the later time. They come from the pens of persons who are unknown to us, and were designed like books which are brought into the market, or otherwise circulated, for all who take any interest in their contents; and more particularly and specially designed to be read aloud in religious meetings for the edification of the community or to serve as a standard wherewith to regulate faith and life.

As a literary device the epistolary form is an ancient one. It is met with alike among Jews, Greeks, and Romans, and was adopted also by Christian writers such as the authors of Acts 16:23-29, 23:26-30, Rev. 2:3; Clem. Hom. 5:9-19, 5:20-26; the epistles of Peter and of Clement to James with which Clem. Hom, is prefaced; that of the Church of Smyrna concerning Polycarp's martyrdom; that of the Christians of Vienne and Lyons with refer ence to the persecution under Marcus Aurelius (see above, 14, 16); and so forth; cp also the epistolary form of the introduction both to the first and to the second work of Lk. (Lk. 1:1-4, Acts 1:1), and also the beginning and the end of the last book in the NT Canon (Rev. 1:4-5a, 22:[18-]21). [Cp EPISTOLARY LITERATURE.]

The letter of edification, on the other hand, is a peculiarly Christian product (cp *Th.T.* 1897, pp. 413-5).

To compose "letters" under another name, especially under the name of persons whose living presentment, or real or supposed spiritual equipment, it was proposed to set before the reader, was then just as usual as was the other practice of introducing the same persons into nar ratives and reporting their "words," in the manner of which we have examples, in the case of Jesus, in the gospels, and, in the case of Peter, Paul, and other apostles, in Acts.

No one saw anything improper in this, or thought of any intentional falsification, deception, the playing of a part in which one had to be always on one's guard against self-betrayal. Any one who had anything to say wrote a "letter" without troubling himself—at any rate not more than other writers—with respect to his work, about a supposed defect in the literary form he had chosen, not even about an address left blank in the epistle when "despatched," as for example in the canonical epistle to the Ephesians; or about the absence of a suitable epistolary beginning, as in the canonical Epistle to the Hebrews; or about the want of an appropriate close, as in the Epistle of James; or about the absence of both, as in the first Epistle of John.

## 19. Estimate of Them

At first no one thought about the matter at all—whether to hold or not to hold such epistles as really proceeding from and intended for their ostensible authors and recipients. Sometimes their real origin was known, sometimes it was guessed, sometimes people were content to remain in the dark. They used the epistles or left them unread, just as they were, indifferently, without asking any question as to their origin, knowing this only, that they were intended for all who chose to give heed to them.

Gradually the position changed as a result of a normal change in the readers mode of thinking, their thirst for knowledge, their reverence for the authoritative word, and their exaltation of it to the dignity of canonical scripture. From the time of Irenaeus onwards the old way of looking at things passed away for centuries,—first with regard to thirteen, anon fourteen, "Pauline," and certain "Catholic," epistles, and others, written by apostolic fathers; next with regard to the whole body of Old-Christian epistles so far as it was taken by the Church under its protection, the most recent not excluded, such as are now found in Acts, Revelation, Clem. Hom., even apocryphal writings such as the Epistle of Paul to the Laodiceans, 3 Cor., that of Jesus to Abgarus. All these epistles now came to be regarded as proceeding from the writers whose name they bore, and to have been originally intended for those who were named as their first recipients in superscription, subscription, address, or tradition.

Here also the rise of the modern spirit wrought a change, and the human mind had to retrace its steps along the path it had for centuries been following. The apocryphal epistles were all of them rejected soon after the Reformation; the genuineness of those embodied in the Clementine Homilies, Rev., and Acts was modestly questioned; some pieces, such as the larger recension of the Ignatian Epistles, and the second Epistle of Clement, formerly classed among the Apostolic Fathers, were no longer deemed to belong there; other epistles, both Catholic and Pauline, were from the time of Semler removed from the position they had so long occupied as possessed of the highest, antiquity and indisputably "genuine."

The process of disintegration steadily went on. The Tubingen school left unchallenged hardly more than the four principal epistles—Rom., 1 and 2 Cor. , Gal. In the end criticism succeeded in removing the veil of error and misunderstanding that concealed the true character of even these (see PAUL, 1, 2-3, 33+). The history of this criticism is the justification of those who hold to it and at the same time the condemnation of those who wholly or in part set it aside. The time seems to be approaching when the question as to "genuineness"—in the sense now usually attached to the word—will no longer be discussed as regards any of the epistles that have come down from the first Christian centuries; it will be enough to be satisfied of their genuine antiquity.

## 20. Pauline and Catholic Epistles

i. The Old-Christian epistle as a literary phenomenon seems, so far as we can discover, to have first made its appearance in progressive Pauline circles. The first examples of it have disappeared unless it be that some portions survive in some of our present canonical "Epistles of Paul" [Epistolai Paulon], also "the apostle" [o apostolos] or "the apostolic" [to apostolikon]; see ROMANS; CORINTHIANS, etc.; PAUL). Perhaps there was an earlier group, to which reference is made in 2 Cor. 10:9-11, cp 1:13, and the present group had not originally the same extent as now.

We know not by whom the collection was made, nor yet what influence his work had upon the traditional text. Perhaps we may suppose that it led to some changes. Probably the collection was not wholly the work of one person, but arose gradually through additions. The oldest account—to judge by what Tertullian says (adv. Marc. v. ) tells of a group of ten epistles used by Marcion (about 140 A.D.). It is known that Hebrews was for a long time set aside in many circles.

ii. A second group of Old-Christian Epistles is that known as Catholic (×). The word must be understood as referring, not to the destination, nor to the ecclesiastical use, but to the contents of these writings. It was not originally intended to convey, as is often still incorrectly supposed, the idea of general or circular letters, nor yet of canonical ones, but only (as a careful examination of the ancient employ ment of the word shows) trustworthy, worthy of acceptance, when judged by the standard of religion and dogma. The group, after long hesitation, was finally made up of seven: Ja., 1 and 2 Pet., 1, 2, and 3 Jn.,and Jude (see JAMES (EPISTLE); PETER (EPISTLES OF); JOHN (SON OF ZEBEDEE), 57-65; JUDE (EPISTLE).

iii. A third group: Epistles of Barnabas (21-22), Clement ( 23-27), Ignatius (28-29), Polycarp (see PHILIPPIANS, 10 14, and above, 14) : is usually included among the writings of the Apostolic Fathers. At a later date was added an Epistle of the Church of Smyrna (see above, 14); on the same grounds might be added the epistle of the churches of Vienne and Lyons (see 16).

## 21. Barnabas

The epistle of Barnabas [barnaba epistole] referred to in CANON 65-73 , GOSPELS, 89, 90, is found in several MSS.

It is met with in x, as also in the Jerusalem codex from which the Didache comes (I); chaps. 5, 7- × in nine other Greek MSS, the so-called [akephaloin] (of pheusa [= LXX]); chaps. 1-17 in an Old Latin version; some sentences are also found in Clement of Alexandria and Origen.

The work professes to be a letter—now by one who is the spiritual father of the "sons and daughters" he addresses (1:1), to whom he feels himself bound by the closest ties, and among whom he has long sojourned (1:3-4); now by one who belongs to their own number, who earnestly addresses the brethren, but not as if he were the teacher who had been placed over them (1:8, 4:69). The epistolary form, however well maintained, and on that account usually accepted without question, is, in view of the contents, seen to be fictitious; in reality the writing is a treatise intended for general use.

The writer's purpose is to instruct, to edify, to communicate under the form of a letter that which he has himself received, in order that his assumed readers, rich in faith, may now arrive also at fulness of knowledge (×). This knowledge or gnosis concerns chiefly the right attitude of Christians towards the OT, the religion of Israel, the divine covenant with the fathers. On these things they need to be enlightened, in connection with the putting into practice of the new religious ethical life. This end is sought to be accomplished by means of a peculiar view—partly allegorical, partly typological, but always arbitrary—of "Scripture" (the OT and some apocrypha).

The epistle admits of being divided into a double introduction (1:2-5, 1:6-8) and two main portions of a doctrinal (2-17) and a hortatory (18-21) character respectively.

The doctrinal part begins by showing that what is of supreme importance is not the offering of sacrifices or the observance of fasts, but a life in conformity with the moral precepts of the Lord (2-3). It is our duty to love righteousness, especially at the present time when the days are evil and the end of the present age is at hand (4:1-6a). We Christians have been ever since the days of Moses the true covenant people (4:6b-14), kept by the Lord, who suffered on our behalf after he had become manifest in the flesh in accordance with what can still be read in Scripture (5). There we can continuously read of his manifestation in the flesh (6). The fasts prescribed in the law, the sacrifice of Isaac, the goat on the great day of atonement, all are types of his passion (7).

So also the red heifer that must be slain and burnt, whilst the ministering servants prefigure the twelve as preachers of the gospel (8). The precept ofcircumcision must be spiritually understood; the 318, circumcised by Abraham, are a type of Jesus (9); the laws concerning foods are to be taken metaphorically (10). At every moment one finds in the OT hints of baptism and of the cross (11-12).

In Jacob and Ephraim we come to see that not Israel but the whole body of Christians are the true heirs of the covenant broken in the days of Moses but renewed in Christ (13-14). The true day of rest is not the Jewish Sabbath, but the eighth day, the first of the new week; the true temple of God is not the building at Jerusalem, but the spiritual temple, of which Christians form a part (15-16). After a short retrospect (17), passing on to another knowledge and teaching [gyosis kai didache], our author depicts the paths of light and of darkness, and stirs up the children of joy and peace to a walk in conformity with the precepts of the Lord (18-21).

As to the (relative) unity of the whole, often denied or disputed since le Moyne (1685) but also frequently defended, no doubt need be entertained; there is no need for supposing chaps. 18-

21 to be a later addition or that the original epistle has been largely interpolated or has undergone one or more redactions. It is obvious, however, that in the preparation of 18-21 the writer has made use of an older form of the Two Paths, as also, there and elsewhere, of the OT, the book of Enoch, 4 Ezra, and perhaps other works besides.

## 22. Authorship, Date

The author's name has not come down to us. Tradition, still clung to by many, suggests Barnabas, the companion of Paul, of whom mention is already made in the [beta] text of Acts 1:23 (see BARNABAS and BARSABAS); but it has no claim on our acceptance and has been often controverted. The tradition is admittedly old, however, and perhaps the name of Barnabas has been always associated with this work.

The unknown author was probably a gentile Christian, by birth a Greek, belonging to the Alexandrian circle. This conclusion is pointed to at least by his language and his manner of scripture interpretation, his ideas and some of his expressions, such as as "novices shipwreck ourselves upon their law" (×, 36). It is also possible, however, to think of him as living somewhere in Syria or Asia Minor not far from the environment within which the epistles of Paul arose. There is nothing to indicate that he was a Jew by birth, or one of the later inhabitants of Palestine.

Notwithstanding his love for gnosis, the author is a practical man who has at heart before all else the edification and the safety of the church. Neither things imminent nor things that lie in the future (×) are of the highest importance, but present things [ta parunta] and to know how to comport oneself among them. See e.g. 1:6-8, 2:1-10, 4:1, 17.

The author belongs neither to the right wing nor to that of Paul, nor yet to that of the writer of Hebrews or that of Marcion. Towards Judaism his attitude is one of freedom; in his view

Christianity came in its place in principle, as early as in the time of Moses; law and prophets are binding on believers, almost always, however, in the metaphorical interpretation only, not the literal, even where a historical occurrence seems to be described.

The date is earlier than that of Eusebius, Origen, Clement of Alexandria, Celsus, or the present form of the Didache; but later than the destruction of Jerusalem in 70 A.D. (chaps. 4, 16); later than the time of the apostles (5:9, 8:3); later than "Paul" (see PAUL, 38-42), including Hebrews; therefore not (as is still often supposed) before the end of the first century (see ACTS, 16), but rather, let us say, between 130 and 140 A.D. It is not possible to gain a more precise determination from chaps. 4 and 16, unless in so far as the silence regarding the building of the temple of Hadrian at Jerusalem, in honour of Jupiter Capitolinus, may be taken as showing that the temple had not yet been erected.

The value of the work, which, looked at either from the aesthetic or from the edificatory point of view, is not great, lies so far as we are concerned in the historical evidence it affords as to the existence of an interesting tendency—not observable elsewhere—in the direction of free thought among the Christians of the first half of the second century, and of a number of views, in the domain of Christian dogma and history, which differ from the usual opinions as to the contents of the Gospel narratives.

The older literature of the subject will be found referred to in the recent editions of the text by Gebhardt-Harnack (i8-8(2)), Hilgenfeld (×), Lightfoot (×). See further Duker and Van Manen, Oud. Chr. Lett. 1870, 1 1-02; Loman, van Manen, Volkraar in Th. 1 , 1884; Steck, Galaterbr., 1888, pp. 310-314; Volter, JPT, 1888, pp. 106-144; Joh. Weiss, ×;A. Link, TLZ, 1889, no. 24; Harnack ×, 1806, pp. 410-413; ACL ii. 1 410-428, 436-7. Cp A. van Veldhuizen, De brief van Barnabas, 1901.

## 23. Clement

Two epistles of Clement to the Corinthians (× [Klementos pros korinthious] A and B), cited as witnesses in CANON, 65, 73, and GOSPELS 87, are found in Cod. Alexandrinus (A), in the Jerusalem MS (J), and in an old Syriac version; the first also in an Old Latin version. It is claimed for them that they were written by Clement, in name of the Church of Rome, to the Church of Corinth in connection with disputes which had arisen there on questions of government. They have in reality the epistolary form, though not written by Clement.

## 24. First Epistle

The first, which from the moment of its recovery from the Cod. Alexandrinus by Patrick Junius [= Young] (Epistolae ad Corinthios, Greece, cum versione et notis Patr. Junii, Oxford, 1633) was received with great distinction and accepted, in accordance with tradition, as the work of the bishop-martyr Clement, a disciple and one of the first successors of the apostles Peter and Paul at Rome, itself claims to have been written by the Church of God at Rome to that at Corinth. The form is not fortuitous; if the contents be considered, it must be regarded as a literary artifice merely.

A "church" cannot write: usually it is held therefore that Clement wrote in name of the church; of this, however, there is no evidence. The writing has the semblance of a letter throughout, and calls itself so (× [epistole] : 63:2; × [epistellomen] and × [epesteilamen] 7:1, 62:1); yet clearly this is not its real character, and probably it was never sent as such. Rather it is a book, in the form of an epistle; to speak more precisely, in the form of a Pauline epistle, prepared for, and made accessible to, all who cared to read it. It is an "exhortation concerning a peace and concord" (×), to use its own words (63:2) about itself; a "writing" [graphe], as Eusebius (HE iii. 385) designates it; an "admonition" [nouthesia], as

Dionysius has it in Eus. ii. 258, designed to be publicly read in the church; cp 2 Clem. 19:1, 1 Clem. 7:1.

The contents do not relate exclusively to the disputes at Corinth, although these figure as having furnished the occasion for the letter. The writing begins, after the superscription and benediction, with an apology, by reason of various troubles, for not having attended to the Corinthians sooner (1:1); next follows an ideal picture of what the Corinthian Church had been (1:2-2:8); its fall is briefly described (3); a series of examples, drawn from the OT and the history of Christianity, is given to show the evils and misery wrought by jealousy and strife (4-6); a declaration that "we"—not the persons addressed merely, but also the church that is writing—are suffering from the same cause is made; wherefore it will be well that we should pay heed to the rule of tradition (×), to attend to what God demands of us and to fix our eyes on the precious blood of Christ (7:1-4).

- This is the beginning of a long sermon in which it is set forth how God has at all times demanded repentance (7:5-8:5);

- how we must turn ourselves to him, giving heed to what we read of Enoch, Noah, Abraham, Lot, Rahab (9-12);

- must be humble (13);

- obedient to God and not to the schismatics (14);

- must cleave unto those who are godly (15)

- and think upon Christ who is described in language taken from the OT (16);

- copying the examples of the prophets and of Abraham, Job, Moses, David (17-19a),

- laying to heart the example of peace and harmony shown in the Divine ordering of the universe (19b-20);

- in all things bearing ourselves Christianly (21-22);

- holding fast our faith in the second coming of Christ and in the resurrection (23-27),

- fearing God and seeking to draw near to him by faith and good works (28-35),

- finding Christ by this road (30-39);

- observing how in Israel all things were orderly done (40-41);

- the appointment of bishops and deacons among Christians came of the will of God (42);

- Moses stilled a contention as to the priestly dignity (43);

- what the apostles have ordained for the regulation of the episcopal office (44a);

- let no regularly chosen leaders of the church be dismissed, let contentions be avoided, love be stirred up (44b-50);

- where needful make acknowledgment of sin, be willing to yield, admonish one another, submit to the presbyters (51-59:2).

- The exhortation then passes over into a prayer (59:3-61),

- followed by a retrospect, renewed exhortation to submission (62-63),

- a benediction (64),

- a word about messengers sent; renewed benediction (65).

All that is here said about contentions at Corinth belongs to the literary clothing of the document. Paul's first epistle to the Corinthians may have suggested it (cp chap. 47). Perhaps too, though this is very far from certain, it is connected with disputes that had recently arisen as to the continuance in office, dismissal, and election of persons for the government of the church. It was the author's main purpose to remove difficulties of this kind wherever they might have arisen. He spoke under the mask of the Church at Rome, as a high authority, with growing emphasis, and finally as if he were one with the Holy Spirit himself (63:2; cp Acts 15:22-29).

The unity of the work has been disputed and the existence of large interpolations has been supposed at various times, though without just cause. No doubt the author, besides drawing much from the OT, has borrowed here and there from various works both Jewish and Christian, possibly also Pagan, without careful acknowledgment to his readers, or perhaps even to himself.

## 25. Authorship

The author is certainly not Clement of Rome, whatever may be our judgment as to whether or not Clement was a bishop, a martyr, a disciple of the apostles. The church of St. Clement at Rome, where the relics of the saint are reputed to rest, is evidently the third building on the site, and not older than 10:59; the underlying second building may possibly be the basilica of which Jerome speaks ( Vir. ill. 15). The first, which in turn underlies this, certainly exhibits traces of its having at one time been dedicated to the worship of Mithras, but not of any connection with the martyr-bishop Clement. The martyrdom, set forth in untrustworthy Acts, has for its sole foundation the identification of Clement of Rome with Flavius Clement the consul, who was executed by command of Domitian. (See the proofs of this in Lightfoot.)

Clement, as bishop of Rome, be he the first, second, or third after Peter, can no longer be maintained in view of the discovery that the Church of Rome (see ROME, CHURCH OF) had no monarchical government at all before Anicetus (156-166?). The disciple of Peter (and Paul) finds no support either in our present epistle or in Phil. 43. He disappears in the diverging versions of the tradition.

The possibility, still firmly maintained by such scholars as Harnack and Lightfoot, that the writing may have been the work of a certain Clement concerning whom nothing is known except what can be gathered from "his" epistle, has no real value; and to connect it with the further supposition that this Clement was an influential member of the governing body of the Roman church—the martyr-bishop of legend—is not to be recommended. The epistle furnishes no ground for it, but rather the reverse.

The oldest tradition as to its origin knows nothing of any such view. Irenaeus (iii. 83) had occasion to refer to it, had he known it, when in that context he mentions the name of Clement; yet he speaks, with some emphasis, just as Dionysius of Corinth does in Eus. HE iv. 23:11, of the epistle as having been sent by the Church of Rome in such a manner as to make it, and it alone, responsible for the contents. The first to express himself distinctly in another sense, and to name Clement of Rome as the writer, is Clement of Alexandria (Strom, i. 7:38).

From the work itself, all we can gather is that the author probably belonged to the Church of Rome. He was an educated man, well acquainted with the OT, and the Pauline and other NT epistles; a friend of peace and order; a warm advocate of the occasionally, perhaps often, disputed rights of the presbyters and deacons once chosen, who had adequately discharged the duties of their office.

## 26. Date

The date, with regard to which we cannot follow Harnack in deducing anything from the lists of bishops, which have been found untrustworthy, cannot be sought as was done by the older scholars, and more recently by Hefele, Wieseler, and Mallinckrodt, in the time of Nero or immediately there after, but considerably later. There is nothing to compel us, with most scholars, amongst whom are Lipsius, Gebhardt-Harnack, Lightfoot, to assign it to the last years of the first century; with Kriiger to leave it open till the reign of Trajan; with Volkmar to fix definitely on 125 A.D.; with Loman on the middle of the second century.

Rather let us say with Steck, somewhere about 140 A.D.; especially on account of the author's acquaintance with the Pauline epistles (including, of course, Hebrews) and also with 1 Peter. Whether he also had read the *Shepherd*, or whether, on the other hand, it was Hermas that had read the epistle of Clement, is not quite clear. It is clear, nevertheless, that Polycarp, Hegesippns, Dionysius of Corinth, and Irenaeus were acquainted with his work.

The value of the epistle, not insignificant from an aesthetic or religious point of view, lies specially in what it tells us regarding the development of Christianity in the writer's time, and regarding the relation between clergy and laity.

## 27. Second Clement

The second epistle was almost immediately on its rediscovery in 1633 received with a certain amount of depreciation; soon it came to be regarded by some as simply a homily which cannot have been written by Clement, and ultimately this view was adopted almost unanimously. The epistle is, nevertheless, equallv with the first, so far as form is concerned, a "letter," although it be as regards contents an edifying treatise designed to be from time to time read in church (19:1, cp 15:1-2, 17:5).

• The writer reminds his readers how they ought to hold high their Christian profession, live in accordance with it, make no Compromise with the world, have no fear of death (1-5);

• not serving two masters—the present world and the world to come (6);

• struggle, seek repentance, believe in the resurrection of the body, do the will of God, have no fear about the future, but rather live in expectation of the great day at every moment, not put off the duty of repentance, make sure that they belong to the true church (7-14).

• Looking back upon what he has written, the writer calls it a "counsel respecting continence" (×). He anew exhorts to fidelity to what has been learned, to diligence in seeking repentance both for oneself and for others, to a joyful confidence in God (15-20).

The unnamed author to whose Voice we are listening here is not Clement of Rome, as Bryennius alone among modern scholars would have it, nor yet another Clement to whom Hermas refers in Vis. 2:4, as Harnack for some time (from 1875) supposed, nor yet is he to be identified with the author of the first epistle we have just been considering (25). It is probable enough, no doubt, that the writer was acquainted with the last-named writing, and was in harmony with it.

This view is confirmed by many obvious points of agreement : its being met with only in conjunction with the first epistle; the later yet still old tradition which unfalteringly assigns both epistles to Clement; and the older tradition in Dionysius (see 31) where, in his epistle to the Romans, he refers to the present epistle (just as Irenaeus did in the case of the first) as proceeding from the Church of Rome, but not, like the first, as written—whatever the words may mean—"through Clement" [dia klementos]; Eus. HE 4:23:11, cp 9).

However the anonymous writer may seem to change his character—now as adviser (15:1), now as presbyter (17:35), now as reader (19:1) it is clear that he is a Christian of gentile origin (16:26), an educated man who interests himself in the growth of the religious life of the community, and who when necessary stands up for the defence of the existing ecclesiastical order.

In date the work belongs to the transition period—approximately, after 140 but before 170 A.D.—towards the middle of the second century. Since we ought, in all probability, to attach no weight to the mention of Soter in Eusebius (loc. cit.), we may say, certainly before about 160 A.D.

The importance of this letter, apart from the value which it possesses for those who are in search of earnest exhortation and edification in the Old-Christian literature, lies mainly in the contribution it makes to our knowledge of Christianity as it was about the middle of the second century, the emphasis here again laid upon conduct as compared with doctrine (though neither is this depreciated), and the demand for good literature to be used along with the OT and gospels in the public meetings of the church.[7]

## 28. Epistles of Ignatius

A large number of epistles of Ignatius, handed down from antiquity in various forms, attracted much attention in their several groups from 1498 onwards. The protracted controversy, not only as to the genuineness and value of these writings, but also as to the relative antiquity of the groups—the longer, the shorter, and the Syriac recension named after Cureton—has at last resulted in a practically unanimous

---

7. The fullest and best studies of the two epistles are those of Lightfoot (Ap. Fathers: S. Clement, 1890 (2)), with which compare Duker and van Manen, OC × 93-263; Hilgenfeld, Cl. A om. 1876 (21; Gebhardt-Harnack-Zahn, Pat. Ap. 187612); Loman, Tk. T, 1883, 14-25; Steck, Gal.-br. 1888, 294-310; Mal-linckrodt. Gel. en V rijh. 1890, 85-143 , Harnack, ACL ii. 1 251- 255, cp Th. l , 1898, 189-193; R. Knopf, Der erste Clemensbr. ( JU, new series, 61); K. X. Funk, Die Apost. Veiter, 1901.

conclusion that only seven epistles of Ignatius, mentioned by Eusebius (HE. 3:36) and preserved in two Greek MSS—or rather, properly speaking, only in one, for the first gives six epistles and the second one more—in an Old Latin version, and partially in Old Syriac, Armenian, and Coptic versions, belong to the category of Old-Christian literature.

Towards the end of the fourth century they were worked over and augmented by the addition of five others, to which in turn at a much later date (11th or 12th cent.) three more were added, in Latin. Moreover, they were translated in an abridged form into Syriac. The text of three of these Syriac abridgments —those to the Ephesians, Smyrnteans, and Polycarp—still treated with too great respect in Lightfoot O, was published by Cureton in 1845.

The original group, cited as evidence in CANON, 65, and GOSPELS, 92, has the aspect of being a collec tion of seven epistles written by Ignatius when, after having been thrown into prison for his Christian pro fession and sentenced, he was on his journey from Antioch to Rome, where he expected to suffer martyrdom. Four of the seven—those to the churches of Ephesus, Magnesia, Tralles, and Rome—appear to have been written at Smyrna; the remaining three—to the Philadelphians, to the Smyrnaeans, and to Polycarp—at Rome.

The first three treat the subject of monarchical church government with great earnestness, warn against heresies, and urge to a Christian life. The fourth treats of martyrdom, of which Ignatius must not be deprived. The filth is chiefly devoted to the subject of church unity, by all the members adhering to the bishop. The sixth deals with docetism, and also with the recognition due to the bishop. The seventh, with the reciprocal duties of the church rulers and people, and of all to one another.

The form of this seeming collection, and of each of the epistles separately, however little prominence be given to the fact even where the genuineness is definitely given up, is artificial. The whole makes up a single complete book, designed for the edification of the readers.

To satisfy oneself of this it is enough to observe the absence of all trace of any such collection having been made of the epistles as has been assumed; their mutual relations as parts of a whole; the reference in the first to the second epistle as a "second tract" [deuteron biblidion] intended for the same readers (Eph. 20:1); the peculiar form of the addresses and super scriptions; the meaning of the words there employed: "who is also Theophorus" ([o kai theophoros] [Philadelphia]), "of Asia" (TTJS Affias), "on the Maeander" (×); the forced character of the assumed relations between writer and readers; the improbability of the details of the journey of Ignatius; its irreconcilability in various respects with the certainly older tradition—as such brilliantly defended by Volter against Lightfoot in 1892—according to which Ignatius died a martyr, not about 107 or 110 at Rome, but in the winter of 115-116, at Antioch, by command of the Emperor Trajan, who was there at that time; the fact that the writer sometimes distinguishes himself from Ignatius; the testimony of Ep. Pol. 9 and 13 regarding Ignatius and his epistles; the points of agreement and difference between Ignatius and Paul.

After the example of Paul, who writes edifying and doctrinal epistles, and is on his journey towards Rome, where he looks forward to martyrdom as probable, our writer makes Ignatius of Antioch, well known as a Christian martyr, bear witness to what lies in his heart regarding the glorv of Christian martyrdom; the need for close adherence on the part of all church members to the bishop and presbyters of the church; the purity of Christian doctrine and the uprightness of a Christian life to be secured in this way. "Ignatius" is not, however, as many with Baur have held, the mere advocate of the bishop or the mere assailant of docetism.

## 29. Authorship

Who this writer may have been it is impossible to ascertain or even to guess. Certainly not Ignatius.

So much was already recognised following in the footsteps of Salmasius and Blondel (1645)–by Daille (1666) in his controversy with Usher and Voss; by Larroque (1674) against Pearson; in modern times by Baur, Schwegler, Hilgenfeld, Volkmar, Bunsen, Duker, van Manen, Keim, Killen, van Loon, against Rothe, Uhlhorn, Junius, Zahn, Lightfoot, Viilter, Reville, Harnack. Thirty years ago it seemed as if the time had wholly passed by in which "genuine" epistles of Ignatius would be spoken of at all. That the position has changed in recent years seems to be due, on the one hand, to the advocacy of Zahn (Ignatius von Antiochien, 1873; Pat. Ap. 1876) and of Lightfoot (Ap. Fathers: S. Ignatius, 1889 ×), whilst on the other, no account has been taken of anything urged on the other side by Dutch and American scholars; also to the readiness to accept various plausible yet baseless suppositions, as full and adequate answers to objections.

It is in reality, however, of no avail, as has been frequently attempted, to separate, in the interests of the supposed "genuineness," the Epistle to the Romans from the others, and to attribute either the former only (so Renan), or the others only (so Volter), to the martyr- traveller. It is also useless and contrary to all tradition to regard Ignatius as having been bishop in the late years of Hadrian (Harnack, Die Zeit des Ignatius-von Antioch, 1878), or to keep his date open to 125 A.D. (Harnack, 1897, ACL 11:1, p. 406, 3); to regard his advocacy of monarchical church government as made on behalf of an ideal only (Jean Reville, tudcs sur les origines de l'épiscopat, 1891; cp van Manen, *Th.T.*, 1892, 625-633: van

Loon, ib. 1893, 278-284); to identify him with a second Ignatius, who lived about the middle of the second century (Volter, *Th.T.*, 1886, 114-136), or with Peregrinus Proteus in the days when he was still a Christian (Volter, *Th.T.*, 1887, 272-320, also Die Ignatianischen Briefe, 1892; cp van Loon, *Th.T.*, 1886, 509-581; 1888, 420-445; 1893, 275-316).

The unknown writer was, to judge by his work, an earnest man with much zeal for martyrdom and all that made for what he thought right in doctrine and life. Perhaps he was a layman, and lived in Rome, at some date intermediate between Eusebius, Origen, Clement of Alexandria, Irenaeus, and "Polycarp," on the one hand, and Peter and Paul, the "apostles," Ignatius (+ 115-116), and a group of Pauline epistles, including Eph., 1 Thess., 1 Tim., Titus, on the other. The importance the writer attaches to acceptance of monarchical church government as a guarantee of purity of doctrine and life, and his animadversions on Marcionite errors, also point to a date near the middle of the second century, though at the same time it does not seem advisable to fix upon circa 175 as van Loon does.

The value of the little work lies in the region of history, particularly in that of the external and internal ordering of the life of the church. It speaks to the existence of a strong desire for vigour and unity in the government of the church in the interests of sound doctrine and life.[8]

---

8. The copious literature will be found registered for the most part in Lightfoot (Ap. Fathers; S. Ignatius, iSSgl 2 )): cp also Duker and van Manen, OCL2 5-154; Zahn, Ign. v. Ant. 1873 and ×, 1876; V. D. Killen, The Ancient Church, 1883×, and The Ignatian Epistles entirely Spurious, 1886; R. E. Jenkins, Ignatian Difficulties and Historic Doubts, 1890; Volter, fgn. Br. 1892; van Loon, Th.T, 1886, 1888, 1893; Harnack, ACL 11.1381-406; Funk, Ap. Viit. 1901.

## 30. Diognetus, Valentinus, Marcion, Themiso

The epistle to Diognetus, cited in GOSPELS, 95, belongs to the
category of Apologies, on which see below, 41.

Epistles of Valentinus, an Egyptian gnostic who lived at Rome
in the middle of the second century, are mentioned by Clement
of Alexandria (Strom, 2:836, 2:20:114, 3:7:59), and were, it
would seem, of a doctrinal character. So also an Epistle of
Marcion, dating from his pre-heretical period, to which
Tertullian refers (adv. Marc. 11:44, de Carne, 2). A catholic
epistle [epistole katholike]) by the Montanist Themiso "in
imitation of the apostle" [memoumenos ton apostolon], 170,
written, according to Apollonius (ap. Eus. HE 5:18:5), for the
enlightenment of those who were opposed to his views, is
known to us only by this reference, and is noteworthy as the
latest example of its kind from the time when "epistles" were
still written without hesitation in imitation of the manner of
the "Apostle"–i.e. , "Paul."

## 31. Dionysius of Corinth

Catholic epistles to the Churches (×) is the name given by
Eusebius (HE 4:23) to seven epistles, written by Dionysius,
bishop of Corinth, about (it is conjectured) ±170 A.D. , by
request, to the Lacedaemonians, Athenians, Nicomedians, the
churches of Gortyna and elsewhere in Crete, at Amastris, and
elsewhere in Pontus, the Cnossians and the Romans.

The book is currently held to have been a collection of actual
letters. To judge, however, by the character of the fragments
preserved in Eusebius, we ought rather to regard it as a
collection similar in kind to the Ignatian (see 28), containing a
series of precepts, suggestions, instructions regarding the true
faith and right manner of life, the constitution and government
of the churches.

That Dionysius himself, and not that—after the practice of those times—a later author, should have written them and published them collectively under Dionysius's name becomes increasingly improbable as soon as we en deavour to do full justice to the complaint in the mouth of Dionysius about the falsification of his epistles; to the reasons given why he, Dionysius, wrote to one group of readers upon one subject and to another upon another, and so forth. Perhaps substantially the same has to be said of an epistle which Dionysius, according to Eusebius (I.c., 13), addressed to sister Chrysoptora.

## 32. Irenaeus

i. An Epistle of Irenaeus to Florinus, presbyter at Rome and a pupil of Valentinus, known from Eusebius (HE 5:20:1 ) and still regarded as genuine by Harnack (ACL 1:593-594) and Kruger (ACL 93), is a later treatise, in epistolary form, on the unity of God, in connection with the question whether God is the author of evil (×). The manifest exaggeration to which Matthes years ago called attention (De ouderdom van het Joh. Ev. 1867, 117, 162-3), coupled with the fact that Irenaeus, moreover, never shows any signs of acquaintance with Florinus, although he would constantly have had occasion to controvert him in adv. Haer. had he known him, and the manner in which the writer poses as Irenoeus in defence of orthodox doctrine, all enable us to perceive clearly that a writer otherwise unknown is speaking to us here and why he is doing so.

ii. In like manner the Epistle to Blastus, connected with that of Irenceus to Florinus, and named only in Eusebius (HE 5:20:1, cp 615), is also, probably, not the work of Irenaeus, but a later treatise on "schism" (irtpl [peri schismatos])

iii. A third epistle, which according to Eusebius (HE 5:24:11) was sent by Irenaeus in name of the brethren in Gaul to Victor of Rome, and which is partially preserved by Eusebius (loc. cit. 12-17), should confidently be regarded as a later treatise about the paschal feast [logos peri tou pascha], an earnest attempt at conciliation between contending parties in the paschal controversy, in which in all probability the name of Irenaeus at first did not figure at all.

## 33. Ptolemy

An Epistle of Ptolemy to Flora, preserved in Epiphanius (Her. 33:3-7), and printed by Stieren (Iren. 1:922-936), and, in an improved text, by Hilgenfeld (ZWT 24 [1881] 214-230), takes the form of a friendly answer to the question : How ought we to think regarding the Law of Moses? Irenaeus, in writing about the gnostic Ptolemy, head of the school of Valentinus in Italy, neither uses this epistle nor shows any knowledge of it—a reason for regarding it as probably a treatise belonging to a somewhat later date than that usually assumed (the middle of the 2nd cent. ). The same inference is suggested by the peculiar use here made of the gospels of Mt. and Jn. , and of the Pauline epistles Rom., 1 Cor., Eph. (Cp A. Stieren, De Irencei adv. Hcer. operis fontibus, etc., 1836, pp. 19-21; De Ptolemcci gnostici ad Floram Epistola, 1843.)

## 34. Apocryphal Epistles

As Apocryphal epistles the following may here be mentioned by way of Appendix :- An interchange of letters between Abgarus and Jesus (see APOCRYPHA, 29, and von Dobschutz, ZWT 1900, pp. 422-486); between Seneca and Paul; between the Corinthians and Paul (= 3 Cor.); from Paul to the Lacedaemonians (see PAUL, 50).

# IV. APOCALYPSES

## 35. Revelations

In Old-Christian literature a fourth class is constituted by the writings usually known as Apocalypses, *Apokalupseis*, or Revelations, most of which are partially or wholly lost. The following are known: a Revelation of John; part of a Revelation of Peter; the Shepherd of Hermas. Of the Revelation of Paul and of the Revelation of Abraham, both mentioned by Epiphanius (*Haer.* 38:2), and both considered to date from the second century, we know little more than the names.

Under this section we may include those fragments of older Christian Revelations which may be held to survive in Matthew 24, Mark 13, Luke 21:5-36, 2 Thessalonians 2:1-12, Barnabas 4:1-6, and the Christian portions of certain originally Jewish writings: 4 Ezra, the Testaments of the XII. Patriarchs, the Sibylline Oracles, etc., and the later or apocryphal Revelations edited by Tischendorf, 1866, and others.

# V. APOLOGIES

## 36. Quadratus, Aristides

The Apologies form a fifth group. One of the oldest, known only in a small fragment (Eus. *HE* 4:3) claims to be by Quadratus and addressed to the Emperor Hadrian on his visit to Athens about 125-126 A.D. So also a writing of Aristides partially (chs. 1, 2) extant in an Armenian version (1878), and wholly in a Syriac version discovered by Rendel Harris in 1889, as also in Greek in the romance *Barlaam and Josaphat* discovered by Armitage Robinson in 1890 (ed. princeps in *Theological Studies* (*TS*) (1:1, 1891).

It has the form of a speech delivered before an unnamed "king" (*basileus*) and may be conjectured to have been published under the title, "Apology of Aristides for the Christians" religion, to Hadrian" (*Tou Aristeidous apologia uper tes ton Christianon theosebeias pros Adrianov*) most likely with the superscription "To the Emperor Caesar Hadrian, Aristides the Philosopher, of Athens" (*Autokratopi Kaisari, Adriano, Aristeides philosophos Athenaios*).

The speaker begins with a short profession of his faith in God (ch. 1). He premises that there are worshippers of so-called gods, as well as Jews and Christians; they fall into various classes as Chaldaeans, Greeks, and Egyptians; and all are in error (2). Their gods have no title to be acknowledged or worshipped (3-13). They belong to the visible, not to the invisible world, and are creatures of God, perishable *stoicheia*, or images of these (3-7).

Amongst the Greeks, they are often represented as human beings displaying all kinds of objectionable attributes, vices and crimes (8-11). Amongst the Egyptians, moreover, as irrational animals, plants, and herbs (12, 13). The Jews know indeed the Almighty, the Invisible who sees all things and has created all things, but although they are nearer the truth they do not serve him with understanding, as is shown by their denial of Christ the Son of God who has come into the world (14). It is otherwise with the Christians. They live in accordance with the commandments of God engraved on their hearts, and are conspicuous in every respect for their praiseworthy conduct (15). The discourse concludes with two sections that seem to have undergone some alteration in transmission to us (16, 17).

So far as the form is concerned, it may well be doubted whether Aristides ever delivered such a discourse, either at Athens or elsewhere. There is, however, no sufficient reason for doubting also, with Harnack (*Theologische Literaturzeitung* [*TLZ*] 1891, nos. 12, 13), the rest of the statement in Eusebius, or for inferring from the superscription in the Syriac version that Aristides delivered his discourse to Antoninus Pius (138-161). We may adhere to the date under Hadrian (117-138), but not earlier than 125-126. With this assumed date agrees what can be inferred from the contents (if the simplicity of the discourse is noted), what the writer adopts from the gospel narratives, and his attitude towards the books he appears to have made use of (see van Manen, *Th.T.* 1893, 1-56).

## 37. Aristo of Pella

A *Dispute of Jason and Papiscus concerning Christ*, attributed to Aristo of Pella, depreciatingly spoken of by Celsus, and defended by Origen, is known to us in a fragmentary way from the writings of Origen and others, and perhaps underlies the *Altercatio Simonis Judaei et Theophili Christiani* which comes to us from the fifth century (Harnack, *ACL* 1 92-95; *PRE* (3) 2 47-48) and the *Discourse between Athanasius* [bishop of Alexandria] *and the Jew Zacchaeus* (Conybeare, *Expos.* 1897, April, 300-323; June, 443-463). It appears to have turned upon the question whether Jesus was the Messiah foretold by the prophets, and to date from 135-170, let us say about 140 A.D.

# Justin

## 38. First Apology

The Christian philosopher, Justin Martyr, born about 100 A.D., baptized about 133, died about 165 (± 163-167), was the author of two apologies which are imperfectly preserved in a single MS. The first vindicates our faith before Antoninus and the Roman senate, according to Eus. *HE* 4:8:3, 4:11:3, 4:18:2. It is divisible into three parts: chs. 2-12, 13-60, 61-67, preceded and followed by an introduction (1) and a conclusion (68:1-2) to which was added at a later date a transcript of Hadrian's letter to Minucius Fondanus (68:3-10) and, later still, letters of Antoninus Pius and Marcus Aurelius.

The orator-author maintains

> (1) that Christians ought not to be persecuted for the name they bear seeing that they are neither without God (*atheoi*) nor guilty of all sorts of evil deeds. He states what their belief really is, declares that Jesus Christ has foretold all things, and announces his purpose of proving, for the instruction of those who do not know it, the truth of his Christian confession (2-12).

> (2) He then proceeds in the second place to show that the Christian religion is rational and leads to a life that is lovely as the precepts of Christ are beautiful (13-22). In ch. 23 he lays down three propositions which he goes on to discuss in their order: what he and his brethren have taught concerning Christ and the prophets who went before is true (24-29); all this was taught by Jesus Christ, the Son of God, made man in accordance with the divine purpose (30-53); before the incarnation men had wandered in error under the influence of evil spirits (54-60).

> (3) In the third portion he treats of baptism, the eucharist, the observance of Sunday (61-67).

The assumed character of a spoken discourse is merely literary form. The book is intended to advocate the Christian cause with all who cared to listen to it, especially with rulers (*oi archontes*) all of whom, not merely one or two emperors, are addressed as "pious and philosophers" (*eusebeis kai philosophoi*). Where and when it was written cannot be determined with certainty. Probably it was at Rome about the middle of the second century.

## 39. Second Apology

In the second apology the speaker, in consequence of a bloody persecution of three Christians under Urbicus, addresses himself to the Romans whose "governors" (*hegoumenoi*) permit or perpetrate such cruelties.

He relates what has happened (chs. 1-2), speaks contemptuously of what a certain opponent called Crescens might be able to do (3); disposes of the advice given to Christians to commit suicide (4); explains why it is that in spite of all calamities they maintain their faith in God (5); that God is unnamable; who Jesus Christ is (6); why Christians cannot accept the Stoical doctrine as to the conflagration of the world and as to fate (7, 8); why they believe in the penal justice of God (9); that philosophers like Socrates in the olden time were also persecuted (10); how it is possible to learn from Hercules at the cross way (11); of the fearlessness of Christian martyrs (12); and that it must be held a fitting thing that answer should be made to the complaints of the Christians (13-15).

This discourse is no mere postscript of the first, as has often been supposed, nor a preliminary argument. Rather is it an independent sequel, with constant reference to what has been said in the first: perhaps a work that at a later date (yet not much later) was separately published when Urbicus was city prefect—that is to say between 144 and 160 (circa 153). Both discourses are of great value for our knowledge of the manner in which in those days Christianity was regarded by mature and thoughtful professors. The first has an additional value on account of what it tells us as to the moral life of the Christians of that period as well as their ecclesiastical customs and practices.

## 40. Dialogue with Trypho

A third apology of Justin, in large measure preserved in the same MS, is known as his *Dialogue with Trypho the Jew*. To

Trypho he tells the story of his own baptism (2-8), and then he goes on to show, in the first place that the Mosaic law has had its day and must now give place to the new law, the law of Christ (9-48), and in the second place that Christ is rightly worshipped by believers along with God, because the prophets had foretold his coming and he is truly the Son of God as is witnessed by his birth, by his death on the cross, his resurrection, and ascension (49+).

This dialogue was, according to ch. 120, written after Justin's *First Apology*, probably still within the reign of Antoninus Pius (138-161), approximately about 155-160.

## 41. Epistle to Diognetus

What is known as the Epistle to Diognetus reached modern times in a single MS which was burned at Strassburg in 1870; it is a particularly fine plea for Christianity (cp, 30) in which an unknown writer, who for a while was wrongly identified with Justin, undertakes to enlighten the equally unknown Diognetus on the religion of Christians, the God in whom they trust, their contempt of the world and of death, their renunciation of the gods of Greece and of the Jewish worship (*deisidaimonia*), their mutual love, and the reason why this new "kind or practice" (*genos, epitedeuma*) of piety has only now entered into the world (ch. 1).

He insists on the worthlessness of the gods made by human hands of perishable matter (2); maintains that the Jews are in error when they think to serve the Creator as if he had need of offerings and desired the fulfillment of a multiplicity of commands (3-4). He then goes on to sketch the Christian manner of life so as to show the excellence of the Christian profession (5-6). Their knowledge of God is through the manifestation of the Word (7). How greatly superior is the Christian revelation to all that ever philosophers formerly taught (8). Before it must come the fullness of transgression

(9). Christian faith brings a rich blessing (10). Finally there follows, from another—somewhat younger—hand, a glorification of the Word and of the preaching of the Word to men (11-12).

The whole was, as plainly appears from the last lines of ch. 1, originally designed, not to be sent as a letter, but to be read and re-read in the religious assemblies of the church. When we compare this anonymous writer with Aristides and perceive how he seems to be acquainted with NT writings without ever quoting them verbatim or as possessing authority, we have reason to assign his date to the second half of the second century.

## 42. Tatian

Tatian, already referred to in 7, was the author of a still extant *Oration to the Greeks* (critically edited by Schwartz in 1888) which may be dated towards the middle of the second century, not later than about 172 A.D. He there expounds what he, the quondam philosopher, deems most proper to be said on behalf of Christianity while criticising and confuting the religion, ethics, philosophy, and art of the Greeks.

## 43. Athenagoras

An extant *Oration of Athenagoras* (also edited by Schwartz, 1891) is represented as having been held before the emperors Marcus Aurelius and Lucius Commodus—that is to say, somewhere between the years 176 and 180. In it the Athenian philosopher (of whom nothing further is known) directs attention to the difference of treatment meted out to Christians and Pagans (1-3); he then proceeds to vindicate Christians from the accusation of being atheists (*atheoi*) (4-30) and of being morally inferior to pagans (31-36), and concludes with a fresh appeal to the supreme rulers (37).

## 44. Miltiades, etc.

Apologies by Miltiades and Apollonius are known to us only by name: that of Melito (circa 170) from a quotation by Eusebius (*HE* 4:26:5-11).

# VI. TEXT BOOKS

## 45. Text Books

Such Old-Christian writings as do not come under the categories already dealt with—Gospels, Acts, Epistles, Revelations, Apologies—can be conveniently grouped under the heading of Text books, as having been written for the instruction of their readers. In this class the first we shall mention is the *Antitheses* or *Separatio legis et evangelii*. Of this we know little more than the name, and that it was the chief work of Marcion; it is mentioned by Tertullian (*adv. Marc.* 1:19). *Four-and-twenty books* of Basilides, or it may be, of one of his followers "upon the Gospel" (*eis to euaggelion*) so Eus. *HE* 4:7:7) or exegetics (*exegetica*, so Clem. Alex. *Strom*, 4:1283). *Letters, Homilies and Psalms*, by Valentinus or his adherents, are referred to by Clement of Alexandria, Hippolytus, Tertullian. A "treatise against all the heresies that have existed" (*suntagma kata pason ton gegenemenon aireseon*), by Justin, is named by himself in *Apol.* 126.

Other works also are, rightly or wrongly, attributed to Justin. Philosophical, doctrinal, polemical, ecclesiastical writings by Isidorus, Apelles, Agrippa Castor, Tatian, Miltiades, Apollinaris, Melito, Theophilus, Rhodon, and others in confutation of heretics or in recommendation of their errors. Greater or smaller treatises wholly or partially incorporated or worked into later *Canones, constitutiones*, confessional writings, episcopal lists, etc. The chief work of this description, known to us since 1883, is the *Didache* (see Warfield, *Bibl.*

*Sacr.* 1886, pp. 100ff.; Hennecke, *Zeitschrift für die Neutestamentlische Wissenschaft* (*ZNTW*), 1901, pp. 58-72).

Five books of "Memoirs" or "Commentaries" (*hypomnemata*) by Hegesippus, begun under Anicetus (154/5-165/7), completed under Eleutherus (173/5-188/9), of which fragments are preserved in Eus. *HE*, are more of a polemical, anti-Gnostic, than of an historical, character.

The much discussed work of Papias was probably a commentary on one or more of our canonical gospels.

"Memoirs" or "Commentaries" (*hypomnemata*)—by Heracleon, according to Origen—collected by Brooke (*TS* 1, 4, 1891) belong to a commentary on the Fourth Gospel. *On the Resurrection of the Dead* (*peri anastaseos nekron*; edited by Schwartz, *TU* 42) was written by Athenagoras in answer to objections to the doctrine of the resurrection and in exposition of the arguments in its favour that can be drawn from the writings of philosophers, or from the constitution and destiny of man.

## 46. Literature

The literature of the subject is immense. It includes all studies, whether older or more recent, on the NT, the Apostolic Fathers and other Christian writers of the first two centuries. For brevity's sake we may refer to the Introductions to the NT; Harnack, *ACL* 1 1893, 2 1, 1897; Krüger, *ACL*, 1895, and "Nachtrage," 1897.

# Paul

*Even leaving aside any comparison with the
Pauline epistles, we cannot regard the contents of
Acts, viewed as a whole, and on their own merits,
as a true and credible first-hand narrative of what
had actually occurred, nor yet as the ripe fruit of
earnest historical research—not even where, in
favourable circumstances, the author might
occasionally have been in a condition to give this.*

# Contents

# Introductory

## 1. The Older View

Paul, an apostle of Jesus Christ, though not one of the original twelve, but only at a later date added by the Lord himself to the circle of his more intimate followers, soon became one of the most zealous, if not the most zealous, of them all. A Jew by birth, brought up in accordance with the strictest precepts of the law, bitterly opposed to the Christianity then beginning to emerge into prominence, as a youth he was one of the witnesses of the martyrdom of Stephen (Acts 7:58-8:3). Anon, while "breathing threatening and slaughter against the disciples of the Lord" (Acts 9:1), his career is arrested and he is converted on the road to Damascus (Acts 9:2-8).

Once a preacher of the gospel, he henceforth, without hesitation or delay, devotes to its service for all the rest of his life all his rare gifts of intellect and heart, his unmatched courage, his immovable fidelity. Finally, after long and indefatigable wanderings, including three great (missionary) journeys, probably about the year 64 A.D., while still in the full vigour of manhood, he suffered martyrdom at Rome. Further details will be found in the Acts of the Apostles, and in his 13 (14) canonical epistles. Apart from one or two comparatively unimportant traditions, these are our sole and abundantly sufficient sources of information.

So thought and spoke almost all scholars of all schools, whether Protestant or Catholic, down to the beginning of the nineteenth century. All that was left for scholarship was to determine as exactly as possible the precise order of the events in detail and the proper light in which to view them, so as to gain a picture as faithful and complete as possible of the great apostle's life and activities. That Acts and the Epistles might be regarded, on the whole, as credible throughout, was questioned by no one.

## 2. Criticism in First Half of the Nineteenth Century

Towards the middle of the nineteenth century the situation was completely altered. Criticism had learned to concern itself seriously with the contents of Acts and to inquire as to the genuineness of certain of the 13 (14) Pauline epistles as read in the NT.

The epistle to the Hebrews had already been excluded from the group by Carlstadt (1520), and among those who followed him in this were Luther, Calvin, Grotius (ob. 1681), and Semler (ob. 1791). E. Evanson in 1792 raised some doubts as to the Pauline origin of Romans, Ephesians, Colossians; J. E. C. Schmidt in 1798 as to that of 1 and 2 Thessalonians; Eichhorn (1804), Schleiermacher (1807), de Wette (1826) as to Timothy and Titus; Usteri in 1824, as also de Wette and Schleiermacher, following Evanson, as to Ephesians. By 1835 F. C. von Baur had given the coup de grace to the "so-called Pastoral Epistles," Kern to 2 Thessalonians in 1839; Semler in 1776, followed by others, denied the unity of 2 Corinthians.

Baur, incidentally in his *Pastoralbriefe* (p. 79), declared that we possess only four letters of Paul with regard to the genuineness of which there can be no reasonable doubt:

Galatians, 1 and 2 Corinthians, Romans. This thesis became the corner-stone of the new building.

## 3. Baur

F. C. von Baur, the founder of what was called, from the university in which he taught, the Tübingen school, laid the foundation in his *Paulus* (1845; 2, after the author's death in 1860, by E. Zeller, 1866-1867; ET by Menzies, 2 vols., 1873-1875). In Baur's view, Acts, and also such epistles as were not from the pen of Paul (Peter, or James) himself, ought to be regarded as "tendency"–writings, designed to make peace or to establish it, as between Peter and Paul, the assumed heads of two parties or schools in early Christianity which were called by their names–Petrinists and Paulinists, Jewish Christians and Gentile Christians; parties which he held to have lived, like Peter and Paul themselves, and for a considerable time after the decease of these great leaders, in bitter hostility towards one another until, so far as they did not lose themselves in various heresies to right or to left, they became merged in one another in the bosom of the Catholic church.

For the historian the all-important task now became that of discerning clearly the unquestionably genuine element in the Pauline Epistles, on which alone weight could be laid. With them could be combined only those elements in Acts which were seen not to be in contradiction with the epistles.

This standpoint, if we leave out of account divergences of subordinate importance, was accepted in Germany and Switzerland by many scholars; among others by E. Zeller, A. Schwegler, K. R. Kostlin, K. Planck, A. Ritschl (1849) [In the second edition of his Entstehung, however, Ritschl abandoned the Tübingen position.] A. Hilgenfeld, G. Volkmar, H. Lang, A. Hausrath, K. Holsten, R. A. Lipsius, C. Weizsacker, H. J. Holtzmann, O. Pfleiderer–we may safely say, in short, by the entire old guard of liberal theology–so, too, in France; in

Holland also, until quite recently, by the whole modern school; and in England among others by W. R. Cassells, the long anonymous author of *Supernatural Religion* (vols. i and 2, 1874; vol. 3, 1877), and by S. Davidson (*Introduction to the Study of the NT*, 2 vols.; l), 1894).

This also was, on the whole, the point of view occupied by E. Hatch when he contributed to *Ency. Brit.*, 18 (1885), the article "Paul," from which the following (4-32) of the present article are taken, a few short notes only being added within square brackets.

×××

# Later Criticism

## 33. Transitional Views

From the first, both in Germany and elsewhere, the Tübingen criticism met with strong opposition as well as with cordial acceptance. The right wing, which protested against it on behalf of tradition, spared (and continues to spare) no effort to recover the invaded territory and to protect it, so far as may be, from further attack. The most powerful champion of this conservative attitude in recent years has been Theodor Zahn, author of the *Einleitung in das neue Testament* (2 vols. 1897-99, ×).

Those who were not so timid about breaking with traditional views or with opinions that had been judged to be no longer tenable, inclined, nevertheless, especially in recent years, to consider that Baur had gone to the extreme limit of criticism and to think that some retreat, along part of the line at least, from his extravagances was necessary. They did not shut their eyes to the great merits of the Tübingen school; but neither would they be blind to their faults and shortcomings which

seemed to admit of being summed up in the single word
"exaggeration." They called themselves by choice the critical
school, and could appropriately enough be described as indeed
"moderately" so. Those who have in recent years gone farthest
in this reactionary direction (or, let us call it, retrogression)
are, in practice, A. Jülicher in his Einleitung in das NT, 1894,
1901[9]. and, in theory, A. Harnack in the "Preface" (which is not
to be confounded with the contents which follow) to his
Chronologie der altchristlichen Litteratur (ACL 2:1, 1897).

×××

## 34. A New School

Later criticism that may fairly enough be called "advanced," in
the sense that its conclusions differ more than those of others
from traditional opinion starts from the same principles as the
"critical school," though its opponents prefer such expressions
for it as "scepticism," the "radical," or the "Dutch school,"
"hypercriticism," "uncriticism" or (as Julicher has it recently)
"pseudo-criticism." The way for it was prepared, not to speak of
Evanson (1792), by Bruno Bauer, A. Pierson, S. A. Naber, and
others. By Bruno Bauer in his three volumes entitled Kritik
der Paulinischen Briefe (1850-52), and again after a silence of
many years in his Christus und die Caesaren (1877; see
especially pp. 37-387); by A. Pierson in De Bergrede en andere
synoptische fragmenten (1878; pp. 98-110); by him and Naber
in their Verisimilia (1886); by others in dissertations and
discourses on various public occasions in Holland of which
some account is to be found in, 1883, pp. 593-618; 1884, pp.

---

9. See Krenkel, Das korperliche Leiden des Paulus, in the ZWT, 1873, p.
238, and in Beitrage z. Aufhellung d. Gesch. u. d. Briefe des A. Paulus
(1890). 4, "der Dorn im Fleische," 47-125; and for various views, Lightfoot,
Galatians, 1892, p. 182; Farrar, St. Paul, vol. 1, Excurs. 10:652 [van Manen,
Paulus, 3:284; Meyer-Heinrici, Kommentar, 2 Cor (8), 1900, pp. 397-402;
Ramsay, St. Paul the Traveller and Roman Citizen 1898, 94 ( "a species of
chronic malaria fever")].

562-3; 1886, pp. 418-444; W.C. van Manen, *Het Nieuwe Testament sedert* 1859, 1886, pp. 89-126, 225-7, 265).

The Pauline question, however, was first brought forward in a strictly scientific form by A.D. Loman of Amsterdam in his *"Quaestiones Paulinae,"* published in *Th.T.* in 1882, 1883, 1886. This broadly-based study, however, in the beginning still intimately connected with the writer's much discussed hypothesis of the symbolical character of the gospel history and the person of Jesus, Loman did not live to complete.

The portions published by him were the "Prolegomena" to a book on the principal epistles of Paul, in which the necessity for a revision of the foundations of our knowledge of the original Paulinism and the expediency, for this purpose, of starting from the Epistle to the Galatians are fully set forth (1882, pp. 141-185, cp 593-616); a first chapter in which the external evidence for and against the genuineness of that epistle is exhaustively discussed (1882, pp. 302-328, 452-487; 1883, pp. 14-57; 1886, pp. 42-55), and a second chapter in which the same question is considered in the light of the Canon (1886, pp. 55-113, cp 319-349, 387-406).

At a later date an unfinished study, *De Brief aan de Galatiers*, was posthumously added to these as Loman's *Nalatenschap* (1899). Meanwhile various scholars–J.C. Matthes, J. van Loon, H.U. Meyboom, J.A. Bruins–had signified their agreement with him wholly or partially, and he was followed in the path of advancing criticism he had opened up, as regards the question of the sources of our knowledge of Paul, his life and his work, though without for a moment committing themselves to Loman's hypothesis respecting the gospel history, by Rudolf Steck of Bern, D.E.J. Völter of Amsterdam, and W.C. van Manen of Leyden.

Steck's well-written book *Der Galater brief nach seiner Echtheit untersucht, nebst kritischen Bemerkungen aus den*

*paulinischen Hauptbriefen* was published in 1888; Völter's
*"Ein Votum zur Frage nach der Echtheit, Integrität u.
Composition der vier paulinischen Hauptbriefe"* was
published in *Th.T.* in 1889 (pp. 265-325), but still remains
unfinished in its revised form *Die Komposition der
paulinischen Hauptbriefe: i. Der Romer- u. Galaterbrief*
(1890). Van Manen, as yet hesitatingly in 1886-87, but decidedly
in 1888 as a contributor to *Th.T.* and other periodicals, and
subsequently in connection with his academical work, has
participated largely in the present discussions.[10]

The same critical principles of the "later criticism"—recently
adopted also by Prof. W.B. Smith of Tulane University, New
Orleans—have likewise been in some measure followed,
however unconsciously in the main, by all those who at one
time or another have sought, by postulating redactions,
interpolations, and additions, to escape from the difficulties in
the way of accepting the Pauline authorship of one or more of
the "principal epistles."

## 35. Its Relation to "Redaction" and "Interpolation" Hypotheses

It will suffice to mention

(1) with regard to all the four epistles: the view of J.H.A.
Michelsen (*Th.T.*, 1873, p. 421) that in these we have the
original epistles of Paul published after his death with
elucidations and notes; also conjectures by Straatman,

---

10. See especially his *Paulus* in three parts: *De Handelingen der Apostelen*
(Acts), 1890; *De brief aan de Romeinen*, 1891; *De brieven aan de
Korinthiers*, 1896; followed by a condensed summary of the results arrived
at in his *Handleiding voor de Oudchristelyke letterkunde*, 1900. For a
somewhat fuller survey of the earlier history of this criticism and of the
reception it met with in the learned world the reader may consult his
articles entitled "A Wave of Hypercriticism" in *Exp.T*, 1898, pp. 205-211,
257-9.

Baljon (1884) and Sulze (*Prot. Kirch.—Ztg.*, 1888, pp. 978-85).

(2) So far as Romans is concerned, we have the conjecture of Semler, Baur, and others, that chaps. 15-16, wholly or in part, do not belong to the fourteen preceding chapters, and, according to many, are not from the hand of Paul; that of C.H. Weisse, that chaps. 9-11, of Straatman, that chaps. 12-14, do not belong to the original epistle; of Laurent (1866), that the epistle at a later date was furnished with a number of marginal glosses; of Renan, that it was issued by Paul in more than one form (e.g., 1-11 + 15, 1-14 + part of 16); of Michelsen (Th.T., 1886-7) that we have to distinguish five or six editions in the original text; of E. Spitta (1893) that it is a combination of two letters written by Paul at different times to the Christians of Rome, one before and one after his visit to that city.

(3) With respect to 1 and 2 Corinthians, we have the conjecture of Semler (1776), E.J. Greve (1794), Weber (1798), C.H. Weisse (1855), Hausrath (1870), Michelsen (1873), Baljon (1884), O. Pfleiderer (1887), W. Bruckner (1890), M. Krenkel (1890), P. W. Schmiedel (1892), J. Cramer (1893), A. Halmel (1894), J. Weiss (1894), H.J. Holtzmann (1894), H. Lisco (1896) that 2 Cor. is made up of two or more pieces which originally did not belong to one another; of Lipsius (1873), Hagge (1876), Spitta (1893), Clemen (1894) that the same holds true of 1 Cor.; and of Straatman (1863-5) and J. A. Bruins (1892) that both epistles contain a vast number of interpolations.

(4) As regards Gal., the same opinion has been held, by Weisse, Sulze, Baljon (1889) and Cramer (1890)—the last two in their commentaries.

## 36. Its Proposed Task

Yet, however obvious in all this be the unconscious preparation for and transition to the criticism spoken of in 34, this last does not occupy itself with such conjectures as those just suggested (in 35), unless perhaps in special cases, and never with the definite object of escaping by such means from difficulties touching what is called the genuineness of the Epistles. It is ready to submit all such hypotheses to a candid examination, but does not value expedients whereby objections can be silenced temporarily. It does not start from the belief that the non plus ultra of critical emancipation has been realised by the Tübingen school; but neither does it think that that school went too far.

For it, there is nothing *a priori* "too far" in this field; and it believes that criticism is ever in duty bound to criticise its own work and to repair its defects. It recognises no theoretical limit whatsoever that can reasonably be fixed. It ranks the critical labours of Baur and his school, notwithstanding all shortcomings and defects, far above those of older and less critically moulded scholars. It wishes nothing better than *mutatis mutandis*, to continue the research pursued by the Tübingen school, and, standing on the shoulders of Baur and others, and thus presumably with the prospect of seeing clearer and farther, to advance another stage, as long a stage as possible, towards a real knowledge of Christian antiquity.

That is not to be attained, in the judgment of this school of critics, by a simple return to the old views, by accepting the opinions of those scholars who busied themselves with researches of this kind before Baur (in the first decades of the 19th century or in the last of the 18th), nor yet by adopting the traditional conceptions current at a still earlier period whether amongst candid Protestants or thinking Roman Catholics. No error committed by a younger generation can ever make to be true anything in the opinions of an older generation which has once been discovered to have been false.

Still less does the criticism with which we are now dealing cherish hopes from any mediating policy of "give and take." It has found that it does not avail, in estimating the Tübingen theory, in one point or another, to plead "extenuating circumstances" in favour of tradition whether churchly or scientific, and to offer here or there an amendment on the sketch drawn by Baur (or others after him) of the state of schools and parties in Old Christianity, or to extend the number of the "indisputably genuine" epistles of Paul from four to six or seven (the "principal epistles" + Philippians, Philemon and 1 Thess.), eight (+2 Thessalonians or Colossians), nine (+ both 2 Thessalonians and Colossians), ten (+ Ephesians), if not even augmented by genuine Pauline fragments in the Pastoral Epistles.

The defects of the "tendency criticism" passed upon the NT writings and other documents of early Christianity which have come down to us, whether the criticism in which Baur led the way or that of others like Volkmar, Holsten, S. Davidson, Hatch (who followed Baur, while introducing into his criticism corrections more or less far-reaching), demand a more drastic course. It is needful to break not only with the dogma of the "principal epistles" in the order suggested by Baur and afterwards accepted by Hatch—Galatians, 1 and 2 Corinthians, Romans—but also with the dogma of there being four epistles of Paul in any order with regard to the genuineness of which no question ought to be entertained.

It was a great defect in the criticism of the Tübingen school that it set out from this assumption without thinking of justifying it. It can be urged in excuse, that at the time no one doubted its justice; Evanson was forgotten and Bruno Bauer had not yet arisen; but none the less the defect cannot be regarded as other than serious. It has wrought much mischief and must be held responsible for the song of triumph now being prematurely uttered even by those whose opposition to criticism is by no means trenchant, the burden of which is, "Tübingen itself has alleged nothing against these epistles."

The latest school of advanced criticism has learned not to rejoice over this but to regret an unfinished piece of work that ought to have been taken in hand long ago and demands to be taken up now. It regrets that Baur and his followers should not have stopped to consider the origin of the "principal epistles." It holds that criticism should investigate, not only those books which have been doubted for a longer or shorter period, but also even those that hitherto—it may even be, by every one— have been held to be beyond all doubt, whether they be canonical or uncanonical, sacred or profane.

Criticism is not at liberty to set out from the genuineness—or the spuriousness—of any writing that is to be used as evidence in historical research as long as the necessary light has not been thrown upon it, and least of all may it do so after some or many writings of the same class have already been actually found to be pseudepigrapha. It was and is in the highest degree a one-sided and arbitrary proceeding to go with Baur upon the assumption of the genuineness of the "principal epistles" as fully established, and in accordance with this to assume that Acts must take a subordinate place in comparison with them.

It is not *a priori* established that Paul cannot be mistaken, at least as long as we do not know with certainty whether he and the writer of the epistles that have come down to us under his name are indeed one and the same. The investigation of Acts must be carried on independently of that of the Epistles, just as that of the Epistles must be independent of that of Acts. This rule must be applied in the case of every epistle separately as well as in connection with the other epistles which we have learned to recognise as belonging to the same group.

The four "principal epistles" are not a fixed datum by which Acts and other Pauline writings can be tested unless one is previously able to prove their genuineness. This point has not been taken into account by the Tübingen school—greatly to their loss. As soon as it is observed, it becomes the task of criticism to subject to a strict examination the principal epistles one by one, from this point of view.

What, then, is the criterion which may be employed in this investigation? None of the so-called external evidences. These do not avail here, however valuable may be what they have to tell us often as to the opinion of antiquity concerning these writings. So much Baur and his followers had already long ago learned to recognise. The "critical school" had confessed it, even by the mouth of those among its adherents who had found themselves nearest to the thorough-going defenders of tradition. Where then must the determining consideration be looked for? In the direction where in such circumstances it is always wont to be found: in the so-called "internal" evidence. It is internal criticism that must speak the last, the so far as possible conclusive, word.

The demand seemed to many too hard, as regarded the "principal epistles." The Tübingen school and the "critical" school alike shrank from making it. The "progressive" criticism which had meanwhile come into being, submitted to the inevitable. It addressed itself to the task imposed. To the question, with what result? The answer, unfortunately, cannot be said to be wholly unanimous. True, this is a disadvantage under which the opposing party labours no less than the other. There is no criticism in the judgments of which no trace can be found of what can be called a subjective side.

## 37. Its View of Acts

Viewed broadly, and with divergences in points of detail left out of account, what the recent criticism now described has to say regarding Acts is in substance as follows. The book professes to be a sequel to the third canonical gospel, designed in common with it to inform a certain Theophilus otherwise unknown to us, or in his person any recent convert to Christianity, more precisely with regard to the things in which he has been instructed (Acts 1:1-5, cp Lk. 1:1-4, 24:36-53). We find in it in accordance with this, a by no means complete, yet at the same time (at least, in some measure) an orderly and continuous sketch of the fortunes of the disciples of Jesus, after his resurrection and ascension; of their appearances in Jerusalem and elsewhere; and in particular, of the life and work of Peter, in the first part (Acts 1-12), and more fully and amply of the life and work of Paul, in the second part (13-28).

Even leaving aside any comparison with the Pauline epistles, we cannot regard the contents of Acts, viewed as a whole, and on their own merits, as a true and credible first-hand narrative of what had actually occurred, nor yet as the ripe fruit of earnest historical research—not even where, in favourable circumstances, the author might occasionally have been in a condition to give this. The book bears in part a legendary-historical, in part an edifying and apologetical character.

The writer's intention is to instruct Theophilus concerning the old Christian past, as that presented itself to his own mind after repeated examination, to increase the regard and affection of his readers for Christianity, and at the same time to show forth how from the first, although hated by the Jews, this religion met with encouragement on the part of the Romans. Of a "tendency," in the strict sense of the word, as understood by the Tübingen school, there is nothing to be seen. The book does not aim at the reconciliation of conflicting parties, Petrinists and Paulinists, nor yet at the exaltation of Paul or at casting his Jewish adversaries into the shade, or at placing him on a level with Peter.

Of the substantial unity of the work there can be no question. We have not here any loose aggregation of fragments derived from various sources. Still less, however, can we fail to recognise that older authorities have been used in its composition. Amongst these are prominent two books which we may appropriately call (a) Acts of Paul, and (b) Acts of

Peter. From a is derived in the main what we now read in 1:23 (D), 4:36-37, 6:1-15, 7:51-8:3, 9:1-30, 11:19-30, 13-28; from b, more particularly, much of chaps. 1-12.

> (a) The first and older of the two books included mainly a sketch of the life and work of Paul, according to the ideas of those Christians who placed him high, and who, as compared with others, deserve to be called progressive. With this was worked in—but not incorporated without change (unless the corrections which can still be traced are to be laid to the account of the author of Acts)—a journey narrative, very possibly the work of Luke the companion of Paul. See 11:27 (D), 16:10-17, 20:5-15, 21:1-18, 27:1-28:16.

> (b) The second book, written in view of the Acts of Paul just described, was an attempt to allow more justice to be done to tradition and more light to be thrown upon Peter.

Perhaps the author of the entire work, as we now know it, in addition to oral tradition, had still other means of information at his disposal (such as Flavius Josephus) and borrowed here and there a detail, but certainly not much, from the Pauline epistles.

Alternately free and fettered in relation to his authorities, the author sometimes used their language, yet, as a rule, employed his own. He followed in their footsteps for the most part, yet frequently went his own way, transposing and correcting, supplementing and abridging what he had found in others. To ascertain the details of the process in every case is no longer possible. On the chief points, a fuller discussion will be found in W. C. van Manen, *Paulus: 1. De Handelingen der Apostelen*, 1890.

The spirit in which Luke set about his work is that of budding Catholicism, which has room alike for "Paul" and for "Peter," and does not shrink from bringing to the notice of the faithful a writing—the Acts of Paul just referred to—devoted to the commemoration and glorification of the apostle of the heretics as Tertullian still called him, albeit clothed in a new dress whereby at the same time reverent homage is rendered to the tradition of the ancients.

Luke's true name remains unknown. His home was probably in Rome; but perhaps it may have been somewhere in Asia Minor. He flourished about the second quarter of the second century. There is no necessity for doubting the correctness of the representation that he is one and the same with the author of the Third Gospel.

In the days when the contents of sacred books were held exempt from criticism, the historical value of Acts was much overrated; more recently under the influence of Tübingen criticism it has been unduly depreciated. It is entitled to recognition in so far as it is a rich source of information as to how the Christianity of the first 30 or 35 years after the crucifixion was spoken about, estimated, and taught, in influential circles, about the years 130-150 A.D. It is entitled to recognition also, in so far as we are still in a position to trace, in what has been taken over with or without alteration from older works, how it was that men of that period thought about implied, or expressly mentioned persons, things, and relations.

In estimating the value of details, it is incumbent on us always, so far as possible, to distinguish between the original historical datum, the valuable substance of a trustworthy tradition, and the one-fold, two-fold, threefold, or it may be manifold clothing with which this has been invested by later views and opinions, and in too many cases, unfortunately, concealed by them, in such a manner that it is not always possible, even for the keenest eye, to discriminate as could be wished between truth and fiction.

## 38. Of the Epistles

With respect to the canonical Pauline epistles, the later criticism here under consideration has learned to recognise that they are none of them by Paul: neither fourteen, nor thirteen, nor nine or ten, nor seven or eight, nor yet even the four so long "universally" regarded as unassailable. They are all, without distinction, pseudepigrapha (this, of course, not implying the least depreciation of their contents). The history of criticism, the breaking up of the group which began as early as 1520, already pointed in this direction. No distinction can any longer be allowed between "principal epistles" and minor or deutero-Pauline ones.

The separation is purely arbitrary, with no foundation in the nature of the things here dealt with. The group—not to speak of Hebrews at present—when compared with the Johannine epistles, with those of James, Jude, Ignatius, Clement, with the Gospel of Matthew, or the Martyrdom of Polycarp, bears obvious marks of a certain unity—of having originated in one circle, at one time, in one environment; but not of unity of authorship, even if a term of years—were it even ten or twenty—be allowed. It is impossible, on any reasonable principle, to separate one or more pieces from the rest.

One could immediately with equal right pronounce an opposite judgment and condemn—e.g., Romans or Corinthians, compared with the rest, as under suspicion. Every partition is arbitrary. However one may divide them, there will always remain (within the limits of each group, and on a comparison of the contents of any two or three assumed classes), apart from corrections of subordinate importance, clearly visible traces of agreement and of divergence—even on a careful examination of the famous four: Romans, 1 and 2 Corinthians, Galatians.

There is no less distinction in language, style, religious or ethical contents between 1 and 2 Corinthians on the one hand,

and Romans and Galatians on the other, than there is between Romans and Philippians, Colossians, and Philemon. On the contrary, in the last two cases the agreement is undeniably greater.

Tradition does not assert the Pauline origin of the "principal epistles" more loudly than it does that of the Pastoral or of the "minor" epistles. External evidences plead at least as strongly, or, to speak more accurately, just as weakly, for the latter as for the former. The internal point just as strongly in the case of Romans, 1 and 2 Corinthians, and Galatians, as they do elsewhere to the one conclusion that they are not the work of Paul. This deliverance rests mainly on the following considerations, each of them a conclusion resulting from independent yet intimately connected researches.

## 39. Their Form

The "principal epistles," like all the rest of the group, present themselves to us as epistles; but this is not their real character in the ordinary and literary meaning of the word. They are not letters originally intended for definite persons, despatched to these, and afterwards by publication made the common property of all. On the contrary, they were, from the first, books; treatises for instruction, and especially for edification, written in the form of letters in a tone of authority as from the pen of Paul and other men of note who belonged to his entourage: 1 Corinthians by Paul and Sosthenes, 2 Corinthians by Paul and Timothy, Galatians (at least in the exordium) by Paul and all the brethren who were with him; so also Philippians, Colossians, and Philemon by Paul and Timothy, 1 and 2 Thessalonians by Paul, Silvanus, and Timothy.

The object is to make it appear as if these persons were still living at the time of composition of the writings, though in point of fact they belonged to an earlier generation. Their "epistles" accordingly, even in the circle of their first readers, gave themselves out as voices from the past. They were from the outset intended to exert an influence in as wide a circle as possible; more particularly, to be read aloud at the religious meetings for the edification of the church, or to serve as a standard for doctrine and morals.

Hence it comes that, among other consequences, we never come upon any trace in tradition of the impression which the supposed letters of Paul may have made—though, of course, each of them must, if genuine, have produced its own impression—upon the Christians at Rome, at Corinth, in Galatia; and the same can be said of all the other canonical epistles of Paul. Hence, also, the surprising and otherwise unaccountable features in the addresses of the epistles: "to all that are in Rome, beloved of God, called to be saints" (Rom. 1:7), "to the church of God which is at Corinth, them that are sanctified in Christ Jesus, called to be saints, with all who invoke the name of our Lord Jesus Christ, in all places, theirs and ours" (1 Cor. 1:2); "to the church of God which is at Corinth, with all the saints in the whole of Achaia" (2 Cor. 1:1), "to the churches of Galatia" (Gal. 1:2).

The artificial character of the epistolary form comes further to light with special clearness when we direct our attention to the composition of the writings. In such manner real letters are never written.

i. In a very special degree does this hold true no doubt of 2 Corinthians. Many scholars, belonging in other respects to very different schools, have been convinced for more than a century and have sought to persuade others that this epistle was not written at one gush or even at intervals; that it consists of an aggregation of fragments which had not originally the same destination.

ii. 1 Corinthians allows us to see no less clearly that there underlie the finished epistle as known to us several greater or smaller treatises, having such subjects as the following:

• Parties and divisions in the church (1:10-3:23), the authority of the apostles (4), unchastity (5-6), married and unmarried life (7), the eating of that which has been offered to idols (8-11:1), the veiling of women (11:2-15 [11:16]), love feasts (11:17-34), spiritual gifts (12-14), the resurrection (15), a collection for the saints (16:1-4)

• Other passages being introduced relating to the superiority of the preaching of the cross above the wisdom of this world (1:18-31), the spirit in which Paul had laboured (2:1-16), the right of litigation between Christians (6:1-11), circumcised and uncircumcised, bond and free (7:18-24), the apostolic service (9), Christian love (13).

iii. With regard to Romans it is even more obvious that the author accomplished his task with the help of writings, perhaps older "epistles," treatises, sayings handed down whether orally or in writing—although we must admit, as in the case of so many other books, both older and more recent, that we are not in a position to indicate with any detail what has been borrowed from this source and what from that, or what has been derived from no previous source whatever, and is the exclusive property of the author, editor, or adapter.

iv. With Galatians the case is in some respects different, and various reasons lead us, so far as the canonical text is concerned, to think of a Catholic adaptation of a letter previously read in the circle of the Marcionites, although we are no longer in a position to restore the older form. We have in view the employment of such words as Peter (Πετρος) alongside of Cephas (Κηφας), of two forms of the name Jerusalem (Ιεροσολυμα alongside of ιερουσσαλημ), the presence of discrepant views (as in 3:7, 3:29 and 3:16) of

Abraham's seed; the zeal against circumcision in 5:2-4, 6:12-13 alongside of the frank recognition that it is of no significance (5:6, 6:15)—the cases in which the ancients charged Marcion with having falsified the text, though the textual criticism of modern times has found it necessary to invert the accusation.

There are to be detected, accordingly, in the composition of the principal epistles phenomena which, whatever be the exact explanation arrived at in each case, all point at least to a peculiarity in the manner of origin of these writings which one is not accustomed to find, and which indeed is hardly conceivable, in ordinary letters.

## 40. Their Contents: Paulinism

The contents of the epistles, no less than the results of an attentive consideration of their form, lead to the conclusion that the "principle epistles" cannot be the work of the apostle Paul.

i. Is it likely that Paul, a man of authority and recognised as such at the time, would have written to the Christians at Rome —men who were personally unknown to him—what, on the assumption of the genuineness of the epistle, we must infer he did write? That he would have taken so exalted a tone, whilst at the same time forcing himself to all kinds of shifts in writing to his spiritual children at Corinth and in Galatia? One cannot form to oneself any intelligible conception of his attitude either to the one or to the other; nor yet of the mutual relations of the parties and schools which we must conceive to have been present and to some extent in violent conflict with one another if Paul really thought and said about them what we find in the "principal epistles."

ii. Even if we set all this aside, however, the doctrinal and religious-ethical contents betoken a development in Christian life and thought of such magnitude and depth as Paul could not possibly have reached within a few years after the crucifixion. So large an experience, so great a widening of the field of vision, so high a degree of spiritual power as would have been required for this it is impossible to attribute to him within so limited a time. It does not avail as a way of escape from this difficulty to assume, as some do, a slow development in the case of Paul whereby it becomes conceivable that when he wrote the "principal epistles" he had reached a height which he had not yet attained fourteen or twenty years previously.

There is no evidence of any such slow development as is thus assumed. It exists only in the imagination of exegetes who perceive the necessity of some expedient to remove difficulties that are felt though not acknowledged. Moreover, the texts speak too plainly in a diametrically opposite sense. It is only necessary to read the narrative of Paul's conversion as given by himself according to Galatians 1:10-16 in order to see this. The bigoted zealot for the law who persecuted the infant church to the death did not first of all attach himself to those who professed the new religion in order to become by little and little a reformer of their ideas and intuitions.

On the contrary, on the very instant that he had suddenly been brought to a breach with his Jewish past, he publicly and at once came forward with all that was specially great and new in his preaching. The gospel he preached was one which he had received directly. It was not the glad tidings of the Messiah, the long expected One, who was to come to bless his people Israel; it was the preaching of a new divine revelation, and this not communicated to him through or by man, but immediately from above, from God himself, God's Son revealed in him. With this revelation was at the same time given to him the clear insight and the call to go forth as a preacher to the Gentiles.

iii. Underlying the principal epistles there is, amongst other things, a definite spiritual tendency, an inherited type of doctrine (Rom. 6:17)—let us say the older Paulinism—with which the supposed readers had long been familiar. They are wont to follow it, now in childlike simplicity, now with eager enthusiasm, or to assail it, not seldom obstinately, with all sorts of weapons and from various sides.

Some have already got beyond this and look upon Paulinism more as if it were a past stage, a surmounted point of view. One might designate them technically as Hyperpaulinists. They are met with especially amongst Paul's opponents at Corinth according to 1 and 2 Corinthians. Others remain in the rear or have returned to the old view, the Jewish or Jewish-Christian view which had preceded Paulinism. They are the Judaisers against whom above all others the Galatians are warned and armed. Both are groups which one can hardly imagine to oneself as subsisting, at least in the strength here supposed, during the life time of Paul. Plainly Paul is not a contemporary, but a figure of the past. He is the object or, if you will, the central point of all their zeal and all their efforts.

iv. Paulinism itself, as it is held up and defended in the "principal epistles," apart from diversities in the elaboration of details by the various writers, is nothing more or less than the fruit of a thorough-going reformation of the older form of Christianity. Before it could be reached the original expectations of the first disciples of Jesus had to be wholly or partly given up.

The conception of Jesus as the Messiah in the old Jewish meaning of the word had to give place to a more spiritual conception of the Christ the Son of God; the old divine revelation given in the sacred writings of Israel had to make way for the newer revelation vouchsafed immediately by God, in dreams and visions, by day and by night, and through the mediation, if mediation it can be called, of the Holy Ghost: the law had to yield to the gospel. For these things time—no little time—was needed, even in days of high spiritual tension such as must have been those in which the first Christians lived and in which many are so ready to take refuge in order to be able to think it possible that the "principal epistles" with their highly varied contents could have been written so soon after the death of Jesus as the theory of Pauline authorship compels us to assume.

v. Writers and readers, as we infer from the contents, live in the midst of problems which—most of them at all events—when carefully considered are seen not to belong to the first twenty or thirty years after the death of Jesus. We refer to questions as to the proper relation between law and gospel, justification by faith or by works, election and reprobation, Christ according to the flesh and Christ according to the Spirit, this Jesus or another, the value of circumcision, the use of clean or unclean things, sacrificial flesh, common flesh and other ordinary foods and drinks, the Sabbath and other holy days, revelations and visions, the married and the unmarried condition, the authority of the apostles, the marks of true apostleship and a multitude of others.

We must not be taken in by superficial appearances. Though Paul is represented as speaking, in reality he himself and his fellow apostles alike are no longer alive. Everywhere there is a retrospective tone. It is always possible to look back upon them and upon the work they achieved. Paul has planted, another has watered (1 Cor. 3:6). He as a wise master-builder has laid the foundation; another has built thereupon (3:10). He himself is not to come again (4:18). He and his fellow-apostles have already "been made a spectacle unto the world, both to angels and to men," God has "set them forth as men doomed to death, lowest and last"—i.e., given them the appearance of being persons of the lowest sort (4:9).

Their fight has been fought, their sufferings endured. It is already possible to judge as to the share of each in the great work. Paul, to whom Christ appeared after his resurrection "last of all," "the least of the apostles," has "laboured more abundantly than they all" (15:8-10); he has run his course in the appointed way (9:26-27), a follower of Christ (even as others may be followers of himself, 11:1), whose walk in the world can readily stand comparison with that of others, even the most highly placed in Christian circles (2 Cor. 1:12, 11:5, 12:11), who has been ever victorious, whom God has always led in triumph, making manifest the savour of his knowledge by him in every place; unto God a sweet savour of Christ, by his coming forward testifying, as in the sight of God, of the sacrifice made by Christ in his death; sufficient for all things (2:14-16); a pattern of long-suffering, patience, and perseverance, who had more to endure than any other man (4:8-10, 6:4-5, 7:5, 11:23-27), an ideal form whose sufferings have accrued to the benefit of others and been a source of comfort to many (4:10-11, 1:4-7).

vi. A special kind of Christian gnosis, a wisdom that far transcends the simplicity of the first disciples and their absorption with Messianic expectations, haunts and occupies many of the more highly-developed minds (1 Cor. 1:17-31, 26:16 and elsewhere). In Romans 9-11 the rejection of Israel is spoken of in a manner that cannot be thought to have been possible before the fall of the Jewish state in 70 A.D. The church is already conceived of as exposed to bloody persecutions, whereas, during Paul's lifetime, so far as is known to us, no such had as yet arisen (Rom. 5:3-5, 8:17-39, 12:12, 12:14, 2 Cor. 1:3-7); she has undoubtedly been in existence for more than a few years merely, as is usually assumed, and indeed requires to be assumed, on the assumption of the genuineness of the epistles.

The church has already, from being in a state of spiritual poverty, come to be rich (1 Cor. 1:5). Originally in no position to sound the depths, consisting of a company of but little developed persons, the majority of its members, though still in a certain sense "carnal," are able to follow profound discussions on questions so difficult as those of speaking with tongues, prophecy, or the resurrection (1 Cor. 12-15). There are already "perfect" ones who can be spoken to about the matters of the higher wisdom; spiritual ones who can digest strong nourishment; understanding ones who have knowledge (2:6-16, 3:1-3, 10:15).

The church is in possession of their traditions (11:2, 11:23, 15:3): epistles of Paul which presented a picture of him different from the current tradition received from those who had associated with him (2 Cor. 1:13, 10:10). There is an ordered church life to the following of which the members are held bound. There are fixed and definite customs and usages—such as regular collections of charitable gifts (2 Cor. 9:13) or the setting apart, when required, of persons whose names were in good repute, and who had been chosen, by the laying on of hands (8:18-19).

In a word, the church has existed not for a few years merely. The historical background of the epistles, even of the principal epistles, is a later age. The Christianity therein professed, presupposed, and avowed, in a number of its details does not admit of being explained by reference to the period preceding the date of Paul's captivity or even that of his death in 64 A.D. Everything points to later days—at least the close of the first or the beginning of the second century.

Necessary limitations of space do not allow of fuller elucidations here. The reader who wishes to do real justice to the view here taken of the question as to the genuineness of Paul's epistles will not stop at the short sketch given here, but will consult the following works among others:

(a) On the subject as a whole, Loman, *Qusestiones Paulinae* in *Th.T.*, 1882, pp. 141-185; cp 593-616, 1886, 55-113; cp 319-349 and 387-406 ; Steck, *Galaterbrief*, 1-23, 152-386.

(b) On Rom. and Cor., Van Manen, *Paulus*, 2 and 3.

(c) On Gal., Steck, *Galaterbrie*; cp Loman, *Quaest. Paul.* in *Th. f*, 1882, pp. 302-328, 452-487; 1883, pp. 14-57; 886, pp. 42-55; and Loman's *Nalatenschap*, 1899;

(d) for a general survey of the entire Pauline group, Van Manen, *Handleiding*, iii., 1-98 (pp. 30-63).

## 41. Paul's Life and Work: Negative Results

To the question as to the bearing of the conclusions of criticism upon our knowledge of the life and activity of Paul, the answer must frankly be that in the first instance the result is of a purely negative character. In truth, this is common to all the results of criticism when seriously applied. Criticism must always begin by pulling down everything that has no solid or enduring foundation. Thus all the representations formerly current—alike in Roman Catholic and Protestant circles— particularly during the nineteenth century—regarding the life and work of Paul the apostle of Jesus Christ, of the Lord, of the Gentiles, must be set aside, in so far as they rest upon the illusory belief that we can implicitly rely on what we read in Acts and the 13 (14) epistles of Paul, or in the epistles alone whether in their entirety or in a restricted group of them.

These representations are very many and—let it be added in passing—very various and discrepant in character: far from showing any resemblance to one another, they exhibit the most inconsistent proportions and features. But, however different they were, they all of them have disappeared; they rested upon a foundation not of solid rock, but of shifting sand.

So, too, with all those surveys of Paulinism, the "ideas," the "theology," the "system" of Paul, set forth in accordance with the voice of tradition, as derived from a careful study of the contents of Acts and the epistles, whether taken in their entirety or curtailed or limited to the "principal epistles" alone. Irrevocably passed away, never more to be employed for their original purpose, are such sketches, whether on a large or on a smaller scale, whether large or narrow in their scope, sketches among which are many highly important studies, especially within the last fifty years. Henceforward, they possess only a historical interest as examples of the scientific work of an older school. They do not and could not give any faithful image or just account of the life and teaching of Paul, the right foundation being wanting.

This, however, does not mean, as some would have us believe, that the later criticism has driven history from the lists, banished Paul from the world of realities, and robbed us even of the scanty light which a somewhat older criticism had allowed us, to drive away the darkness as to the past of early Christianity. These are impossibilities. No serious critic has ever attempted them or sought to obscure any light that really shone. The question was and is simply this: what is it that can be truly called history? Where does the light shine? To see that one has been mistaken in one's manner of apprehending the past is not a loss but a gain. It is always better, safer, and more profitable, to know that one does not know, than to go on building on a basis that is imaginary.

## 42. Positive Results, Foundations

The results of criticism, even of the most relentless criticism, thus appear to be after all not purely negative. Though at first sight they may, and indeed must, seem to be negative, they are not less positive in contents and tendency. The ultimate task of criticism is to build up, to diffuse light, to bring to men's knowledge the things that have really happened.

As regards Paul's life and work, now that the foundations have been changed, it teaches us in many respects to judge in another sense than we have been accustomed to do. Far from banishing his personality beyond the pale of history, criticism seeks to place him and his labours in the juster light of a better knowledge. For this it is unable any longer in all simplicity to hold by the canonical Acts and epistles, or even to the epistles solely, or yet to a selection of them. The conclusion it has to reckon with is this:

> (a) That we possess no epistles of Paul; that the writings which bear his name are pseudepigrapha containing seemingly historical data from the life and labours of the apostle, which nevertheless must not be accepted as correct without closer examination, and are probably, at least for the most part, borrowed from Acts of Paul which also underlie our canonical book of Acts (see above, 37).

> (b) Still less does the Acts of the Apostles give us, however incompletely, an absolutely historical narrative of Paul's career; what it gives is a variety of narratives concerning him, differing in their dates and also in respect of the influences under which they were written. Historical criticism must, as far as lies in its power, learn to estimate the value of what has come down to us through both channels, Acts and the Epistles, to compare them, to arrange them and bring them into consistent and orderly connection. On these conditions and with the help of these materials, the attempt may be made to frame some living conception of the life and work of the apostle, and of the manner in which the figure of the apostle was repeatedly recast in forms which superseded one another in rapid succession.

Towards this important work little more than first essays have hitherto been made. The harvest promises to be plentiful; but the labourers as yet are too few. We must, for the time being, content ourselves with indicating briefly what seem to be the main conclusions.

## 43. The Historical Paul

Paul was the somewhat younger contemporary of Peter and other disciples of Jesus, and probably a Jew by birth, a native of Tarsus in Cilicia. At first his attitude towards the disciples was one of hostility. Later, originally a tent maker by calling, he cast in his lot with the followers of Jesus, and, in the service of the higher truth revealed through them, spent the remainder of a life of vicissitude as a wandering preacher. In the course of his travels he visited various lands: Syria, Asia Minor, Greece, Italy.

Tradition adds to the list a journey to Spain, then back to the East again, and once more westwards till at last his career ended in martyrdom at Rome. With regard to his journeys, we can in strictness speak with reasonable certainty and with some detail only of one great journey which he undertook towards the end of his life: from Troas to Philippi, back to Troas, Assos, Mitylene, Samos, Miletus, Rhodes, Patara, Tyre, Ptolemais, Caesarea, Jerusalem, back to Caesarea, Sidon, Myra, Fair Havens, Melita, Syracuse, Rhegium, Puteoli, Rome (Acts 16:10-17, 20:5-15, 21:1-18, 27:1-28:16).

Perhaps at an earlier date he had been one of the first who, along with others of Cyprus and Cyrene, proclaimed to Jews and Gentiles outside of Palestine the principles and the hopes of the disciples of Jesus (Acts 11:19-20). Possibly, indeed probably, we may infer further details of the same sort from what Luke and the authors of the Epistles have borrowed from the "Acts of Paul," as to the places visited by Paul, and the measure of his success in each; in which of them he met with opposition, in which with indifference; what particular discouragements and adventures he encountered; such facts as that he seldom or never came into contact with the disciples in Palestine; that even after years had passed he was still practically a stranger to the brethren dwelling in Jerusalem; that on a visit there he but narrowly escaped suffering the penalty of death on a charge of contempt for the temple, which would show in how bad odour he had long been with many.

As regards all these details, however, we have no certain knowledge. The Acts of Paul, so far as known to us, already contained both truth and fiction. In no case did it claim to give in any sense a complete account of the doings and sufferings of the apostle in the years of his preaching activity. The principal source which underlies it, the journey narrative, the so-called "We-source," is exceedingly scanty in its information. It says not much more, apart from what has been already indicated about the great Troas-Philippi-Troas-Rome journey, than that Paul, sometimes alone, sometimes in company with others, visited many regions, and preached in all of them for at least some days, in some cases for a longer period.

It does not appear that Paul's ideas differed widely from those of the other "disciples," 1 or that he had emancipated himself from Judaism or had outgrown the law more than they. Rather do one or two expressions of the writer of the journey-narrative tend to justify the supposition that, in his circle, there was as yet no idea of any breach with Judaism. At any rate, the writer gives his dates by the Jewish calendar and speaks of the "days of unleavened bread" (i.e., after the Passover), Acts 20:6, and of "the fast" (i.e., the great Day of Atonement in the end of September), 27:9. He is a "disciple" among the "disciples." What he preaches is substantially nothing else than what their mind and heart are full of, "the things concerning Jesus" (τα περι του ιησου).

It may be that Paul's journeyings, his protracted sojourn outside of Palestine, his intercourse in foreign parts with converted Jews and former heathen, may have emancipated him (as it did so many other Jews of the Dispersion), without his knowing it, more or less—perhaps in essence completely— from circumcision and other Jewish religious duties, customs, and rites. But even so he had not broken with these. He had, like all the other disciples, remained in his own consciousness a Jew, a faithful attender of temple or synagogue, only in this one thing distinguished from the children of Abraham, that he held and preached "the things concerning Jesus," and in connection with this devoted himself specially to a strict life and the promotion of mutual love.

What afterwards became "Paulinism," "the theology of Paul," was not yet. Still less does it ever transpire that Paul was a writer of epistles of any importance; least of all, of epistles so extensive and weighty as those now met with in the Canon. So also there is no word, nor any trace, of any essential difference as regards faith and life between him and other disciples. He is and remains their spiritual kinsman; their "brother," although moving in freedom and living for the most part in another circle.

For doubting, as is done by E. Johnson, the formerly anonymous writer of *Antiqua Mater* (1887), the historical existence of Paul and his activity as an itinerant preacher outside the limits of Palestine, there is no reason. Such doubt has no support in any ancient document, nor in anything in the journey-narrative that, in itself considered, ought to be regarded as improbable; on the other hand, it is sufficiently refuted by the universality of the tradition among all parties regarding Paul's life and work (cp Van Manen, *Paulus*, 1:192-200).

## 44. The Legendary Paul

It is true that the picture of Paul drawn by later times differs utterly in more or fewer of its details from the original. Legend has made itself master of his person. The simple truth has been mixed up with invention; Paul has become the hero of an admiring band of the more highly developed Christians; the centre, at the same time, of a great movement in the line of the development of the faith and expectations of the first disciples; the father of Paulinism—that system which, at first wholly unnoticed by the majority, or treated with scorn and contempt (cp 4, n. 2), soon met with general appreciation, and finally found world-wide fame, however at all times imperfectly understood.

It is difficult, or almost impossible, to indicate with distinctness how far Paul himself, by his personal influence and testimony, gave occasion for the formation of that which afterwards came to be associated with his name, and which thenceforward for centuries—indeed inseparably for all time, it might seem—has continued to be so conjoined, though very probably, if not certainly, it had another origin. We find ourselves here confronted with a question involving a problem similar to that relating to the connection between John, originally a simple fisherman of Galilee, one of the first disciples of Jesus, and John the Divine, the father of the illustrious Johannine school which speaks to us in the Fourth Gospel and in the three epistles bearing his name.

## 45. In Acts of Paul

The following seems certain: Paul, of whom so little in detail is known, the artisan-preacher, who travelled so widely for the advancement and diffusion of those principles which, once he had embraced them, he held so dear, was portrayed in a no longer extant work which can most suitably be named after him Acts of Paul, based partly on legend, partly on a trustworthy tradition to which the well-known journey-narrative may be reckoned.

There he comes before us, now enveloped in clouds and now standing out in clear light; now a man among men, and now an ideal figure who is admired but not understood. At once the younger contemporary of the first disciples, and yet as it seems already reverentially placed at a distance apart from them; a "disciple" like them, yet exercising his immediate activity far outside their circle; full of quite other thoughts; in a special sense guided by the Holy Spirit; a "Christian" who bows the knee before the Son of God and is entrusted with "the gospel of the grace of God" (Acts 20:24); in the main, perhaps, so far as his wanderings and outward fortunes are concerned, drawn from the life, yet at the same time, even in that case, in such a manner that the reader at every point is conscious of inaccuracy and exaggeration, and finds himself compelled to withhold his assent where he comes across what is manifestly legendary.

So in the story of Paul's conversion, his seeing of Jesus in heaven, his hearing of Jesus' voice, his receiving of a mandate from him (Acts 22:21, 26:16-18); the word to Ananias that he is to be instructed by Jesus himself and filled with the Holy Ghost (9:16-17); the representation of Paul as receiving visions and revelations (22:17-21, 16:9-10, 18:9-10, 27:23); the record of how he was wont to be led by the Holy Spirit (13:4, 16:6-7, 19:21, 20:22, 21:4, 21:10-12); the description of his controversy with Elymas Barjesus, whom he vanquishes and punishes with blindness (13:6-12); the healing of the lame man at Lystra and the deification that followed (14:8-18); the vision of the man of Macedonia at Troas (16:9); the casting out of the evil spirit at Philippi (16:16-18); the liberation from prison at the same place (16:25-34); the imparting of the Holy Ghost to disciples of the old school at Ephesus by the laying on of hands (19:1-7); the cures there wrought and castings out of evil spirits (19:11-12), the vengeance of the evil spirit who recognises indeed the superiority of Paul, but not that of other men (19:16); the giving up and burning of precious books at Ephesus (19:19); perhaps also the affair of Eutychus at Troas (20:7-12), and the details respecting Paul's sojourn at Melita (28:1-10).

We are here already a good distance along the road upon which a younger generation, full of admiration for its great men, yet not too historically accurate, is moving, setting itself to describe the lives of Peter, Paul, Thomas, John, and others, in the so-called apocryphal Acts, or, more particularly (Gnostic), "circuits" (Περίοδοι).

Luke also moves in the same direction, but with this difference, that his Paul (see Van Manen, *Paulus*, 1:164-169), under the influence of the current in which his spiritual life is lived, stands nearer again to Peter, yet in such a manner that it is still more impossible to present before one's mind an image of anything recorded of him among the often discrepant and mutually conflicting details, not a few of which are manifestly incorrect (id., 1:169-176).

The writer of the Acts of Paul never shows any acquaintance with epistles of Paul, however much one might expect the opposite when his way of thinking is taken into account. On the contrary, the "historical details" in the Epistles, or at least a good part of them, appear themselves to be taken from the Acts of Paul, since they are not always in agreement with what Luke relates in his second book, although they are manifestly speaking of the same things.

Luke must have modified, rearranged, supplemented, perhaps also in some cases more accurately preserved, what he and the writers of the epistles had read in the book consulted by them, a work lost to us, or, if you will, surviving in a kind of second edition as the Acts of the Apostles. In this lost Acts of Paul, Paul had become (in contrast to what, even by the admission of the journey-narrative, he really was) the hero of a reforming movement, the exponent of wholly new principles in the circle of those who wrought for the emancipation of Christianity from the bonds of Judaism and its development into a universal religion.

## 46. Home of Paulinism

Where that circle, under the patronage of Paul, must be looked for cannot be said with certainty. Probably it was in Syria, more particularly in Antioch; yet it may have been somewhere in Asia Minor. We may be practically certain, at all events, that it was not in Palestine; it was in an environment where no obstruction was in the first instance encountered from the Jews or, perhaps still worse, from the "disciples" too closely resembling them; where men as friends of gnosis, of speculation, and of mysticism, probably under the influence of Greek and, more especially, Alexandrian philosophy, had learned to cease to regard themselves as bound by tradition, and felt themselves free to extend their flight in every direction.

To avail ourselves of a somewhat later expression: it was among the heretics. The epistles first came to be placed on the list among the Gnostics. The oldest witnesses to their existence, as Meyer and other critics with a somewhat wonderful unanimity have been declaring for more than half a century, are Basilides, Valentinus, Heracleon. Marcion is the first in whom, as we learn from Tertullian, traces are to be found of an authoritative group of epistles of Paul. Tertullian still calls him "*haereticorum apostolus*" (*adv. Marc.* 3:5) and (addressing Marcion) "apostolus *vester*" (1:15).

## 47. Paulinism Characteristic of Epistles

Whencesoever coming, however, the Paulinism of the lost Acts of Paul and of our best authority for that way of thinking, our canonical Epistles of Paul, is not the "theology," the "system" of the historical Paul, although it ultimately came to be, and in most quarters still is, identified with it. It is the later development of a school, or, if the expression is preferred, of a circle, of progressive believers who named themselves after Paul and placed themselves as it were under his aegis. The Epistles explain this movement from different sides, apart from what some of them, by incorporating and working up older materials, tell us in addition as to its historical development and the varying contents of its doctrines.

> i. Romans, with its account of what the gospel, regarded as a religious doctrine, is (1:18-11:36), and of what those

who profess it are exhorted to (12-15:13), throws a striking light upon what Paulinism is, both dogmatically and ethically, for the Christian faith and life.

ii. 1 Cor. shows in a special way how deeply and in what sense Paulinism has at heart the practice of the Christian life, as regards, for example, parties and disputes within the church (1:10-3:23), the valid authority in it (4), purity of morals (5 and 6:12-20), the judging of matters of dispute between Christians (6:1-11), their mutual relations, such as those of the circumcised and the uncircumcised, of bondmen and freemen (7:18-24) the married and the unmarried life (8-11:1), the veiling of women (11:2-15 [11:2-11:16]), the love feasts (11:17-34), spiritual gifts (12-14), and the collection for the saints (16:1-4), along with which only one subject of a more doctrinal nature is treated: the resurrection (15).

iii. 2 Corinthians gives above all else the impression how the person and work of Paul in the circle addressed, or, rather, throughout the Christian world, had to be defended and glorified (1:3-7, 1:16, 10-13:10); and, in a passage introduced between its two main portions, how the manifestation of mutual love, by the gathering of collections for the saints, must not be neglected (8-9).

iv. Galatians gives us an earnest argument on behalf of Paul and the view of Christianity set forth by him, particularly his doctrine of justification by faith, not by the works of the law; as also for the necessity for a complete breach with Judaism.

v. In Ephesians it is the edification of "Pauline" Christians that comes most into prominence. So also in Philippians, although here we have also a bitter attack on the apostle's enemies, and, in close connection with this, a glorification of his person and work (3:1-4:1). In Colossians, along with edification and exhortation, the doctrinal significance of Christ is expatiated upon (1:13-22, 2:11-15); also that of

"Paul" (1:23-2:5); and an earnest warning is given against doctrinal errors (2:6-23).

vi. In 1 and 2 Thessalonians, respectively, the condition of those who have fallen asleep (1 Thess. 4:13-18) and the exact time of the parousia (5:1-11) on the one hand, and the things which may yet have to precede that event (2 Thess. 2:1-12), on the other, are discussed.

vii. The Pastoral Epistles occupy themselves chiefly with the various affairs of the churches within "Pauline" circles; Philemon with the relations which ought to subsist between slaves and their masters in the same circles.

Here we have variety enough, and many historical traits which, once arranged in proper order, can supply us with a conception of what Paul, through all the vicissitudes of earnest opposition and equally earnest support among Christians, finally became first in narrower, anon in wider circles, and at last in the whole Catholic world—the apostle (ο Απόστολος), the equal of Peter, or, strictly speaking, his superior.

## 48. History of Paulinism

At the outset we find Paul standing outside the circle of the Catholic church just coming into being, but held in honour by Marcion and his followers. Already however, Luke in virtue of the right he exercises of curtailing, expanding, modifying aught that may not suit his purpose in the material he has derived from other sources, has in Acts given "Paul" a position of pre-eminence.

Older fragments, whether of the nature of "acts" or of the nature of "epistles," that had passed into circulation under Paul's name were, in whole or in part, taken up into writings on a larger scale, and remodelled into what are now our canonical "Epistles of Paul." A Justin can still, it would seem, pass him over, although spiritually Justin stands very close to Paul and shows acquaintance with him. Irenaeus in his turn has no difficulty in using the Pauline group of Epistles, at least twelve of the thirteen—Philemon is not spoken of, nor is there as yet any word of Hebrews—as canonical, although not from predilection for their contents, but simply because he wishes to vanquish his great enemies, the Gnostics, with their own weapons. That in doing so he frequently had failed to understand "Paul" is clearly manifest (see Werner, *Der Paulinismus des Irenaeus*, 1889).

Tertullian advances along the path opened by Irenaeus. Without really having much heart for the Paul of the Pauline Epistles, he brings out the "apostle of the heretics" against the heretics, though, as regards "history," he holds to the older view that Christianity owed its diffusion among the nations to the activity of the Twelve. In association with these in their solitary greatness no one deserves for a moment to be mentioned, not even the historical Paul, unless, indeed, as their somewhat younger contemporary, "*posterior apostolus*," who might be regarded as having sat at their feet (*adv. Marc.* 4:2 52; see van Manen, *Paulus*, 2:262-276).

In the so-called Muratorian Canon, among the authoritative writings of the NT, thirteen epistles of Paul are enumerated. Apollonius, about the year 210, brings it against the Montanist Themiso as a particularly serious charge that some forty years previously he had ventured to write an epistle in imitation of the apostle (μιμουμενοσ τον Αποστολον; i.e., Paul; Eus. HE 5:18:5). In truth, from that time onwards, in orthodox circles no one doubted any longer the high authority of "Paul" the assumed writer of the thirteen (fourteen) epistles. It was only with regard to Hebrews that a few continued to hesitate for some time longer.

For our knowledge of Paulinism the thirteen epistles are of inestimable value. They are, when thus regarded, no less

important than they were when they were considered—all of
them, or some of them—as unimpeachable witnesses for the life
and activities, especially the Christian thoughts and feelings, of
the historical Paul, the only slightly younger contemporary of
Peter and other original disciples of Jesus.

## 49. Post-"Pauline" Epistles

In a complete study of Paulinism there come into consideration
also Hebrews, 1 Peter, James, and other writings which breathe
more or less the same spirit, or, as the case may be, take a
polemical attitude towards it.

> i. Hebrews, as being the expression of an interesting
> variation from the older Paulinism; a doctrinal treatise,
> rich in earnest exhortations, given forth as a "word of
> exhortation" in the form of an epistle of Paul, though not
> bearing his name.

> ii. 1 Peter, as being a remarkable evidence of attachment
> to "Paul" among people who know that the group of letters
> associated with his name is closed, although they desire to
> bear witness in his spirit; in point of fact, a letter of
> consolation written for those who stand exposed to
> persecution and suffering.

> iii. James, as an instance of seriously-meant imitation of a
> Pauline epistle, written by someone who had
> misunderstood and was seeking to controvert Paul's view
> of the connection between faith and works (2:14-26).

## 50. Apocryphal Epistles, Acts, etc.

On the other hand, there is a great deal that must be regarded
as the product of a later time, and, however closely associated
with the name of Paul, as lying beyond the scope of the present
article.

i. (a) Epistle to the Laodiceans.—Antiquity knew of such an epistle, alongside of (b) the Epistle *ad* Alexandrines, mentioned in the Muratorian Canon (63-65) with the words added "*Pauli nomine fictae ad haeresem Marcionis,*" "feigned in the name of Paul to the use of the heresy of Marcion." This Epistle to the Laodiceans, mentioned also in Jerome (*Vir.* 111. 5, and elsewhere) was very probably our Epistle of Paul to the Ephesians, just as that to the Alexandrians was probably our Epistle to the Hebrews, or, it may be, a Marcionite redaction of it.

(c) Another Epistle of Paul to the Laodiceans occurs in many Latin MSS of the NT, and in old printed editions of the NT; in Luther's Bible, Worms, 1529; in the Dutch of 1560 by L.D.K. (probably Leendert der Kinderen); in 1600, after a copy by Nicolaus Biestkens van Diest; in 1614, Dordrecht, Isaack Jansz. Canin; and in English, cp Harnack, ACL 1(1893) 33-37. See, further, Anger, *Ueber den Laodicenerbrie,* and Lightfoot, *Colossians* ×, who also gives a convenient summary of the views which have been held respecting this letter (Hatch). The writing is composed of NT words of Paul, probably to meet the demand for an epistle to the Laodiceans raised by Colossians 4:16, and actually dating from the fifth, perhaps even from the fourth century.

ii. An epistle from the Corinthians to Paul and the apostle's answer (= 3 Cor.) which is brought into connection with the epistle named in 1 Corinthians 5:9, were included in the Syrian Bible in the days of Aphraates and Ephraim, and centuries afterwards were still found in that of the Armenians.

They occur also in a MS of the Latin Bible dating from the fifteenth century and have been repeatedly printed, the best edition being that of Aucher (*Armenian and English Grammar,* 1819, p. 183). "An English translation will be found in Stanley, Epistles of St. Paul to the Corinthians, × (Hatch). There are German and French translations in Rinck (1823) and

Berger (1891). They appear to belong to the third century and are conjectured to have been written against the Bardesanites, originally in Greek or Syriac, perhaps as portions of the *Acta Pauli*. ×

iii. Fourteen epistles of Paul and Seneca are given in a number of later MSS; first named and cited by Jerome, VT 12, although hardly by that time read by very many.

The correspondence is reproduced in most editions of Seneca, e.g., ed. Haase, 1878, vol. iii. 476-481 and discussed by (among others) Funk, "*Der Briefwechsel des Paulus mit Seneca,*" *Theol. Quartalschr.*, 1867, p. 602; Lightfoot, *Philippians*, 327; Kreyher, *Seneca u. seine Beziehungen zum Christenthuni*, 1887; Harnack, ACL 1 763-765. Their genuineness is not for a moment to be thought of.

iv. Other special writings of a later date relating to Paul are found (apart from the Ebionite Acts of the Apostles already alluded to, mentioned by Epiphanius, *Haer.* 30:16, and the *Acta Pauli* = Παυλοω πραξεις [also lost] mentioned by Origen, perhaps identical with the work called *Pauli Praedicatio* in Pseudo-Cyprian) in the Acts of Peter and Paul; the Acts of Paul and Thecla; the Apocalypse of Paul; × [*Anabatikon Paulon*] mentioned in Epiphanius.

The Acts of Peter and Paul, as also those of Paul and Thecla, are printed in Tischendorf (*Acta Apostolorum Apocrypha denuo ediderunt* R. A. Lipsius et M. Bonnet, 1, 1891; the Revelation of Paul in Tischendorf (*Apocalypses Apocryphae*). [References to the literature of the Apocalypse of Paul in Lat. Syr. Gk. and Ar. will be found in Catalogue of Syr. MSS Univers. of Camb. (1901), × of all three by A. Walker, *The Apocryphal Gospels, Acts, and Revelations*, (1870).][11]

---

11. The best and most exhaustive discussion of the contents of these writings, alike with regard to Paul's life and activity, and with regard to his relation to Peter and other disciples of Jesus, though too exclusively under

## 51. Literature

"The literature which bears upon St. Paul is so extensive that a complete account of it would be as much beyond the compass of this article as it would be bewildering to its readers." So, rightly, Hatch at the close of his article Paul in *Ency. Brit.* ×, 1885.

    i. For the life of Paul Hatch cited A. Neander, Pflanzung, etc., ×

    ii. With regard to the theology of Paul, in addition to several of the works already named: ×

To these may be added C. C. Everett, *The Gospel of Paul*, 1893, and a number of other studies in books and periodicals; general works on Old Christianity, such as [W. R. Cassels] *Supernatural Religion*, 3 vols. 1875-1877; R. J. Knowling, *The Witness of the Epistles*, 1892; C. Weizsäcker, *Das Apostolische Zeitalter*), 1892, ET 1894-1895; J. B. Lightfoot, *Dissertations on the Apostolic Age*, 1892; F. J. A. Hort, *Judaistic Christianity*, 1898, and *The Christian Ecclesia*, 1898; O. Cone, *Paul: the Man, the Missionary, and the Teacher*, 1898; the various works on New Testament Introduction, such as those of Credner (1836); Reuss, 1874 ×; ET, 1884; Bleek-Mangold, ×); Hilgenfeld, 1875 ; B. Weiss, 1897(8) ; ET, 1880, i88g(2) ; G. Salmon, 1896(7); S. Davidson, 1894); H.T. Holtzmann, 1892(3); W. Bruckner, 1890; A. Jülicher, 1901); Th. Zahn, 1900(2); the commentaries on Acts and the Pauline Epistles, such as those in the later editions of Meyer, in the *Hand-Commcntar zum* × 1899; Acts in 1901), or in the International Critical Commentary (in which Romans [1895], Ephesians and Colossians [1897], Philippians and Philemon [1897], have

the influence of the Tübingen construction of history (see van Manen, *Th.T.*, 1888, pp. 94-101), is given by R. A. Lipsius in his standard work *Die apokryphen Apostelgeschichten u. Apostellegenden*, 1883-1890 (reviewed in *Th.T.*, 1883, pp. 377-393 ; 1884, pp. 598-611 ; 1888, pp. 93-108 ; 1891, pp. 450-451), with which cp also the Prolegomena to the second edition of the *Acta* i, 1891, and × 1664-666.

already appeared); C. J. Ellicott, *Crit. and Exeget. Comm. on St. Paul's Epistles* [except Romans and 2 Corinthians], 1889-1890, etc., and cp the bibliographies in ACTS and the separate articles on the several epistles in this work. For advanced criticism see further the discussions already referred to (34) by Bruno Bauer, Pierson, Naber, Loman, Steck, Volter, and van Manen.

The student who wishes further information upon the Pauline literature of recent years is recommended to consult the sections *Apostelgeschichte und apostolisches Zeitalter* and *Paulus* under the heading Literature of the New Testament in the *Theologisches Jahresbericht* (vol. xix., edited by Holtzmann and Kruger, was published in 1900), which regularly, for the last nineteen years, has given a survey of the principal publications mainly German, but not to the exclusion of foreign works of the preceding year. A selection of the most recent literature relating to Paul, which is to be from time to time revised and supplemented, will be found in a list of the best books for general New Testament study at the present time in *The Biblical World*, July 1900, pp. 53-80. Cp *Theological and Semitic Literature* for the year 1900, a Supplement to the *American Journal of Theology*, April 1901, especially the *NT and The First Three Centuries*, pp. 35-49.

# The Epistle to Philemon

*There is a surprising mixture of singular and plural both in the persons speaking and in the persons addressed. This double form points at once to some peculiarity in the composition of the epistle. It is not a style that is natural to anyone who is writing freely and untrammelled, whether to one person or to many.*

## 1. History

The Epistle to Philemon (*pros Philêmona*; so Tish. WH with ℵ, A and other MSS, but fuller superscriptions also occur mainly to indicate that the Epistle was written by the apostle Paul and at Rome) is the name of a short composition which has come down to us from antiquity as the thirteenth in the NT collection of "Epistles of Paul." Tertullian (AM 5.21) is the first who expressly mentions the writing as included by Marcion among the ten epistles of Paul accepted by him, adding the remark that this was the only epistle whose brevity availed to protect it against the falsifying hands of the heretic (*soli huic epistolae brevitas sua profuit ut falsarias manus Marcionis evaderet*).

It retained its position undisturbed, although now and then (as, for example, by Jerome) its right to do so had to be vindicated against some (*plerique ex veteribus*) who thought the honour too great for an epistle having no doctrinal importance. Others did not fail to praise this commendatory letter of the apostle on behalf of a runaway slave as a precious gem showing forth Paul's tenderness and love for all his spiritual children, even those who were the least of them if judged by the standard of the world.

F. C. Baur was the first (*Pastoralbriefe*, 1835; *Paulus*, 1845) who found himself led by his one-sided preoccupation with the four "principal epistles" to raise difficulties with regard to the Epistle to Philemon. Its close relationship to Ephesians, Philippians, Colossians, especially the last-named, which he found himself unable to attribute to Paul, was too much for him, although in this case his "tendency-criticism" failed him. The considerations he urged in addition were certain *hapax legomena*, the romantic colour of the narrative, the small probability of the occurrence, some plays upon words and the perhaps symbolical character of Onesimus—points which, all of them, can be seen set forth in detail *Paulus*, Vol 2, 88-94.[12]

Those who did not adopt the Tübingen position in its entirety, but endeavoured to rescue at least some of the "minor" Pauline epistles—such critics as Hilgenfeld and S. Davidson—either argued for the genuineness or sought a way out of the difficulty of maintaining its genuineness as a whole by a hypothesis of interpolations. So Holtzmann, *ZWT*, 1873, 428-41 (with regard to vv. 4-6, controverted by Steck, *JPT*, 1891, 570-584), and W. Brückner, *Chron. Reihenfolge*, 1890, 200-3 (as regards vv. 5f., controverted by Haupt, Komm., 1897, 10).

The conservative school carried on its opposition to Baur and his followers with greater or less thoroughness in various

---

12. Thorough-going disciples of the Tübingen school followed in the footsteps of their leader although with occasional modifications in detail. Rovers (*Nieuw Testamentische letterkunde*, 1888) saw in the epistle a concrete illustration of what is laid down in Colossians as to the relation between masters and slaves. Pfleiderer (*Paulinismus*, 1890, 42f), although impressed by the simplicity and naturalness of motive of Philemon, could not get over its agreement with Colossians, and, taking refuge in the consideration that Onesimus seemed to betray an allegorical character, ended by regarding the epistle as a symbolical illustration of the relation between Christian slaves and their masters as set forth in Colossians 3:22-4:1. Similarly, Weizsäker (*Apos. Zeitalter*, 1892, 545) who found himself compelled in view of Colossians to regard Philemon "as an illustrative example of a new doctrine bearing on the Christian life, the allegorical character of which is already shown by the very name of Onesimus."

introductions and commentaries, the most recent being that of M. R. Vincent (*Comm.*, 1897, 160) who, after briefly summing up the objections, proceeds: "It is needless to waste time over these. They are mostly fancies. The external testimony and the general consensus of critics of nearly all schools are corroborated by the thoroughly Pauline style and diction and by the exhibition of those personal traits with which the greater epistles have made us familiar."

So also Zahn (*Einleitung*, 1900, Vol. 1, 322), with the usual pathos, and adding a couple of notes, observes: "That this epistle also, with its fullness of material which could not have been invented (note 7), should without any support from tradition and without any adequate reason whatever having been suggested for its invention, have been declared to be spurious, does not deserve more than a passing mention (note 8)."

On the other hand, the criticism which refused to accept as an axiom the doctrine of the four "principal epistles" of Paul (see PAUL, §§ 30, 32, 34) did not make itself much heard. Bruno Bauer was quite silent, and its other representatives contented themselves, as a rule, with the declaration—sometimes more, sometimes less, fully elaborated—that we do not possess any epistles of Paul at all.  R. Steck wrote the treatise already referred to (*JPT*, 1891) in which he concentrated attention upon the double character of the epistle, as a private letter and as a writing apparently intended for the Pauline church; repeated some of the objections of Baur and others; maintained that the ultimate design of the author was to "present vividly" the apostle's attitude to the slavery question, as seen in 1 Corinthians 7:21f.; and took special pains to emphasize the view that the unknown writer had made use, in his composition, of a correspondence between Pliny and Sabinianus preserved in the *Epistles* of Pliny (9.21-24) to which Grotius had long ago called attention (see below, § 4). Van

Manen (*Handleidung*) devoted two sections to a statement of his views as to Philemon.

## 2. Contents

Paul a prisoner of Christ Jesus and brother Timothy, so we learn from the epistle, address themselves with words of blessing to the persons named (vv. 1, 2a, 3), or otherwise Paul alone does so to Philemon (2b). Next Paul goes on to say to Philemon that he thanks God always for his well-known love and his exemplary faith (vv. 4-7), upon which he, as Paul *presbutês* (the aged) and a prisoner of Christ Jesus, beseeches him to receive his son Onesimus, whom he sends to him, though he would willingly have kept him beside himself, as a beloved brother (vv. 8-16).

Whatsoever expenses may have been incurred the apostle promises to defray (vv. 17-20). He might enjoin; but he trusts to the goodwill of Philemon of whose hospitality he hopes ere long to be able to partake (vv. 21-22a) through the mediating prayers of all of them (*dia tôn proseuchôn humôn*, 22b). Next he conveys to him the greetings of Epaphras, his fellow-prisoner in Christ Jesus, and of Mark, Aristarchus, Demas, Luke, his fellow-workers (vv. 23, 24), and the epistle closes with a word of blessing upon all (v. 25).

On the assumption of the correctness of the received tradition regarding the canonical epistles of Paul, and of the identity of the Onesimus of Philemon 10 with the person named in Col 4:9, the statement usually met with is that Onesimus, a runaway slave, Christianised by Paul and sent back by the apostle to his master with our present "letter to Philemon," originally belonged to Colossæ, where also lived his master Philemon, a man of wealth inasmuch as he owned a slave (!), who, either from Ephesus or perhaps at Ephesus itself (for we cannot be certain that the apostle ever visited Colossæ), had been converted by Paul.

Anyone, however, who will allow the epistle to tell its own story must receive from it a somewhat different impression. There is in it no information as to who Philemon was—he is mentioned in the NT nowhere else and is known only by later tradition—nor as to where he was living when Paul, according to Philemon 10-20 sent back to him his former slave Onesimus, after he had Christianised him and so made him a brother of the master who could be spoken of as a beloved fellow-worker of Paul and Timothy, owing his conversion to Christianity to the former (vv. 1, 19).

The reader is not further advanced in his knowledge when Philemon is named by the tradition of a later age as a presbyter, a bishop, a deacon, or even an apostle, and Onesimus is reputed to have been bishop of Ephesus. For the unpreoccupied reader this little document of ancient Christianity represents itself in various lights, now as a letter written by Paul and Timothy to Philemon, Apphia, Archippus, and a domestic church (vv. 1, 2a, 3, 22b, 25), now as written by Paul alone to Philemon (vv. 2b, 4-22a, 23, 24).

Sister Apphia and Archippus, the fellowsoldier of Paul and Timothy according to v. 2, are nowhere else met with in the NT, unless Archippus be, as many suppose, identical with the person named in Colossians 4:17—which may or may not be the case. That Apphia and Archippus should be respectively the wife and the son of Philemon, as many are ready to assume, is a gratuitous supposition which has no solid ground, and has against it the strangeness of the collocation "Apphia the sister, Archippus our fellow soldier and the church in the house that is yours, Philemon (*sou*)."

## 3. Composition

There is a surprising mixture of singular and plural both in the persons speaking and in the persons addressed. This double form points at once to some peculiarity in the composition of the epistle. It is not a style that is natural to anyone who is writing freely and untrammelled, whether to one person or to many. Here, as throughout the discussion, the constantly recurring questions as to the reason for the selection of the forms, words, expressions adopted find their answer in the observation that the epistle was written under the influence of a perusal of "Pauline" epistles, especially of those to the Ephesians and the Colossians.

Take the examples in which one or more persons near Paul are named as the writers: Colossians 1:1 as Philemon 1, "Brother Timothy." Again, why does Paul call himself in Philemon 9 *desmios Christou Iēsou*, and not as elsewhere *doulos* or *apostolos*? The answer is found in Ephesians 3:1; 4:1.

What is meant by the inclusion of other names besides that of Philemon among the addressees? For an answer see 1 Corinthians 1:2; 2 Corinthians 1:1. Archippus comes from Colossians 4:17, the epithets *sunergos* and *sunstratiōtēs* from Philippians 2:25, the "church which in the house of" from Colossians 4:15, the prayer in v. 3 from Romans 1:7; 1 Corinthians 1:3; 2 Corinthians 1:2; Galatians 1:3; Ephesians 1:2; or Philippians 1:2, the thanksgiving and commemoration of v. 4 from Romans 1:8, 9; 1 Corinthians 1:4; Ephesians 1:16, 5:20; Philippians 1:3; Colossians 1:3.

The continual hearing of Philemon's love and faith towards all the saints (v. 5) comes from Ephesians 1:15; Colossians 1:4, the expression hon *egennēsa* (v. 10) from 1 Corinthians 4:15; cf. Galatians 4:19. The sending of Onesimus in vv. 10f. comes from Colossians 4:8 or Ephesians 6:21f., although in these passages it is Tychicus, a free man, the phrase *pros hōran* of v. 15 from 2 Corinthians 7:8; Galatians 2:5, the "brother beloved" and "servant of the Lord" of v. 16 from Colossians 4:7, 9, the "reckoning" of v. 18 from Philippians 4:15, the "I, Paul" in v. 19 from Galatians 5:2, Ephesians 3:1, the phrase "with my hand" from 1 Corinthians 16:21, Galatians 6:11, Colossians 4:18, the names in vv. 23f. from Colossians 1:7, 4:10, 12, 14, although now Epaphras takes the place of Aristarchus, "the fellow-prisoner," as Onesimus a slave takes the place of the free man, the "brother beloved," in Colossians 4:9. The final benediction comes from Philippians 4:23.

## 4. Authorship

Such phenomena are adverse to the supposition that Paul can have written the epistle. The thing is possible indeed, but certainly not probable. Rather may we say that no one could repeat himself so or allow himself to be restricted to such a degree by the limitations of his own previous writings. Nor can we think of Paul, however often we are told that he did so, as having put a private letter, after the manner here observed, into the form of a church epistle.

We need not pause to conjecture what was the relation between him and Philemon, or where the latter had his home—whether in Colossæ, Ephesus, Laodicea, somewhere else in Asia Minor, or perhaps even somewhere beyond its limits; nor yet as to the circumstances and date of his conversion by the apostle, or as to the reason why the runaway slave Onesimus, who as yet was no Christian, should have betaken himself precisely to Paul the prisoner—at Caesarea, shall we say, or at Rome?

The romantic element in the story does not need to be insisted on. It is to be put to the credit of the writer who may very well perhaps have made use of the story which has been so often compared with it (see above; Pliny, *Epist.* 9.21-24). A freedman (*libertus*) of Sabinianus makes his escape and seeks refuge with Pliny, who was known to him as a friend of Sabinianus who also lives in Rome, whereupon Pliny sends him back with a commendatory letter in which he pleads for the runaway from the standpoint of pure humanity.

Our unknown author makes the freedman into a slave whom he brings into contact, at an immense distance from his home, with Paul, Philemon's spiritual father, who converts Onesimus also, and thereupon sends him back with a plea for the slave from the standpoint of Christian faith and Christian charity. He has thus presented us with an ideal picture of the relations which, in his judgment, that is according to the view of Pauline Christians, ought to subsist between Christian slaves and their masters, especially when the slaves have in some respect misconducted themselves, as for example by secretly quitting their master's service. One might also add that he thus has given a practical commentary on such texts as Colossians 3:22-25, Ephesians 6:5-9, 1 Corinthians 7:21-22 (see Steck).

The author's name and place remain unknown. He is to be looked for within the circle from which the "Epistles of Paul" to the Ephesians, Philippians, and Colossians emanated; nor can Philemon be much later in date.

Probably it was written in Syria or, it may be, in Asia Minor about 125-130. In any case, later than Paul's death about 64 CE, and at a time when men had begun to publish letters under his name, when also they had formed the habit of adorning him with titles of honour such as "bondman (δεσμιος) of Christ Jesus," "aged" (πρεσβυτης), "being such an one as Paul. etc." (τοιουτος ον ος Παυλος, κ.τ.λ.). The "I, Paul" (*egô Paulos*) implies a name of high authority (v. 19), when further the Christology of the church had already so far developed that it was possible to use convertibly the designations Christ, Jesus, Christ Jesus, Jesus Christ, and to speak of him as the fountain of grace and peace as God himself is (vv. 3, 25) and as "the Lord" who is the centre towards whom all the thinking and striving of believers is directed (vv. 3, 5-9, 20, 23). On the other hand, it is of course earlier than Tertullian's *Marcion*.

## 5. Value

If the epistle can no longer be regarded as a direct product of
Paul's spirit, so full of Christian charity, it nevertheless
remains to show by an example what Christianity at the time of
its composition had been able to achieve as a guiding and
sanctifying force in the case of certain special problems of life,
and what the several relations were amongst believers of that
time.

# The Epistle to the Philippians

*Thorough criticism has no other course open to it but that of condemning any method which ties the hands in a matter of scientific research. Before everything else it demands freedom.*

There fall to be considered two Old-Christian documents—those bearing the names of Paul and Polycarp respectively.

## Paul's Epistle

### 1. History of Criticism

The first of the two constitutes one of the NT group of "Epistles of Paul" (*epistolai Paulou*), "to Philippians" (*pros Philippêsious*) being the shortest form of the title. Down to 1845—or, shall we say, to 1835?—no one had doubted its right to this position. Men saw in it an expression, greatly to be prized, of the apostle's love for a church which he had founded, written while he was languishing in prison, probably in Rome, and sent by the hand of Epaphroditus who had been the bearer of material and spiritual refreshment for Paul, had fallen sick, and was now on the point of returning to his home in Philippi. The only point on which doubt seemed possible was as to the place of composition—whether Caesarea or Rome.

Paulus (1799), Böttger (1837), Thiersch, and Böhmer declared for Caesarea; elsewhere the voice was unanimous: "the apostle's testament; written in Rome" (Holtzmann). "The testament of the apostle and the most epistolary of all epistles." Then came F. C. von Baur with his thesis that only four of the epistles of Paul (Galatians, 1 and 2 Corinthians, Romans) could be accepted as indisputably genuine—a thesis that he employed as a criterion in determining the genuineness of all the rest (*Die sogennante Pastoralbriefe*, 1835, p. 79; *Paulus*, 1845). Tried by this standard Philippians had, in Baur's view, to be at once rejected (*Paulus*, 458-475).

The replies of Lünemann (1847), B. Brückner (1848), Ernesti (1848 and 1858), de Wette (1848), and others were not effective. Indeed, the support given to Baur by Schwegler (1846), Planck (1847), Köstlin (1850), Volkmar (1856) did not advance the question more than did Baur's own reply to Ernesti and others published in *Theol. Jahrbb.* 1849 and 1852, and afterwards incorporated in *Paulus* (1866-7), 2.50-88. Hoekstra (*Th.T.*, 1875) and Holsten (*JPG*, 1875-6) sought to base the Tübingen position as to Philippians upon the solid foundation of a more strict and searching exegesis, rejecting all that in their judgment could not be relevantly urged, and adding such other arguments as seemed to them to have weight.

Both these critics. however, still started from the genuineness of the four "principal epistles." So Hitzig, Hinsch, Straatman, Kneucker, Biedermann, and various others ranged themselves more or less decidedly upon the same side.

At the same time, not merely among thoroughgoing apologists, but also among friends of the Tübingen school, such as Hilgenfeld, Schenkel, Pfleiderer, Lipsius, Hatch (*Ency. Brit.*, 9/1885), S. Davidson (*Intr.* 3/1894), and others, there were very many who found themselves unable to accept the result of Baur's criticism so far as the Epistle to the Philippians was concerned. Without realising it very clearly, both advocates and opponents of the genuineness found their stumbling-block, from the beginning, in the axiom of the genuineness of the "principal epistles" of Paul. Of necessity, however closely attached to Baur and his school, or however little bound to one another by common principles, they at once fell into two groups—each of them, in itself considered, most singularly constituted—which felt compelled to maintain or to reject the Pauline origin of our epistle, in the one case because it did not appear to differ from the principal epistles as a whole more than did these from each other, in the other case because assuredly, whether in few or in many respects, it seemed when compared with them to breathe another spirit, and in language and style to betray another hand.

A way of escape has been sought—but unsuccessfully—by means of the suggestion, first made by le Moyne in 1685 and afterwards renewed by Heinrichs (1803), Paulus (1812), Schrader (1830). and Ewald, that the epistle was not originally a unity.[13]

A newer way, at first allowed to pass unnoticed, was shown by Bruno Bauer (*Kritik der paulinischen Briefe*, 1852, 110-117; cf. *Christus und die Cäsaren*, 1877, 373f.), when he determined to make his judgment upon this epistle independently of that upon the four "principal epistles," his main conclusion being that it was not earlier than the middle of the second century. He was followed, so far as his leading principle was concerned, by Loman, Steck, and van Manen. Loman, however, did not go more closely into the question of the origin of Philippians. Steck intimated his adhesion in an incidental statement in his *Galatians* (p. 374) that in Philippians we hear some "echoes" of the controversy between

---

13. C.H. Weisse (*Beitrag z. Kritik der Paul. Briefe*, 1867) saw in it, besides some later insertions, two epistles: Phil 1:1-3:1a and the fragment 3:1b-4:23. Similarly Hausrath (*NTliche Zeitgeschichte*, 3, 398f) saw one letter written after the first hearing, and a second some weeks later after the gift of money from Philippi. W. Brückner (*Chron. Reihenfolge*, 1890) assumed various interpolations; Völter (Th.T., 1892) a genuine and a spurious epistle which have been fused together in that which we now possess. Names and titles will be found more fully in Holtzmann, *Einleitung* (1892), 266-272; S. Davidson, *Introduction* (1894); Vincent, *Commentary* (1897); Zahn, *Einleitung* (1900), 1, 369-400; and other writers of introductions and commentaries.

Paulinism and the older party of the followers of Jesus. (Van Manen's view was set forth in his *Handleiding*, 3, §§ 34, 36).

Thorough criticism has no other course open to it but that of condemning any method which ties the hands in a matter of scientific research. Before everything else it demands freedom. Exegesis must not be content to base itself on results of criticism that have been arrived at in some other field; rather is it the part of exegesis to provide independent data which may serve as a foundation for critical conclusions. The Epistle to the Philippians, like all other Old-Christian writings, requires to be read and judged entirely apart and on its own merits, independently of any other Pauline epistles, before anything can be fitly said as to its probable origin.

## 2. What Philippians Seems to Be

The writing comes before us as a letter, not of course of the same type as those commonly written at the period, of which we have recently received so many examples in the *Oxyrhynchus Papyri*, but as a letter of the sort that we know from the New Testament, and especially from the Pauline group; a letter, to judge from the opening sentence, written by Paul and Timothy, but, to judge from all that follows, by Paul alone. In it we find Paul speaking, as a rule, as if he were a free man, yet sometimes, particularly in 1:7-17, as if he were a prisoner.

He is full of sympathetic interest in those whom he is addressing. He tells them that his thoughts are continually about them and their excellences (1:3-11; 2:12), how he yearns to see them once more (1:8, 26; 2:24, 26), how they are properly speaking the sole object for which he lives, his joy and his crown (1:24; 4:1).

The epistle purports to be addressed to all the saints in Christ Jesus at Philippi with the bishops and deacons (1:1; 4:5), known and loved brothers, disciples, and friends of the apostle; still, the impression it gives is rather as if it had been written for a wider circle of readers, among whom the Philippians play no other part than that of representing the excellent Christians addressed, who nevertheless required to be spoken to seriously about many and various things that demanded their unremitting attention.

## 3. Contents

The writer, as Paul, declares his thankfulness to God for the fidelity of his readers to the gospel, and his earnest yearning after them all and their continued spiritual growth (1:3-11). He refers to the misfortunes that have recently happened to him and to that which in all probability lies before him, pointing out how his bonds have served to promote the cause of Christ both amongst unbelievers and amongst the brethren, and how Christ to his great joy is being preached, whatever be the reasons and however diverse be the ways; how he is in a strait between his desire to be released and his desire to go on with life, whilst in any case hoping to be able to glorify Christ in his body (1:12-26).

Next, he exhorts his readers, whether he be present or absent, and especially in the latter case, to let their manner of life be worthy of the gospel of Christ, after the example of him who, being in the form of God, had humbled himself by taking the form of a bondservant, being found in fashion as a man, and becoming obedient even to the death of the cross (1:27-1:18).

He then proceeds to speak of his intention to send Timothy—joint author of the epistle, according to 1:1—whom he highly commends, and Epaphroditus his "brother," "fellow-worker" and "fellow-soldier," and at the same time the "messenger" (*apostolos*) and "minister" (*diakonos*) of the Philippians to the need of Paul. Epaphroditus has been sick nigh unto death, and sore troubled because they had heard he was sick, and yet he is recommended to the Philippians as if he were a stranger (2:19-30).

The writer, as Paul, goes on, abruptly, to a vigorous onslaught on his enemies, prides himself upon his Jewish birth, glories in his conversion, describes his unremitting effort towards the Christian goal, and exhorts to imitation of his example. For those whom he addresses he is himself is a "type," his conversation a "conversation in heaven" (3:1-4:1).

Lastly, comes a new series of exhortations, to Euodia and Syntyche, Syzygus and all the other brethren, to conduct themselves in all things in accordance with the word and example of Paul who is addressing them (4:2-9); an expression of thanks for the gift, received from them by the hand of Epaphroditus, which has recalled the memory of previous kindnesses, and has been welcome at this time, although not indispensable (4:10-20); greetings to and from all the saints, and a benediction (4:21-23).

## 4. Difficulties

Some things here are certainly not easily intelligible or very logical, whether we regard the form or the substance. We may point, for example, to the unusual although genuinely "Pauline" "Grace to you and peace from God our Father and (the) Lord Jesus Christ" in the *exordium* (1:2), and "Now unto our God and Father be the glory for ever and ever, Amen" at the close (4:20), followed by the prayer "The grace of our Lord Jesus Christ be with your spirit" (4:23) instead of the well-known customary formula of salutation and greeting. The address, moreover, to "all the saints of Christ Jesus at Philippi, with the bishops and deacons" (1:1) seriously raises the question, Who are they? Where do they live?

Contrast, too, the double authorship (Paul and Timothy) of the epistle as seen in 1:1 with the fact that from 1:2 onwards Paul alone speaks and in 2:19 speaks of Timothy as if he had nothing to do with the epistle. Observe also the peculiarly exaggerated manner in which the Philippians are addressed, as if they and they alone were by way of exception Christians, worthy to absorb the apostle's every thought, and as if it was for them alone that he lived and endured, and how, once more, towards the end (4:5) he names them in a singularly lofty tone as "ye Philippians." How he again and again praises himself, holds himself up as a pattern, as the best example that can be given for the imitation of his disciples and friends: not only when he speaks so ecstatically of his thanksgivings and prayers, the significance of his sufferings and possible death, the tie between him and his present or absent readers (1:2-30; 2:1, 12, 16f., 27f.), but also when he boasts of his pure Hebrew descent, his faith, his unceasing effort to be perfect, and to walk as an example (3:5-21; 4:9-14).

Note how the writer salutes *"every* saint in Christ Jesus" and sends greetings from *"all* the saints, especially those that are of Caesar's household" (4:21f), he being a prisoner yet apparently in free communication with the people of the Praetorium, the imperial guard in Rome to whose charge he has been committed (1:7, 13f., 17). Consider how impossible it is to picture clearly to oneself his true relation to the supposed readers at Philippi, the circumstances by which he and they are surrounded, the occasion for writing or sending the epistle, unless a considerable part of its contents be left out of account.

All is confused and unintelligible as long as one thinks of it as an actual letter written in all simplicity and sent off by Paul the prisoner at Rome to his old friends at Philippi after he has been comforted and refreshed by their mission of Epaphroditus to him. Wherefore, in that case, the bitter attack and the self-glorification so intimately associated with it (4:2-21)? Wherefore the Christological digression (2:6-11), with the substance of which (on the assumed data) one might presume the reader to have been already long familiar? Why the proposal to send Timothy "shortly" (*taxeôs*), whilst yet the writer himself hopes to come "shortly," and Epaphroditus is just upon the point of setting out (2:19, 24f.)?

Could not Epaphroditus, if necessary by letter, have sent the wished-for information touching the Philippians which is spoken of in 2:19? What was Epaphroditus in reality? a fellow-worker of Paul? Or a messenger of the friendly Philippians (2:25)? Why did he need to be warmly recommended to the Philippians as if he were a stranger, though they had already been full of solicitude on account of the illness from which he has now happily recovered (2:26-30)? How can this give occasion for the exhortation to hold "such" in honour (2:30)?

Even Euodia and Syntyche, Syzygus and Clement (4:2f), simple though they seem, have long been the subjects of various perplexing questions. Who were they? symbolical or real persons? In what relation did they stand to one another, to Paul, to the community addressed? Why the reminiscence of what Philippi had previously done for the apostle (4:15f.)? Only to give him an opportunity to say that he valued the good-will of the givers more than their gift (4:17)?

## 5. Not a Letter

The solution of these and other riddles of a like nature raised by the Epistle lies in the recognition that it is not really a letter, in the proper sense of that word (see above, § 2), but an edifying composition in the form of a letter written by Paul to the church of Philippi and intended to stir up and quicken its readers. Or rather, let us say, its hearers; for epistles of this sort were designed first and foremost to be read in the religious meetings of the congregation.

No more precise determination of the occasion for the composition and sending of the epistle—such as is usually sought in the receipt of the gift alluded to (for the first time) in

4:10-18 (cf. 2:25, 30)—can be given. The writer knows the proper form of a Pauline epistle, and he follows it without troubling himself as to whether everything that he says exactly fits its place or not.

Hence his naming of Timothy as joint writer of the Epistle (1:1) although he makes no further mention of him, apart from 2:19, 23, where he speaks of him as if he were a third person. Hence, too, his vague expression "all the saints in Christ Jesus at Philippi" and the strange addition, explicable only from 1 Corinthians 1:2 and 2 Corinthians 1:1 "*With* the bishops and deacons" (1:1), his benedictions (1:2; 4:23), his greetings (4:21f.), his thanksgiving for, and high praise of, the church he is addressing, which yet has to be admonished with such earnestness; his exaltation of Paul and his relation to "the whole Praetorian Guard and all the rest" (1:13), his intercourse with them that are of Caesar's household (4:22); his praise of Timothy (2:20-22), of Epaphroditus and of the always attentive Philippians (2:25-30; 4:10-18); in a word, everything that strikes the reader as strange and perplexing as long as he is endeavouring to regard the Epistle as a genuine letter of Paul to the church he had founded at Philippi.

His "Philippians" are ideal Christians of the good old times to which the living generation may acceptably have its attention directed, and at the same time they are the "you" amongst whom are found faults and shortcomings, and even "dogs," "evil workers," and "concision" (3:2). The aim of the writer is no other than to edify, to incite to patience and perseverance by pointing to the example of Paul and others, including the church addressed, with its illustrious past.

## 6a. Composition

The author is acquainted with the canonical Epistles to the Romans, the Corinthians, the Galatians, perhaps also the Ephesians, as is shown by the "parallel" pass-words and allusions, to which defenders as well as assailants of the "genuineness" are accustomed to point in order to prove either the identity of the writer with the author of the "principal epistles" or his dependence on those writings. A careful examination makes it evident that many of the phenomena can be accounted for only by imitation.[14]

---

14. For example: the naming of Timothy (1:1) as a joint writer of the epistle although its further contents show that he was not so (cf. 2 Cor 1:1); the expression "with the bishops and deacons," alongside all of the saints at Philippi (1:1; cf. 1 Cor 1:2; 2 Cor 1:1); the expression "Jesus Christ" in 1:2 after "Christ Jesus" in v. 1 (cf. Rom 1:7; 1 Cor 1:3; 2 Cor 1:2; Gal 1:3; Eph 1:2); the calling of God as a witness of the sincerity of Paul's desire towards his readers (1:8; cf. Rom 1:9); the expression "test the things that differ" (*dokimazein to diaferonta*, 1:10), elsewhere only in Rom 2:18 (cf. 12:2); the bonds (*hoi desmoi*) of the prisoner, who nevertheless seems to walk at liberty (cf. *ho desmois*, Eph 3:1); the strange word (and therefore unexplained by *elpis*) "expectation" (*apokaradokia*) in 1:20, elsewhere only in Rom 8:19; the great importance attached, without any apparent reason, to Paul's coming (1:26; cf. Rom 1:10-13).

In addition, the expression "the same love, etc." (*tēn autēn agapēn...*) in 2:3-4 as compared with the exhortation, originally standing by itself, "to mind the same thing" (*to auto fronein*) cf. 2 Corinthians 13:11; Romans 12:16; the use of such words as *morphē* ("form"), *arpagmos* ("robbery," or "a thing to be "grasped"), *isa* ("equality"), *kenousthai* ("empty himself"), *huperupsoun* ("greatly exalted") in 2:6-11, even though perhaps not borrowed from our existing Pauline epistles; the *likeness* of men (2:7), cf. the *likeness* of sinful flesh in Romans 8:3; the words in 2:10f. borrowed from the OT in accordance not with the text of Is 45:23 LXX but with that of Rom 14:11; the stringing together of purely Pauline expressions (such as *hōste*, *hupēkousate, pollō mallon, hē parousia*, and *hē apousia mou*) in 2:12 for which no reason is apparent from the context; the echo of Romans 7:18 in 2:12f.; the expression "to run in vain," "to labour in vain," "praise the day of Christ" in 2:16 (cf. Gal 2:2; 4:11; 2 Cor 1:14).

Also the sending of Timothy and the praise accorded to him in 2:19-22 (cf. 1 Cor 4:17; 16:10); the assurance in 2:24, very strange in the connection in which it occurs, that the writer himself will speedily come (cf. 1 Cor 4:19); the "supposed to be necessary" and "speedy" sending of Epaphroditus in 2:25, 28 (cf. 2 Cor 9:5; 8:22); the unintelligible imperative (*prosdechesthe*) in

Perhaps the special features connected with Paul's sojourn as a prisoner in Rome, as also the allusion to succour previously received by him from the Philippians according to 4:5f., may be both borrowed from some written source; if this be so, the source in question cannot, in view of the discrepancies, be the canonical book of Acts, but must be rather a book of "Acts of Paul" which underlies it (see Van Manen, "Pauline Epistles," § 37).

## 6b. Not Patchwork

However many the traces of the writer's use of earlier materials, it does not seem advisable, and certainly in no case is it necessary, to regard his work as a chance or deliberate combination of two or more epistles or portions of epistles. The epistle as a whole does not present the appearance of patchwork. Rather does it show unity of form; we find a letter with a regular beginning and ending (1:1f., 4:20-23); a thanksgiving at the outset for the many excellences of the persons addressed (1:3-12; cf. Rom 1:8-12; 1 Cor 1:4-9) not withstanding the sharp rebukes that are to be administered later; personalia; exhortations relating to the ethical and religious life; all mingled together yet not without regard to a certain order.

---

2:19, with reference to the highly appreciated Epaphroditus (cf. Rom 16:2); the deviation after "such" (*toioutoi*) in 2:30 (cf. *ta auta* in 3:1) otherwise than as referring to what occurred elsewhere in some previous passage in the group of epistles to which this originally belonged; the keenness of the attack in 3:2-6, 19, which is fully in harmony with much in 2 Corinthians 10-13 and Galatians, but not with the present epistle; the unintelligibleness of the assurance "for we are the circumcision" in 3:3, so long as we do not bear in mind such words as those in Romans 2:25, 28f.; the necessity for explanation of "glorifying in Christ Jesus and not trusting in the flesh" (*kauxômenoi en Christou "Iêsou kai ouk en sarki pepoithotes*) in 3:3, by referring to such texts as Romans 2:17, 23; 11:1; 2 Corinthians 11:21-23; Galatians 1:13f., and so forth.

Here and there some things may be admitted to interrupt the steady flow of the discourse; 3:1 or 3:1b raises the conjecture of a new beginning; the "things" spoken of here are not different from those which we meet with elsewhere in other Pauline epistles—even in Romans, 1 and 2 Corinthians, Galatians. There also, just as here, we repeatedly hear a change of tone, and are conscious of what seems to be a change of spirit. Yet even apart from this, to lay too great stress upon the spiritual mood which expresses itself in 3:2-6 as contrasted with that of 1:3-11 or, on the whole, of 1-2, would be to forget what we can read in 1:15-17; 2:21 and the calm composure shown in chs. 3f.

No unmistakable trace can be shown of conjunction or amalgamation of two or more pieces of diverse origin, apart from what admits of explanation from use having been made of existing writings—say, the reading of certain Pauline epistles. Rather does everything, even that which has been borrowed, reach the paper through the individual brain and pen of the writer. Witness the unity of language and style which becomes all the more conspicuous whenever we compare the work with, for example, a Johannine epistle or a chapter from the synoptical gospels.

There is but one so-called conclusive proof that there were originally more than one epistle—whether genuine or not genuine—of Paul to the Philippians: the much discussed testimony of Polycarp (*Pol. Phil.* 3.2). There we read of Paul that he had not only in his time orally instructed the Philippians but also written them "letters, into which if you look carefully you will be able to have yourselves built up into the faith that has been given you" (*epistolas, eis as ean egkruptête, dunêthêsesthe oikodomeisthai eis tên dotheisan humin pistin*). It is not necessary, however, as is done by some scholars, to explain the plural number (letter[s]) by reference to Latin idiom *(epistolae)*, or, with others, to think that Polycarp is exaggerating.

The text in 13.2 clearly shows that he well knows the difference between *epistolê* and *epistolai*; in 11.3, (*qui estis in principio epistulae ejus*) that he knows of but one epistle of Paul to the Philippians; in 11.2, that he regards 1 Corinthians 6 as belonging to the instruction given by Paul to the Philippians, whilst we moreover meet with other traces of acquaintance with Pauline epistles. The inference lies to our hand: the plural form (*epistolai*) in 3.2 is to be explained by the writer's intention of pointing to a group of epistles by Paul which his readers might read for edification, and which the Philippians also might regard as written for them. A remarkable evidence indeed, not of the earlier existence of more than one epistle of Paul to the Philippians, but of the way in which in the middle of the second century the group of Pauline epistles was regarded—not as a chance collection of private letters, but as one destined from the first for the edification of various churches.

After what has been said it is hardly possible to think of Paul as the writer of Philippians.

## 7a. Paul Not the Author

In itself considered it is possible indeed that the apostle should have written in the form of a letter to a particular church a composition which was in truth no real letter, but a writing designed for purposes of general edification. This is not impossible; but it is hardly at all probable. The same remark applies to the writer's method of borrowing one thing and another from extant "Pauline epistles" even if sometimes the borrowing amounts perhaps to no more than a slight unconscious reminiscence of what he had at some time read. Possible also, but still less probable, is it that he should have written in so impalpable a manner regarding his then surroundings—his recent vicissitudes, what might be awaiting him in the future, his relation to the community addressed, what was happening within it—and above all that he should write in so exalted a tone of himself as an "example" whose sufferings are significant for them all.

What finally puts an end to all doubt is the presence of unmistakable traces of the conditions of a later period. Amongst these are to be reckoned in the first instance all that is vague and nebulous in the supposed historical situation, the firmly held conception of "Paul," his "bonds," his presence and absence. More particularly, everything points to a considerably advanced stage in the development of doctrine. Christianity has freed itself from Judaism. "Saints" may be called so, not because of their relation to the law, nor as children of Abraham, but in virtue of their standing "in Christ Jesus" (1:1; 4:21). Righteousness, or the fruit of righteousness, is attained not through the law but "through Jesus Christ" (1:11; cf. 3:9). Not the Jew but the believing Christian belongs to the true Israel (3:3).

It is no longer Jesus who is by preference spoken of—the expression occurs only twice (2:10, 19; according to Tischendorf's text); usually it is "Christ Jesus," or "Christ," sometimes "Jesus Christ." God is in a special sense his father (1:2).

> **Editor's Note:** By "Tischendorf's text," Van Manen
> refers to the Codex Sinaiticus, a remarkable 4th
> century manuscript that Lobegott Friedrich
> Constantin von Tischendorf had rescued not long
> earlier from obscurity in a monastery at the foot of
> Mount Sinai.

His "day" is spoken of (1:6, 10; 2:16), the righteousness obtained through him (1:11), the abundance that is had in him (1:26). He can be the subject of preaching (1:15, 17f.); *the* life (1:21); his spirit a stay for believers (1:19), and he himself glorified in the body of the apostle (1:20). In him is comfort

(2:1), he is the highest object of human striving (2:21), whose work must be done (2:30), in whom alone can there be glorying (3:3), for whom everything may well be sacrificed (3:7), the knowledge of whom is worth all else (3:8), who lays hold of those who are his (3:12), in whom is the calling of God (3:14), to be hostile to whose cross is the saddest of all things (3:18), who is to be looked for from heaven as Lord and Saviour (3:20), who shall make us like unto himself (3:21), in whom we must stand fast (4:1), whose "thoughts" (*noêmata*) we must have (4:7), through whom or in whom God blesses us (4:19), whose grace may be invoked upon us (4:23), our Lord at whose name every knee must bow (2:10f.), who came down from heaven, who was in the form of God and who humbled himself, became man, suffered and died, and was glorified above all (2:6-11).

The church already possesses its "bishops and deacons" (1:1), its factions, its parties and schools (1:15, 17; 3:2), its good old times (1:5; 2:12). The unity of the faith is in danger (1:27*f*.; cf. 2:2f.), there is suffering on account of the faith (1:29f.), there is an aiding of prisoners (2:25, 30), with regard to which we find a testimony in Lucian's *De Morte Peregrini.*

In a word: all points back to an Old-Christian development that cannot at so early a date as 64 A.D., the assumed death-year of Paul, have attained to such a degree of maturity as we see it here possessing. Let it not be said, however, on this account, that the unknown writer who conceals himself behind the name "Paul" or, if you will, "Paul and Timothy," was a forger or fraudulent person.

Nothing gives us the smallest title to cast any such imputation on his character. He simply did what so many had done before him, and so many others were to do after his day; more from modesty than from any arrogance or bluntness of moral sense did such men write under the name of someone whom they esteem, in whose spirit they wish to carry on their labours, and under whose spiritual protection, as it were, they wish to place their literary efforts. The "Paul" whom this author brings before his reader is the motive—indispensable or at least desirable—for glorying over against those who are accustomed to exalt themselves over well-known predecessors, as we learn from 2 Corinnthians 5:12.

## 7b. The Real Author

The author himself lived at a later date; we know not where. Presumably in the same circle as that in which the "principal epistles" had their origin, and not long after the production of these, probably in Syria or Asia Minor, about the year 125 A.D. In any case not earlier than the beginning of the second century and not later than the testimony of Polycarp already cited, dating from the middle of the century, or indeed, when we bear in mind Marcion's use of the letter, not later than 140 A.D.

What we can securely infer from the epistle itself is no more than this: that it appeared after the "principal epistles," and in dependence on them, yet by another hand than any of those which we find at work there, as is shown by the divergences by which, not withstanding many things they have in common, its language and style are distinguished. Our author, like the writers of the "principal epistles," belonged to the Pauline School. Yet he was, so far as we can judge, less dogmatically inclined than these writers, or at least than the authors of Romans and Galatians. Rather was he one who directed his thoughts by preference to the practice of the Christian life.

He knows well of conflicting tendencies and divergent schools and parties, yet he glides lightly over them and in the character of Paul unhesitatingly places himself above them all (1:18), if only his readers are obedient and adhere to that which has once been taught (2:12; 3:16f.; 4:9). Questions of doctrine leave him unmoved, if only his readers will bear in mind the watchwords: struggle, ceaseless struggle (3:12-16); a walk in accordance with the gospel of Christ, in unity of the spirit

(1:27); after the pattern given by Paul *(passim,* especially 1:21-26; 2:17f.; 3:17; 4:9-13), Timothy, Epaphroditus (2:19-30), and other Philippians of the good old days (1:3-11; 4:10-18), only thinking the thoughts which were in Christ Jesus (2:5).

## 8. Value

The historical as distinguished from the abiding religious and ethical value of this writing, even though it makes no contribution to our knowledge of the life of Paul, is not slight. It throws light for us upon the history of Paulinism and the course of this quickening practical movement within Christianity during the first half of the second century.

×××

# Polycarp's Epistle

## 10. Text

The Epistle of Polycarp to the Philippians has long held a place, by universal consent, among the writings of the "Apostolic Fathers." Its title in that group (according to Zahn) runs: *tou agiou Polukarpou episkopou Zmurnês kai hieromartuos pros Philippêsious epistolê.* In Lightfoot it is simply *pros Philippêsiuos.* Neither the longer nor the shorter title can be regarded as original. The epistle is now extant in its entirety only in a faulty Latin rendering by the same hand as that which translated the longer recension of the Ignatian Epistles. We know the Greek text of chs. 1-9 from nine MSS, which all go back to the same ancestor, and are usually called *akephaloi* because they contain the Greek text of the acephalous "Barnabas" 21—i.e., of Barnabas 5:7 (*ton laon k.t.l.*). Ch. 13 is found in Eusebius *HE* 3:36.14-15.

## 11. Form and Contents

The work is in the form of an epistle written by "Polycarp and the presbyters who are with him," or by Polycarp alone, to the church of God at Philippi which had invited him to write the epistle (3.1; 13.2), we are not told how or why. The "presbyters" are mentioned as joint writers of the epistle only in the exordium; for the repeatedly recurring "we" elsewhere does not necessarily imply them. "Polycarp" speaks in chs. 1-14 to "brethren," to whom his attitude is after the manner of "Paul" in his epistles. He declares his joy at their friendly reception of Ignatius and his companions on their journey to Rome (1), gives some exhortations (2), declares that he cannot compare himself with Paul (3), gives directions and precepts for married women and widows (4), for deacons, youths (i.e., laymen) (5), presbyters, himself and others (6). He warns against docetism and exhorts to faithful adherence to the views that have been handed down (7).

He points to the perseverance of Christ Jesus, the blessed Ignatius, Zosimus, Rufus, Paul and the rest of the apostles (8f.), urges his readers to follow their example (10), laments the falling away of the former presbyter Valens and his wife, yet desires that they should be gently dealt with (11). He incites to the examination of the scriptures, to a holy walk, to prayer for others (12). He will take care, on the request of the Philippians and Ignatius (see *Ign. Poly.* 8), that letters should be sent to Antioch in Syria, and says a word in commendation of the epistles of Ignatius accompanying his own; also of Crescens, the bearer, and his sister (13f.).

## 12. Is Polycarp the Author?

The author of this epistle, according to tradition, was Polycarp, a disciple of the apostles, especially of John, who made him bishop of Smyrna, where about 166 or 167-168 A.D. he suffered martyrdom at an advanced age. The difficulties, however, in the way of our accepting this tradition are insuperable. In the first place, it has to be asked what motive was there for Polycarp, the bishop of the church at Smyrna, to address such an epistle at all to the church at Philippi—with which, so far as we can trace, he had nothing to do? What is said in 3.1 (cf. 13.2) about the epistle having been invited is manifestly invention.

Further, we must not overlook that, though doubtless the writing gives itself out to be a letter, it is in reality nothing of the sort, but rather, in the author's own language, a treatise "concerning righteousness" (*peri tês dikaiosunês*, 3.1; cf. 9.1). The form is taken from the Pauline "epistle," on the whole coinciding most with that of the Pastoral letters, or those of Ignatius, though also now and then showing affinities with the First Epistle of Clement to the Corinthians. Its dependence on all these continually strikes the eye.

Now, it is, in itself considered, certainly possible, yet at the same time it is not at all likely, that Polycarp, under his own name or as "Polycarp and the presbyters that are with him," should have written a treatise "concerning righteousness" in the form of an epistle to the church at Philippi. Rather does it lie in the nature of the case that a third person should have made use of his name in this manner.

The same observation has to be made upon the circumstance that the writer, in the character of Polycarp, refers to the charge laid upon him by Ignatius. Ignatius himself, however, in his letter to Polycarp (8.1) had said that on account of his hasty departure from Troas for Neapolis he was no longer able to write to all the churches, wherefore he, Polycarp, must now instead send letters "to the churches in front"—a fiction upon which the real Polycarp could hardly have proceeded, though for a third party this would have presented no difficulties. Or if it be held that we are not at liberty to speak of fiction in this connection because Ignatius had really said what we read in the passage cited above, how then could his friend Polycarp have passed over his words, have written a treatise in an epistle to the Philippians, and in the so-called letter assume the appearance of having written, not to please Ignatius, but because the writing had been called for by the persons addressed (3.1; cf. 13.2)?

There are other difficulties also. The date of Polycarp's death is unknown.[15]

The oldest tradition we possess regarding the date of Polycarp is that given by Irenaeus (*AH* 3:3-4, written about 180), who speaks of him as one whom he had known in his earliest youth (*en tê prôtê hêmôn hêlikia*), who at that time was bishop of the church of Smyrna, and of whose successors "down to the present time" (*hoi mexri nun diadedegnenoi ton Polukarpon*) he is able to speak. To what is said by Irenaeus here and elsewhere, as also in the Epistle to Florinus wrongly attributed to him (see Van Manen, Old-Christian Literature, § 25).

---

15. The tradition that speaks of 166 or 167-8 as Polycarp's death-year rests upon some indications of Eusebius (*Chron.* and *HE* 4.14f.; 5.5, 20), yet it appears to be inadmissible. The same authority, however, speaks (*HE* 3.36) of Polycarp not only as a contemporary of Ignatius and Papias, but also as already in the third year of Trajan (98-117) bishop of Smyrna and at that time in his full vigour. For this reason many scholars—such as Hase, Wiseler, Duker, Keim, Uhlborn [et. al.]—have during ever so many years not hesitated to use their freedom in this connection, and have assigned as the death-year of Polycarp various dates between 147 and 178.

More particularly, however, many scholars since Waddington (1867)—such as Renan, Aubé, Hilgenfeld, Harnack, Völter, Lightfoot, and Zahn—have fixed upon the year 155-6 as the date, basing their conclusion on what they read in the *Martyrium Polycarpi*, ch. 21. Unfortunately it is not possible to place reliance even on this passage. The purport of the supposed statement is uncertain; it requires a number of guesses to be made before it can be taken in the sense that is desired; and in the most favourable event yields a statement that stands and falls with the twofold, far from probable, view (1) that ch. 21 is an integral part of the main work, although it was still unknown to Eusebius and Jerome; (2) that the *Martyrium* itself is as old as it claims to be, and was written within a year after the martyrdom of Polycarp (see Van Manen, Old-Christian Literature, § 14).

Eusebius has nothing new of any consequence to add, beyond his indications as to the death-year in 167-8, which are certainly not to be accepted. Irenaeus names no such year.

We should certainly not go very far astray if, in view of what Irenaeus tells us about Polycarp, we were to seek his death about the middle of the second century. At that date the Ignatian letters, with which our present epistle is connected, had not yet been written (see Van Manen, Old-Christian Literature, § 22), and thus the latter cannot have been the work of Polycarp.

It is of no avail to attempt, as some scholars have done, to meet these difficulties by assuming our present epistle to be greatly interpolated, so that in its original form it can still be regarded as older than the Ignatian Epistles. The assumption of the many interpolations required finds no support in the MS tradition nor yet in the textual phenomena or in external testimony—as has been rightly pointed out by Zahn and Lightfoot among others.

## 13. Author Unknown

The conclusion remains—notwithstanding Zahn and Lightfoot, who (albeit supported by Harnack) have not succeeded in proving the "genuineness"—that our "Epistle of Polycarp to the Philippians" is the work of an unknown hand, in the spirit of the Epistles of Ignatius, though not, in view of the differences in style and language, by the same author, as a sequel to that group, and not, as has been conjectured, with the object of recommending them, or of controverting docetism.

The "Pauline" epistles are much more strongly recommended (3.3) than the Ignatian (13.2); and the polemic against docetism in ch. 7 comes too little into the foreground for us to be able to regard it as one of the main objects of the writing. The epistle is a well-meant, though by no means important, composition of the edifying order, made up in great part of borrowed words, and in no respect showing much independence, written after Polycarp's death about the middle of the second century, and before Irenaeus, who (*AH* 3.3.4) praised it as "an able epistle" (*epistolē ikanōtatē*) from which we can learn the manner of Polycarp's faith and how to preach the truth; probably, therefore, about 160 A.D.

# Epistle to the Romans

*We may, in truth, safely dispense with further comparison between our epistle and any real letters from ancient times, so impossible is it to regard it as an actual epistle, to whatever date, locality, or author we may assign it.*

Old Christian literature is acquainted with two epistles to the Romans–that of Paul and that of Ignatius. As regards the latter, the reader is referred to what has been said under "Old-Christian Literature," §§ 28f. The "Epistle of Paul to the Romans" has come down to us from antiquity not as a separate work but as one of the most distinguished members of a group– the "epistles of Paul" (*epistolai Paulou*)–in which its title in the shortest form (א, ABC, etc.) is "to Romans" (*pros 'Rômaious*).

## 1. History of Criticism: Traditional View

From the beginning (first by Marcion, about 140 A.D.) the work, as an integral part of the authoritative "Apostle" (*ho Apostolos, to apostolikon*)–i.e., Paul–in other words as a canonical writing, was tacitly recognized as the work of the Apostle Paul. This continued without a break until 1792. Justin took no notice of Paul; Irenaeus and Tertullian–the latter with a scornful *"haereticorum apostolus"* on his lips–laboured to raise the "apostle" in the estimation of the faithful (cf. "Paul," § 48); but no one ever thought of doubting the genuineness of the letters attributed to the apostle–or of defending it. During the whole of that period the question did not so much as exist.

## 2. Theories of Composition

There is indeed a very old discussion—perhaps it had already arisen even in the second century—as to the existence of the epistle in two forms, a longer and a shorter, even after omission of the two last chapters (15, 16). Origen taxes Marcion with this last omission; but Origen's older contemporary Tertullian says nothing of that, though he several times reprimands the heretic for having tampered with the text of chs. 1-14. The probability is that Tertullian had no acquaintance with chs. 15-16. At any rate, he made no citation from them in his polemic against Marcion *(Adv. Mar.* 5.13-14), although in its course he leaves none of the previous chapters (1-14) unreferred to and speaks of one expression—*tribunal Christi* (14:10)—as written *in clausula (epistulae)*.

In recent times the tradition of the text as regards chs. 15-16 has frequently come under discussion. The conclusion is not only that the chapters in question were unknown to Marcion and probably also to other ancient witnesses, including Irenaeus and Cyprian, but also that there were in circulation at an early date MSS in which the doxology Romans 16:25-27 either occurred alone immediately after 14:23 or was entirely wanting (cf. Sanday-Headlam, *Romans* [1895], lxxxixff.; S. Davidson, *Introduction*, 1894).[16]

---

16. To these facts were added, at a later date, considerations based on the contents of chs. 15-16 tending to show that they hardly fitted in with chs. 1-14. Semler (1767), soon afterwards supported by Eichhorn (*Einleitung in das NT*, 1827), held ch. 15 to be by Paul but not to have originally belonged to the Epistle to the Romans. Baur (Paulus, 1845), followed, in the main, among others by Schwegler, Zeller, and S. Davidson, and controverted by Kling, De Wette, and others, maintained the piece to be spurious. Since Baur, many scholars have endeavored to steer a middle course by seeking—in very divergent ways, it is true—for the close of the letter supposed lost, in chs. 15, 16. In these various attempts an important part was always played by the conjecture, first put forth by Schulz (1829), that in Romans 16:1-20 what we really have is an epistle of Paul to the Ephesians.

In this direction—that of holding more Pauline epistles than one to have been incorporated with each other or amalgamated together to form the canonical Epistle to the Romans—the way had already been led (leaving chs. 15 and 16 out of account) by Heumann in 1765.[17]

Thus, there has been no lack of effort on the part of scholars to satisfy themselves and each other of the composite character of

---

17. Heumann argued, according to Meyer (*Kommentar*, 1859), for the "strange hypothesis" that a new Epistle to the Romans begins at ch. 12, whilst ch. 16 contains two postscripts (vv. 1-24 and 25-27) to the first. Eichhorn (*Einleitung*, 1827) guessed that Paul in reading over the epistle after it had been written by an amanuensis made various additions with his own hand. C. H. Weisse (1855) held Romans 9-11 to be a later insertion. He found, moreover, a number of minor insertions in the Epistle, and finally concluded that chs. 9-10+16:1-16, 20b, probably had belonged originally to an Epistle of Paul to the Ephesians. Laurent (*NT Studien*, 1866) supposed Paul to have written with his own hand a number of notes to his Epistle to the Romans which subsequently by accident found their way into the text.

Renan (*St. Paul*) was of the opinion that Paul had published his Epistle to the Romans in several forms—e.g., chs. 1-11+15; chs. 1-14+16 (part); out of these forms the epistle known to us ultimately grew. Straatman (ThT., 1868, 38-57), controverted by Rovers (Ibid., 310-325), came to the conclusion that chs. 12-14 do not fit in with what precedes; that these chapters along with ch. 16 belong to an Epistle of Paul to the Ephesians; and that the close of the Epistle to the Romans, properly so called, is found in ch. 15. Spitta (1893) contended, and at a later date (1901) reaffirmed, though with some modifications of minor importance, that our Epistle to the Romans is the result of a fitting-together of two epistles written by Paul at separate times, one before and one after his visit to Rome, and addressed to the Christians there. The first and longer, a well rounded whole, consisted of 1:1-11:36, 15:8-33, 16:21-27; the second, partly worked into the first, has not reached us in its entirety; we recognise with certainty only the portions: 12:1-15:7 and 16:1-20.

Pierson and Naber (*Verisimilia*, 1886), controverted by Kuenen (*ThT.*, 1886), point to a number of joinings and sutures, traces of manipulation and compilation, in the traditional text of the Epistle to the Romans, with a view to proving its lacera condition, Michelsen (*Th.T.*, 1886-7) sought to distinguish in that text five or six editions of Paul's Epistle, in the course of which various far-reaching modifications may be supposed to have been the traditional text. Equally decided, however, at least with most of them, is the opinion that nevertheless the text is, for the most part, and in the main, from the hand of Paul. This conviction was for a long time tacitly assumed, rather than explicitly expressed. So even by Baur, Weisse, and Straatman, while it was brought to the foreground, with friendly yet polemical emphasis, as against the representatives of "advanced criticism," by Spitta.

As regards the others mentioned above, most hesitation was to be noticed in Pierson-Naber, Michelsen, and Völter; but even these, one and all, continued to speak of an original letter, written by Paul to the Romans. Not a few writers continued simply to maintain the *prima facie* character of the canonical epistle or, as occasion offered, to defend it in their notes and discussions, commentaries and introductions.[18]

## 3. Pauline Authorship Questioned

The first to break in all simplicity with the axiom of the genuineness of our canonical epistle to the Romans, although without saying so in so many words, was E. Evanson. He appended to *The Dissonance of the four generally received Evangelists* (1792) some considerations against the justice of the received view which regarded Paul as author of the epistle— considerations based upon the contents themselves and a

---

made. Sulze (1888) pressed still further for the recognition of additions and insertions. Völter repeated his "Votum" (Th.T., 1889) in a separate publication (Komposition der paul. Hauptbriefe, 1890), and sought to prove again that our canonical Epistle to the Romans is the fruit of repeated redaction and expansion of a genuine epistle of the apostle.

18. For details, *pro et Contra*, and some guidance through the extensive literature, the student may consult Holtzmann, Einleitung (1892), 242-6; Sanday-Headlam, Romans (1895), lxxxixff.; Zahn, *Einleitung* (1900), 1, 268-299. For a more complete though not always accurate account of the doubts regarding the unity of the work, Clemen, *Die Einheitlichkeit der paulin. Briefe* (1894); cf. Th.T. (1895), 640ff.

comparison between them and Acts (pp. 256-261). Controverted by Priestley and others, Evanson's arguments soon fell into oblivion.

Sixty years afterwards, Bruno Bauer (*Kritik der paulin. Briefe*, 1852, 3, 47-76) took up the work of Evanson, without, so far as appears, being acquainted with the writings of that scholar. He was not successful, however, in gaining a hearing–not at least until after he had repeated his doubts in more compendious form in his *Christus u. die Caesaren* (1877, pp. 371-380).

Soon afterwards A.D. Loman (*"Quœstiones paulinae"* in *Th.T.*, 1882) developed the reasons which seemed to him to render necessary a revision of the criticism of the epistles of Paul which was then current. Without going into details as regarded Romans, he declared all the epistles to be the productions of a later time. Rudolf Steck (*Der Galaterbrief nach seiner Echtheit untersucht, nebst kritischen Bemerkungen zu den paulinischen Hauptbriefen,* 1888) came to the same conclusion and took occasion to point out some peculiarities connected with the Epistle to the Romans.

The same investigation was more fully carried out, and substantially with the same result, by W. C. van Manen *(Paulus II. De brief aan de Romeinen,* 1891; cf. *Handleiding, voor de Oudchr. letterkunde,* 1900, ch. 3, §§ 34-36), and Prof. W. B. Smith of Tulane University, Louisiana, has recently begun independently to follow the same path. The *Outlook* (New York) of November, 1900, contained a preliminary article by him, signed "Clericus" (a misprint for "Criticus"), and in the *Journal of Biblical Literature,* 1901, a series of articles bearing the author's own name was begun—the first entitled "Address and Destination of St. Paul's Epistle to the Romans," and the second "Unto Romans: 15 and 16."

The newer criticism has made itself heard and goes forward on its path in spite of much opposition and strife, applauded by some, rejected by many. For its character and aims see "Paul," §§ 34-36; cf. §§ 37-48.

Its desire is to read "the Epistle of Paul to the Romans" as well as the rest of the canonical books without any fear of the ban that lies upon aught that may perchance prove to be contrary to tradition, whether ecclesiastical or scientific; uninfluenced by any antecedent presumption as to the correctness of the current views as to contents, origin, or meaning of the text as it has come down to us, however highly esteemed be the quarter—Tübingen or any other—from which they have reached us; free, too, from the dominion of any conviction, received by faith merely, and held to be superior to any test of examination, as to the epistle being indubitably the work of Paul and of Paul alone. It seeks to read the epistle in the pure light of history, exactly as it appears after repeated examination has been made on every side, as it at last presents itself to the student who really wishes to take knowledge of the contents with as little prejudice as possible.

## 4. What "Romans" Seems to Be

Coming before us, as it does, as a component part of the group known as "the Epistles of Paul," handed down from ancient times, Romans appears indeed to be neither more nor less than an epistle of the apostle, written probably at Corinth and addressed to the Christians at Rome, whom he hopes to visit ere long after having made a journey to Jerusalem. Both superscription and subscription, as well as tradition, indicate this, even if we leave out of account the words "in Rome" (*en 'Römë*) and "to those in Rome" (*tois en 'Römë*) which are wanting in some MSS in 1:7, 15.

We have only, in connection with the superscription and subscription, to look at the manner in which the epistle begins and ends (1:1-15; 15:14-16:27), at the way in which the writer throughout addresses his readers as brethren (1:13; 7:14; 8:12; 10:1; 11:25; 12:1; 15:14f., 30; 16:17), stirs them up, admonishes them and discusses with them, as persons with whom he stands on a friendly footing, and has opened a correspondence on all sorts of subjects. The appearance of Tertius as amanuensis (16:22) need cause no surprise, it being assumed that perhaps Paul himself may not have been very ready with the pen.

## 5. Contents

If we turn for a little from a consideration of the literary form to occupy ourselves more with the contents, the first thing that strikes us is the conspicuously methodical way in which the writer has set forth his material. After an address and benediction (1:1-7), an introduction (1:8-15), and a statement of what he regards as the essential matter as regards the preaching of the gospel—a thing not to be ashamed of but to be everywhere preached as a power of God for the salvation of every believer whether Jew or Greek (1:16f.)—come two great doctrinal sections followed by an ethical section. The first doctrinal section, 1:18-8:39, is devoted to the elucidation of the truth that the gospel is the means for the salvation of Jews and Greeks, because in it is revealed the righteousness of God from faith to faith; the other, chs. 9-11, to an earnest discussion of what seems to be a complete rejection of the Jews by God; the third, the ethical section (12 :1-15:13), to a setting forth of the conduct that befits the Christian both towards God and towards man in general, and towards the weak and their claims in particular.

In substance the doctrine is as follows. Sin has alienated all men, Jews and Gentiles alike, from God, so that neither our natural knowledge of God nor the law is able to help us (1:18-3:20). A new way of salvation is opened up, "God's righteousness has been manifested" (*dikaiosunê Theou pephanerôtai*) for all men without distinction, by faith in relation to Jesus Christ (3:21-31). It is accordingly of no importance to be descended from Abraham according to the flesh; Abraham in the higher sense is the father of those who believe (4). Justified by faith, we have peace with God and the best hopes for the future (5).

Let no one, however, suppose that the doctrine of grace, the persuasion that we are under grace, not under the law, will conduce to sin or bring the law into contempt. Such conclusions can and must be peremptorily set aside (6-7). The emancipated life of the Christian, free from the law of sin and death, is a glorious one (8). Israel, the ancient people of the promises with its great privileges, appears indeed to be rejected, yet will finally be gathered in (9-11). The life of Christians, in relation to God and man, must in every respect give evidence of complete renewal and absolute consecration (12:1-15:13). Finally, a closing word as to the apostle's vocation which he hopes to fulfil in Rome also; a commendation of Phoebe, greetings, exhortations, benedictions, and an ascription of praise to God (15:14-16:27).

## 6. Difficulties: Not a Letter

If, at a first inspection, the work presents itself to us as an epistle written by Paul to the Christians at Rome, on closer examination it becomes difficult to adhere to such a view. Difficulties arise on every side. To begin with—as regards the form that is assumed. We are acquainted with no letters of antiquity with any such exordium as this: "Paul, bond-slave of Jesus Christ, called an apostle, separated unto the gospel of God... to all those who are in Rome... grace to you and peace from God our father and the Lord Jesus Christ;" nor with any conclusion so high-sounding as the doxology of 16:25-27, or the prayer for the grace of our Lord Jesus Christ which is heard in 16:20 (or 16:24). In every other case the epistles of antiquity invariably begin plainly and simply.

Greetings are indeed conveyed both from and to various persons; but never are so many introduced as in Romans 16:3-16, where in fact at the end *all* the churches salute. A letter-writer may, at the outset, seek to bring himself into closer relationship with his reader or to make himself known more exactly; but in the many examples of real letters that have come down to us from ancient times we nowhere find anything even approaching the amplitude of Romans 1:2-6. Nor yet does any real letter, whether intended for few or for many, so far as we are in a position to judge, ever give us cause—because by its length or its elaborate method it resembles a treatise arranged in orderly sections—to regard it as a book, as our canonical Epistle to the Romans does, with its great subdivisions (already taken account of under § 5).

## 7. Style of Address

We may, in truth, safely dispense with further comparison between our epistle and any real letters from ancient times, so impossible is it to regard it as an actual epistle, to whatever date, locality, or author we may assign it. How could anyone at the very beginning of a letter, in which, too, the first desire he writes to express is that of writing solemnly, earnestly, directly, allow himself to expatiate, as this writer does, in such a parenthesis? He speaks as a didactic expounder who, for the most part, directly and as concisely as possible, deals with a number of disputed points, with regard to which the reader may be supposed to be in doubt or uncertainty because in point of fact they have gained acceptance within certain circles.

These expositions relate to nothing more or less than such points as the relation of the Pauline gospel to the OT (v. 2), the descent of the Son of God from the house of David (v. 3), the evidence of the Messiahship of Jesus derived from his resurrection (v. 4), the origin and the legitimacy of the Pauline preaching (v. 5). At the same time the readers (who have not yet been named and are first addressed in v. 7) are assured that they belong to the Gentiles (*ethnê*), with reference to whom Paul has received his apostleship, although, according to 1:10-13, he has never as yet met them and consequently has not been the means of their conversion. All this within a single parenthesis. In such wise no letter was ever begun.

The writer addresses himself to "all" the members of a wide circle—let us say in Rome; even if the words "in Rome" (*en Rômê*) and "those who are in Rome" (*tois en Rômê*), according to some MS authorities, do not belong to the original text, their meaning is assured by the superscription "to Romans" (*pros Rômaious* ; cf. 15:22-29) and by the unvarying tradition as to the destination of the "epistle." The Paul whom we meet here addresses his discourse to a wide public, and utters in lofty tones such words as these:

- "O man, whoever thou be who judges, etc." (2:1);

- "O man, who judges, etc." (2:3);

- "If thou bearest the name of a Jew, etc." (2:17);

- "Nay but, O man, who art thou that replies against God?" (9:20); "But I speak to you that are Gentiles" (11:13);

- "say . . . to every man that is among you, etc." (12:3);

- "Who art thou that judges the servant of another?" (14:4); "But thou, why dost thou judge thy brother?" (14:10);

- "For if because of meat thy brother is grieved, etc." (14:15); etc.

Often the argument proceeds uninterruptedly for a long time without any indication of the existence of a definite circle of persons to whom it is addressed. Yet, on the other hand also, the abstract argumentation gives place to direct address, the word of admonition or exhortation spoken to the brethren (*adelphoi*), whether named or unnamed—the mention of whom, however, when it occurs, is a purely oratorical form and no natural expression of the existence of any special relation between the writer and his assumed readers. Of the passages coming within the scope of this remark (some of them, already noticed in §4), none presents any peculiarity in this respect. On the contrary, every one of them produces uniformly the same impression; in this manner no real letter is ever written.

The last chapter has nothing of the character of a postscript to a letter already completed, although the letter appears to end with 15:30-33. Strange, in the sense of being not natural but artificial, is the appearance in 16:22 of Tertius ("I, Tertius, who write the epistle"), the secretary of Paul, who, however, seems himself to have had a hand in the letter, since we find him saying in 15:15, "I wrote to you." Strange especially is Tertius' greeting of the readers in his own name, in the midst of the greetings which Paul seems to be transmitting through him (vv. 21, 23).

The contents of the epistle, largely consisting of argument and discussions on doctrinal theses, differ as widely as possible from what one is wont to expect in a letter—so widely that many have long laboured at the task of making a suitable paraphrase of the "textbook" while retaining their belief in its epistolary character (See, e.g., the specimen in Holtzmann, *Einleitung*, 237; cf. S. Davidson, *Introduction*, 1, 113-116).

## 8. The Supposed Readers

In vain do we make the attempt in some degree to picture to ourselves what the relation was between the supposed author and his readers. Acts supplies no light. There we read that when Paul is approaching Rome the brethren go to meet him, not because they had previously had a letter from him, but because they have heard various things regarding his recent fortunes (28:14f). As for the Jews of the metropolis, they have heard nothing either good or bad concerning him (v. 21).

Tradition, apart from the NT, has equally little to say about the epistle, whether as to its reception or as to what impression it may have made. The document itself says something, but only what adds to the confusion. The truth of the matter seems unattainable. Scholars lose themselves in most contradictory conjectures as to the occasion and purpose of the writing. Who the supposed readers of the epistle were can only be gathered from its contents. But these are so different in many aspects that it is possible to say with equal justice that the church in Rome was Jewish-Christian, Gentile-Christian, or a mixture of the two.[19]

It may be added here that the work is throughout addressed to "brethren" of all kinds, and sometimes it seems also to have been intended for Jews and Gentiles who stood in no connection whatever with Christianity. Did anyone ever give to a particular letter an aim so general, without realising that his letter had ceased to be a letter at all in the natural meaning of the word, and had become what we are accustomed to call an open letter, an occasional writing, a book? Everything leads to the one conclusion (that) the epistolary form is not real, it is merely assumed. We have here to do, not with an actual letter of Paul to the Romans, but rather with a treatise, a book, that with the outward resemblance of a letter is nevertheless something quite different.

## 9. A Kind of Unity

The same conclusion results from a closer examination of the whole as it lies before us, whenever we direct our attention to the connection of its several parts. The relative unity of the book there is no reason for doubting. It is not, however, unity of the kind we are accustomed to expect in a book written after

---

19. See, among others, Weiss, *Kommentar* (1889), 19-33; Holtzmann, *Einleitung*, 232-241; Lipsius, *Handkommentar zum NT* (1891), 70-76; Sanday-Headlam (1895), xxxviii-xliv; Steck, *Galaterbrief* (1888), 359-363; Van Manen, *Paulus*, 2, 20-25.

more or less careful preparation, in accordance with a more or less carefully considered and logically developed plan; not unity such as is the outcome of a free elaboration of the materials after these have been more or less diligently collected, and fully mastered by the writer. Least of all, a unity such as we look for in a letter, whether we think of it as written at one sitting or as written bit by bit and at intervals. It is rather a unity of such a sort as reminds us of that of a synoptical gospel, with regard to which no one doubts that it is the result of a characteristic process of redaction and remaniement, curtailment, correction, and supplementation by the help of older pieces drawn from other sources. It is such unity as we find in reading Acts, although we do not hesitate for a single moment to realise that Luke has made an often very palpable use of written sources.

There is unity of language and style, of thought, of feeling, of opinion; but at the same time there are, not seldom, great diversities in all these respects. The result, obviously, of the unmistakable circumstance that the writer of the canonical epistle has made continual and manifold use of words, forms of expression, arguments, derived from sources known to him, whether retained in his memory or lying before him in written form.

## 10. Failures to Find Unity

Proof of the justice of this view is supplied by the various attempts made by earlier and later exegetes to expound the epistle as a completely rounded whole—attempts in which it is found necessary at every turn to resort to the assumption of all sorts of conceivable and inconceivable figures and forms of speech, and thus to conceal the existence of joints and sutures, hiatuses, and unintelligible transitions. More particularly is this seen in the scientific line taken by Heumann, Semler, Eichhorn, Weisse, Straatman, Völter, Michelsen, Spitta, and so many others (cf. above § 2), who have argued, and continue to argue, for the view that more than one epistle of Paul lies concealed in the apparently homogeneous canonical epistle, or for the view that there have been interpolations, more or less numerous, on an unusually large scale. In the last resort, on an (as far as possible) unprejudiced reading of the text which has come down to us—a reading no longer under the dominion of a foregone conclusion, to be maintained at all hazards, that here we have to do with the original work of the Apostle Paul, sent by him to the church at Rome—we shall find that what lies before us is simply a writing from Christian antiquity presenting itself as such a work, which we must try to interpret as best we can.

## 11. Signs of Composition

The traces of additions and redactions in the various sections and subsections of the epistle are innumerable. It would be superfluous, even if space allowed, to go through all the details on this matter. A few examples may suffice. Compared with the first part (1:18-8:39), the second (9-11), although now an integral portion of the work, betrays tokens of an originally different source. There is no inherent connection between them, although this can, if desired, be sought in the desire to set forth a wholly new doctrinal subject in a wholly new manner. In the second we no longer hear of the doctrine of justification by faith; the treatment of the subject enunciated in 1:16f. is no longer continued.

What takes its place is something quite different and wholly unconnected with it; a discussion, namely, of the doctrinal question, "Why is it that the Gentiles are admitted and Israel excluded from salvation?" This discussion is directed not, like the contents of the first part, ostensibly to Christian Jews, but to Gentiles. There is nothing in the first part that anywhere suggests any such affection for Israel as is everywhere apparent throughout the second part, and especially in 9:1-3; 10:1; 11:1, 25-36; nothing that comes into comparison with the solemn declaration of 9:1 in which the writer bears witness to his great sorrow and unceasing pain of heart concerning Israel.

This exordium points to a quite different situation, in which "Paul" requires to be cleared of the reproach of not concerning himself about God's ancient people. Hence the wish expressed by him that he might become "anathema from Christ" for his brethren's sake, his "kinsmen according to the flesh" (9:3). Hence his zeal here and in 11:1 to declare himself an Israelite, of the seed of Abraham, the tribe of Benjamin. Hence also the summing-up of the ancient privilege of Israel, "whose is the adoption and the glory and the covenants" (9:4f.), in comparison with which the simple statement that they were entrusted with the oracles of God (3:2) sinks into insignificance.

In the first part a quite different tone is assumed towards the Jew (*Ioudaios*, 2:17), with whom the speaker appears to have nothing in common. There we find Jew and Greek placed exactly on an equality (1:16; 2:9f., 3:9); the idea of the Jews that as such they could have any advantage over the heathen is in set terms controverted (2:11-3:21), and it is declared that descent from Abraham, according to the flesh, is of no value (ch. 4). In 9-11, on the other hand, we have earnest discussion of the question how it is possible to reconcile the actual position of Israel in comparison with the Gentile world with the divine purpose and the promise made to the fathers.

Here, too, a high-pitched acknowledgment of the privileges of Israel, the one good olive-tree, the stem upon which the wild olive branches—the believing Gentiles—are grafted; Israel in the end is certain to be wholly saved, being, as touching the election, beloved for the fathers' sake (*kata tēn exlogēn agapētoi dia tous pateras*, 9:4f., 31; 10:2; 11:7, 17f., 26, 28). In the first part, a sharp repudiation of the law in respect of its powerlessness to work anything that is good (3:20f., 27; 4:15; 6:14; 7:5f., etc.); in the second a holding up of the giving of the law (*nomothesia*) as a precious gift (9:4). In the first part the earnest claim to justification by faith (5:1), to being under grace (6:4), to a walk in newness of spirit (7:6); in the second the assurance that "if thou shalt confess with thy mouth Jesus as Lord, and shalt believe in thy heart that God raised him from the dead, thou shalt be saved" (10:9).

Observe, again, the difference in respect of language. The words "just," "justify," "be justified" (*dikaioun, dikaioun, dikaiousthai*) nowhere occur in chs. 9-11, nor yet the expression "both Jews and Greeks," except in 10:12 where apparently it is not original, or at least has no meaning after the words "for there is no distinction" (*ou gar estin diastolē*). The words "Israelite" and "Israel" are not met with in 1-8, whilst in 9-11 the first occurs thrice and the second eleven times. On the other hand, we have "Jew" nine times in 1-3, but only twice in 9-11, and in both cases its occurrence seems probably due to the redactor.

The "adoption" (*huiothesia*), which, according to 8:15 (cf. Gal 4:5; Eph 1:5) is a privilege of all Christians, whether Jews or Greeks, recurs in 9:4 in connection with a supposed predestination of Israel as the son of God; the word is the same but it sounds quite differently. In 1-8 Christ is seven times called the Son of God, and in 9-11 never. On the other hand, he is probably called God in 9:5, but nowhere in 1-9. While in 1-8 we find no other form of the verb "say" (*erein*) than "shall we say" (*eroumen*), in 9:19f. we also have "thou wilt say" (*ereis*) and "shall the thing say?" (*erei*). If the occurrence of the expression "what then shall we say" (*tu oun eroumen*) in 9:14, 30, as well as in 4:1, 6:1; 7:7; 8:31, points to oneness of language, it has nevertheless to be noted that in 1-8 it never, as in 9:30, is followed by a question, but always by a categorical answer.

A speaker who says that Israel "following after a law of righteousness did not arrive at [that] law" (*diōkōn nomon dikaiosunês eis nomon ouk efthasen*, 9:31) understands by "law" (*nomos*) something quite different, and at the same time is following a quite different use of language, from one who declares that the Jew sins "under law" (*ennomos* or *ennomô*); shall be judged "by law" (*dia nomou*, 2:12); doeth not "the things of the law" (*ta tou nomou*, 2:14), is not justified "by works of law" (*ex ergôn nomou*), comes to knowledge of sin "through law" (*dia nomou*, 3:20) and lives "under law" (*hupo nomon*, 6:14). Only the latter is thinking of the Mosaic law, about which the former would not speak so depreciatingly. In chs. 9-11, as Steck (*Galaterbrief*, 362) justly remarks, a much more superficial use is made of the proof from scripture, "and the whole representation and language is somewhat less delicate."

## 12. The Third Part; 12:1-15:13

The third part of the epistle (12:1-15:13) seems to be closely connected with that which precedes. Observe the "then" (*oun*, 12:1), and notice how the writer harks back to 9-11 in his declaration (15:8) that Christ has been made a minister of the circumcision with reference to the promise of God, and to 1:16f. or 1:18-8:39 in the same declaration supplemented with the statement (15:9) that Christ appeared also that the Gentiles might glorify God for his mercy. But the connection, when more closely examined, will be found to be only mechanical. There is no real inward connection. No one expects a hortatory passage such as this after 11:33-36. Nor yet, where some would fain place it, after ch. 8 or ch. 6. The exhortations and instructions given in 12:1-15:13, however we put the different parts together, stand in no relation to the preceding argument; the same holds good of the exordium 12:1f.

Though usual, it is not correct to say that Paul first develops his doctrinal system in 1:18-11:36, and then his ethical in 12:1-15:13; or even to say in the modified form of the statement that he follows up the doctrinal with an ethical section.

Exhortations are not wanting in the first part, nor doctrines in the last. The truth is that in 1:18-11:36 the doctrinal element is prominent, just as the hortatory is in 12:1-15:13. In other words, the two pieces are of different character. They betray difference of origin. 12:1-15:13 is, originally, not a completion of 1-11, thought out and committed to writing by the same person, but rather—at least substantially—an independent composition, perhaps, it may be, as some have conjectured, brought hither from another context. It has more points of agreement with certain portions of the Epistles to the Corinthians than with Romans 1-11. Compare, in general, the manner of writing and the nature of the subjects treated.

## 13. Chapter 15

The conclusion of the canonical epistle 15:14-16:27 must be accepted, as such, notwithstanding the objections urged by Semler, and those who follow him, in rejecting chs. 15 and 16 as not original constituents of the writing sent by Paul to the Romans. It nevertheless shows many evidences of compilation by the aid of various pieces at the redactor's disposal, a process to which reference has already so often been made that it seems superfluous to dwell long upon it now.

Let the reader but observe the disconnected character of the five pieces of which ch. 16 consists, each of which either has no relation to the preceding, or is in contradiction with it. The recommendation of Phoebe in vv. 1f. hangs in the air. The greetings of vv. 3-16 presuppose a previous residence of Paul at Rome and a circle of acquaintances formed there, notwithstanding the positive statements on the subject in 1:8-13 and 15:22f. The warning against false teachers in vv. 17-20 finds no point of attachment in what precedes. The greetings of others in vv. 21-23 raise unanswered questions, not the least of these being those which arise in view of the existence of the already complete list in vv. 3-16, and the mention of all the churches at the close. The detached character of the doxology in vv. 25-27 is shown by the fact that in many MSS it occurs after 14:23.[20]

## 14. Improbability of the Traditional Theory

The examples cited, along with others which might be adduced (cf. van Manen, *Paulus*, 2, 34-101) show conclusively that the "epistle" has been compiled with the help of previously existing

---

20. In detail compare such expressions as "beseech... by" (*parakalô . . . dia*) in 12:1 with 1 Corinthians 1:10, 2 Corinthians 10:1, whereas "beseech" (parakalein), however Pauline, is found neither in Romans 1-11 nor in Galatians; the "mercies" (*oiktirmoi*) of God in 12:1, but nowhere named in Romans 1-11; "this age" (*ho aiôn houtos*) in 12:2 with 1 Corinthians 1:20; 2:6, 8; 3:18; 2 Corinthians 4:4, but not found in Romans 1-11. Compare also the representation that the Christian can still be renewed by the renewing of the mind (*anakainôsis tou noos*) in 12:2 with the assurance that though the outer man perish, "that which is within us is renewed every day" (*ho esô hêmôn [anthrôpos] anakainoutai hêmera*) in 2 Corinthians 4:16, whereas Romans 1-11 knows nothing of this "renewal," and could hardly have introduced it alongside its doctrine that the Christian is dead so far as sin is concerned (6:2) so that he now stands in the service of newness of spirit (7:6).

Compare again, the assurance that God gives to each a measure of faith (*ekastô metron pisteôs*) in 12:3 with "only as the Lord has supplied to each" (*ei mê ekastô hôs memeriken*) in 1 Corinthians 7:14, "according to the measure of the limits which God has apportioned to us as a measure" (*kata to metron tou kanonos, ou emerisen hêmin ho Theos metrou*) in 2 Corinthians 10:13; and also with the declaration that not every one receives faith through the spirit (1 Cor 12:9), as also that there is a still more excellent way than that implied in the spiritual gifts of which faith is one—namely love (1 Cor 12:31—not only are the words "apportion" (*merizein*) and "measure" (*metron*) unknown in Romans 1-11, but so also is "love" (*agapê*) in the sense of love to God and one's neighbor, and (equally so) a faith (*pistis*) which is not regarded as the beginning of a new life, in comparison with which love is not required simply because that and everything else that is needed is already possessed where faith is.

Consider also the distinction between various spiritual gifts (12:6-8) compared with 1 Corinthians 12:4-11 and 28-30; the whole attitude towards self-exaltation (12:3-8) compared with 1 Corinthians 4:6f. and 12:12-30; the exhortations to the practice of love, zeal, and purity (12:9-21; 13:8-14)

documents. There are also other reasons, however, against accepting the voice of tradition regarding the origin of the work. Now and then the contents themselves reveal quite clearly that they cannot be from Paul (ob. 64 A.D.), so that we have no need to dwell upon the improbability of supposing that Paul, a tentmaker by calling and personally unknown to the Christians at Rome, addressed to that place an epistle so broad and so deep, written in so exalted and authoritative a tone; nor upon the question as to how it was possible that such an epistle should, so far as appears, have failed to make the slightest impression, whether good or bad, at the time, and was doomed to lie for more than half a century buried in the archives of the Christian church at Rome in impenetrable obscurity, until

---

compared with 1 Corinthians 13; 14:1-20, 39; 15:58; 5:11; 6:9-11, 16-20, where amongst other things, the occurrence of "cleave" (*kollasthai*) in Romans 12:9 and 1 Corinthians 9:16f., but found nowhere else in the Pauline writings, is to be noticed; the occurrence also of "taking thought for thing honourable in the sight of all men" (*pronooumenoi kala enôpion pantôn anthrôpôn*) in 12:17 as compared with the only parallel expression "for we take thought of things honourable not only in the sight of the Lord but also in the sight of men" (*provooumen gar kala ou monon enôpion kuriou alla kai enôpion anthrôpôn*) in 2 Corinthians 8:21 (cf. Prov 8:4); the term opheilein ("to owe") in 13:8, used several times in 1 and 2 Corinthians, but never in Romans 1-11; the special exhortations to subjection to authority and to due discharge of one's various obligations (13:1-7) indicative of a peaceful environment and hardly in keeping with the persecutions suggested by the closing verses of ch. 8, but on the other hand quite in accord with the special admonitions and exhortations of 1 Corinthians 1:10ff., 6, 6:1-11; 11:2-15; etc.; what is said in ch. 14 regarding the use of certain meats, the observance of sacred days, and the respect for the weak, with regard to which no word is found in 1-11, but which reminds us throughout of 1 Corinthians 3-10, not only by reason of the similarity of such expressions as "eat" (*esthiein*), "food" (*brôma*), "cause to stumble" (*skandalizein*), "a stumbling-block to the brother" (*proskomma tô adelphô*), "not to eat flesh" (*mê phagein krea*), etc., but also very specially by reason of the agreement in the central thought that to the fully developed Christian all things are allowed, but that he must give no offence to the weak brother and therefore ought rather to act as if he were still in bondage to ancient customs and usages.

suddenly it re-emerged to light, honoured and quoted as an authority by—the Gnostics!

Evanson long ago (1792) pointed to the fact that the church addressed in it was apparently of long standing, and to the silent assumption in 11:12, 15, 21f. that the destruction of Jerusalem in 70 A.D. was a thing of the past. As regards the first of these points, he compared what is said in Acts and called attention to the fact that nothing is there said of any project of Paul's to visit Rome before he had been compelled by Festus to make appeal to the emperor (25:10-12), nor yet anything about an Epistle to the Romans or about any Christian community of any kind met there by the apostle (28:11-31). Yet even if we leave Acts out of account as being incomplete and not in all respects wholly trustworthy, what the epistle itself says and assumes with regard to the Christian church at Rome is assuredly a good deal more than, in all probability, could have been alleged about it at so early a date as 59 A.D., the year in which it is usually held to have been written by Paul.

## 15. Reflection of a Later Age

The faith of the Roman church is supposed to be known "throughout the whole world"; and Paul is filled with desire to make its acquaintance in order that so he may be refreshed (1:8, 12). The faith of both rests on the same foundation. The Christians of Rome are Pauline Christians. Like him they are justified by faith (5:1); reconciled with God (5:11); free from the dominion of sin and now in the uninterrupted service of God (8:18-22); no longer under the law but under grace, so that they now live in newness of spirit and not in oldness of the letter (6:15; 7:6).

They are well acquainted with Paulinism. They know it as a definite form of doctrine and have fully and freely given their assent to it—"You were servants of sin but you became obedient from the heart to that form of teaching where unto you were delivered" (6:17). It is possible to speak to them without any fear of misunderstanding, about "faith" (*pistis*) and "grace" (*charis*), "righteousness" (*dikaiosunê*) and "love" (*agapê*), "believing" (*pisteuein*) and "being justified" (*dikaiousthai*), "being justified by faith" (*dikaiousthai ek pisteôs*) and "by works of law" (*ex ergôn nomou*), "sinning without the law" (*hamartanein anomôs*) and "under the law" (*ennomôs* or *en nomô*), "being delivered up" (*paradothênai*) and "dying for men" (*apothanein huper abthrôpôn*), "redemption" (*apolutrôsis*), "being baptised into Christ" (*baptisthênai eis Xriston*), "being crucified with Christ" (*sustaurousthai* [*Christô*]), "living after the flesh" (*zên kata sarka*), "after the spirit" (*kata pneuma*), "to God" (*tô Theô*), "in Christ" (*en Christô*).

It is possible to use such expressions as: "for there is no distinction" (*ou gar estin diastolê*: 3:22); "but where there is no law neither is there transgression" (*ou de ouk estin nomos oude parabasis*: 4:15); "but where sin abounded, grace abounded more exceedingly" (*ou de epleonasen hê hamartia, hupereperisseusen hê Charis*: 5:20); "to be under law," "under grace" (6:14); "spirit of adoption," "Abba, Father," (8:15); to throw out such questions as these: Whether or not there be with respect to Jews and Greeks "respect of persons with God"? (2:11); Has the Jew as such any advantage over the Greek, when both have sinned? (3:9-20); In how far does any importance at all still attach to circumcision? (2:25-29); What value has the law? (2:12-29; 3:19-22, 27-31; 7:1-6); Does faith ever make it void? (3:31); In what sense may we pride ourselves on having Abraham as our father? (ch. 4); Must we not think that the doctrine of grace leads to continuance in sin? (6:1); Is not the conviction that we are not under law but under grace conducive to sin? (6:15); Can the law be held responsible for sin because by means of the law we were brought to the knowledge of sin? (7:7).

## 16. A Developed Faith

All this is unthinkable at so early a date as the year 59 A.D. There is, moreover, the one great simple fact which overrides these considerations, and thrusts them, so to speak, into the background—this, namely, that the Paulinism with which we are made acquainted in the Pauline Epistles, and particularly in that to the Romans, is of more recent date than the historical Paul.

Compared with what the first disciples of Jesus believed and professed, it is not merely a remarkable divergence; it is in point of fact a new and higher development from the first Christianity. It presupposes, to speak with Loman, "a richly developed stage of theological thought." It has learned to break with Judaism and to regard the standpoint of the law as once for all past and done with, substituting in its place that of grace as the alone true and valid one. The new life "under grace" stands in sharp antithesis to the old one "under the law" (6:14). It knows, and it is, a new divine revelation; it has a theology, a christology, and a soteriology, which bear witness to a more advanced thinking and to a deeper experience of life than could possibly have been looked for within the first few years after the crucifixion.

It is a remarkable forward step, a rich and far-reaching reform of the most ancient type of Christianity; now, a man does not become at one and the same moment the adherent of a new religion and its great reformer. All attempts to escape the difficulty so far as Paul is concerned break down in presence of the obvious meaning of Galatians 1:11-23, as was shown years ago by Blom against Straatman (*Th.T.* 1875, 1-44).

It is of no avail continually to hark back to the possibility—which, in fact, no one denies—of a development in Paul's mind during the years that elapsed between his conversion and the writing of his epistles. The Paulinism of the epistles in question is, on their own showing, in its main features at least (with which we are here concerned) as old as the Christian life of Paul; but such a Paulinism is even for thoughtful believers in the supernatural inconceivable as having come into existence immediately after Paul had become a Christian. Let the student read and ponder the sketch of Paulinism given by van Manen in *Paulus*, 2, 126-140; 211-217.

## 17. Kinship with Gnosis

The kinship of Paulinism (especially in the form in which it occurs in the Epistle to the Romans) with gnosis, which has been recognised and remarked both by older and by younger critics—amongst others, by Basilides, Marcion, Valentinus, Irenaeus, Tertullian, Holsten, Hilgenfeld, Scholten, Heinrici, Pfleiderer, Weizsäcker, Harnack (cf. van Manen, *Paulus*, 2, 154-166)—leads also to the same conclusion: that Paul cannot have written this epistle. As to the precise date at which (Christian) gnosis first made its appearance there may be some measure of uncertainty: whether in the last years of Trajan (ob. 117 C.E.), as is commonly supposed, or perhaps some decades earlier; in no event can the date be carried back very far, and certainly not so far back as to within a few years of the death of Jesus. With regard to this it is not legitimate to argue, with Baljon (*Geschichte*, 77), that in the Pauline gnosis "no doctrine of a demiurge, no theory of aeons is found." It is years since Harnack (*DG* 2 1, 196f.) rightly showed that the essence of the matter is not to be looked for in such details as these.

## 18. Other Signs of a Later Age

In addition to the assumed acquaintance (already remarked on) of the readers of the epistle with the Pauline gospel, there are other peculiarities that indicate the church addressed as one of long standing. It is acquainted with various types of doctrine (6:17). It can look back upon its conversion as an event that had taken place a considerable time ago (13:11). It has need of being stirred up to a renewal of its mind (12:2) and of many other exhortations (12-14). It has in its midst high-minded persons whose thoughts exalt themselves above the measure of faith given them (12:3).

It does not seem superfluous to remind them that each belongs to the other as members of one body endowed with differing gifts. There are prophets, ministers, teachers, exhorters, givers, rulers, and those who show mercy, and it appears to be necessary that each should be reminded of what he ought to do or how he ought to behave.

The prophet must keep within the limits of the faith that has been received, and be careful to speak according to the proportion of that faith (12:6); the minister, the teacher, and the exhorter must each busy himself exclusively with the work entrusted to him; the giver must discharge his task with simplicity, the ruler his with diligence; he that shows mercy is to do so with cheerfulness (12:4-8). The mutual relations must be considered anew and carefully regulated, both in general (12:9-21; 13:8-10), and, in particular, with respect to the special "necessities of the saints," the duty of hospitality, the attitude to be maintained towards persecutors (12:12ff.), the public authority, and the fulfilment of the duties of citizenship (13:1-7).

A vigorous exhortation to vigilance and an earnest warning against revellings and drunkenness, chambering and wantonness, strife and envy, are not superfluous (13:11-14). There are weak ones in the faith, who avoid the use of wine and flesh (14:1f., 21); others who hold one day holy above others, and as regards their food consider themselves bound by obsolete precepts regarding clean and unclean (14:5f., 14f., 20). Others again who regard all these things with lofty disdain, making no distinction between clean and unclean food, deeming that they are free to eat and drink as they choose, and that all days are alike; but these, just because of the freedom they rejoice in, give offence to many brethren and are the cause of their moral declension (14:5f., 13, 15, 20-23).

These divergent practices have already continued for so long that the writer, so far as the first two (wine and flesh, clean and unclean) are concerned, is in perplexity between them himself, and has no other plan than to raise himself above them all in order to urge a general point of view—a genuinely "catholic" one—of "give and take," in which the principle of freedom is recommended and its application urged in the fine maxims: let no one give offence, let each one be fully persuaded in his own mind, all that is not of faith is sin (14:5, 13, 23).

The church is exposed to persecution; it suffers with Christ. It has need of comfort. What is said in this connection cannot be explained from any circumstances at Rome known to us before Nero and the time of the great fire in 64 [A.D.]. It points rather to later days when Christians were continually exposed to bloody persecutions. See 5:3-5; 8:17-39; 12:12, 14.

One decisive proof that in our epistle we are listening to the voice of one who lived after the death of Paul in 64 A.D. is to be found in the manner in which the question of the rejection of Israel is handled in chs. 9-11. That question could not thus occupy the foreground or bulk so largely in the minds of Christian writers and readers as long as Jerusalem was still standing, and there was nothing to support the vague expectation of its approaching overthrow which some entertained. The allusions to the great events of the year 70, the overthrow of the Jewish commonwealth, and the expectations which connected themselves with this event are manifest. Anyone who will read what is said, particularly in 11:11-22, about the downfall of the Jews (*to paraptôma autôn*), about the branches that have been broken off (*exeklasthêsan kladoi*) and the "cutting off" (*apotomia*) which has come upon those who are fallen (*epi tous pesontas*), can be under no misapprehension on this point.

## 19. Summary

If we now sum up the points that have been touched on in §§ 6-18, we need have no hesitation in deciding that the arguments are convincing: our canonical Epistle to the Romans is not what it seems to be, not a letter written by the apostle and sent to a definite church; it is a tractate, a book, designed to be read aloud at Christian meetings, a piece to be read in church (*kirchliches Vorlesungsstück*), or homily, as Spitta has phrased it. It is a book written in the form of a letter, not written after the kind of preparation with which we write our books, but compiled rather in a very peculiar manner by use of existing written materials wherein the same subjects were treated in a similar or at least not very divergent way.

We can best form some conception of the method followed here by studying the text of one of the synoptical gospels with an eye to the method in which it was presumably composed; or by tracing in detail the manner in which such authors as the writer of the present epistle make use of the OT. They quote from its words alternately verbatim and freely, often, too, without any reference to the OT context, so that we can trace the question only by comparison of the text we possess which has been wholly or partly followed (cf. van Manen, *Paulus*, 2, 217-9).

The study of the "epistle" from the point of view of its probable composition enables us to distinguish what treatises or portions of treatises were probably made use of before the text came into existence in its present form. In this way the work as a whole makes us acquainted with underlying views then prevalent, and accepted or controverted by our author—on the universality of sin and its fatal consequences (1:18-3:20); on righteousness by faith (3:21-31); on the connection between this and Abraham as father of the faithful (ch. 4); the fruits of justification (ch. 5); three objections against Paulinism (6:1-14; 6:15-7:6; 7:7-25); the glories of the new life in Christ (ch. 8); the rejection of the Jews (chs. 9-11); what is the duty of Christians towards God and man generally, and towards the weak and the principles held by them in particular (12:1-15:13).

Such views, however greatly they may vary in purpose and scope, all belong to one main direction, one school of thought, the Pauline. We give them this name because we gain our best and most comprehensive acquaintance with the school from the "epistles of Paul," just as we speak of the Johannine School and the Johannine tendency, although we know nothing about the connection between the school or tendency on the one side, and the well-known apostolic name connected with it on the other. To suppose that the school originated from the historical Paul, as was formerly maintained by Steck, is possible; but the supposition finds no support in any historical facts with which we are acquainted (cf. *Paulus*, 2, 222-227).

## 20. The Author

What is certain, at any rate, is that the canonical epistle is not by Paul. A writing that is so called, but on closer examination is seen to be no epistle but rather a compilation, in which, moreover, are embedded pieces that plainly show their origin in a later time, cannot possibly be attributed to the "Apostle of the Gentiles." In this connection, however, it is inappropriate to speak of deception or forgery or pious fraud.

There is not the slightest reason for supposing that our author had the faintest intention of misleading his readers, whether contemporaries or belonging to remote posterity. He simply did what so many others did in his day; he wrote something in the form (freely chosen) of a tractate, a book, or an epistle, under the name of someone whom he esteemed or whose name he could most conveniently and best associate with his work, without any wrong intention or bad faith, because he belonged or wished to be thought to belong, to the party or school which was wont to rally under his master's standard.

His own name remained unknown; but his *nom de plume* was preserved and passed from mouth to mouth wherever his work was received and read. What reason was there for inquiring and searching after his real name if the work itself was read, quoted, copied, and circulated with general approval? The work might bear evidence of the artist so far as concerned person, surroundings, sufferings. In this case, according to the epistle, he was a Christian, one of the Pauline School, a polished and educated man with a heart full of zeal for the religious needs of humanity: a Paulinist, however, of the right wing.

## 21. His Method

He raises himself above the different shades of opinion which he knows so well by letting them find alternate expression, by letting the voice now of the one and now of the other be heard. He gives utterance to words so sharply explicit as these: "by the works of the law shall no flesh be justified in his sight" (3:20); "now are we delivered from the law wherein we were held" (7:6); but also to other words, so friendly in their tone as regards the very same law: "not the hearers ... but the doers of the law shall be justified" (2:13); "the law is holy," "spiritual" (7:12, 14). He asseverates that there is no distinction between Jew and Greek (3:22); that there is with God no acceptance of persons (2:11); and that the privileges of the Jew are many (3:1f.); that Israel is in a very special way the people of God (9:4f.; 11:1).

He says that to be a son of Abraham after the flesh signifies nothing (4:1ff.), and that to be of the seed of Abraham is a specially great privilege (11:1). He recognises at one time that the wrath of God is now manifest upon the sins of men (1:18), and at another that this is yet to come (2:5-8). He speaks of it as a matter of experience that the Christian has broken with sin for good and has become a wholly new creature (5:1-7:6 and ch. 8), and also lays down a quite different doctrine to the effect that he is still "sold under sin," continually doing the thing he would not, and he longs for emancipation from the body (7:7-25). He embraces the doctrine of a redemption of man from a power hostile to God on the ground of the love of the Father (3:24; 5:1; 8:3, 32), and with this he associates the thought of an atoning sacrifice on behalf of the sinner offered to God by Christ "in his blood" (3:2-5).

Paul is to him the called Apostle of the Gentiles (1:1, 5, 13f.; 15:16,18); but also warmly attached to the Jews and ready to do everything for them (9:1-3; 10:1; 11:1); in possession of the "first fruits of the spirit," always working "in the power of God's spirit," but also in the manner of the original apostles "in the power of signs and wonders" (15:19). He recognises Jesus as God's son, who has appeared "in the likeness of sinful flesh" (8:3, 32); but he also says that he is of Israel according to the flesh (9:5), and that he was first exalted to the dignity of divine sonship by his resurrection (1:*3f.*; 15:12). He speaks with the same facility of "Jesus," "Jesus Christ," and "our Lord Jesus Christ" as he speaks of "Christ" and "Christ Jesus."

For him all distinction in the use of these various designations has practically disappeared. Not seldom do we find him affirming and denying on the same page. He knows how to give and take, when to evade arguments, and when to meet them. Already we perceive in him something of the "catholic" spirit which rises above the strife of parties; which serves the truth and promotes the unity of believers, by siding now with the right wing, now with the left, by gliding over thorny points, and boldly thrusting difficulties aside.

## 22. The Writer's Origin

As for origin, he was probably a Greek. He thinks in Greek, speaks Greek, and seems to have used no other books than those which he could have consulted in Greek (cf. *Paulus*, 2, 186-190). His home we can place equally well in the East or in the West. In the East, and particularly in Antioch or elsewhere in Syria, because Paulinism probably had its origin there. The catholic strain, on the other hand, within the limits of the Pauline movement, seems rather to have proceeded from Rome.

The possibility is not excluded that the main portions of the letter, or if you will, of a letter, to the Romans, were written in the East, and that the last touches were put to it in Rome or elsewhere in the West; in other words, that it was there that the epistle took the final form in which we now know it. There is a considerable number of writings which passed over from the hands of the Gnostics into those of "catholic"-minded Christians, and in the transition were here and there revised and corrected, brought into agreement, somewhat more than appeared in their original form, with the prevailing type of what was held to be orthodox (cf. *Paulus*, 2, 227-230).

## 23. Date

The author has not given us the date of his work, and we can guess it only approximately. Broadly speaking, we may say, not earlier than the end of the first nor later than the middle of the second century. Not before the end of the first century, because after the death of Paul (about 64 A.D.) time enough must be allowed to admit of epistles being written in his name as that of a highly placed and authoritative exponent of Christianity—the representative, not to say the "father," of Paulinism, a forward-reaching spiritual movement, a deeply penetrating and largely framed reform of that oldest Christianity which embodied the faith and expectations of the first disciples of Jesus after the crucifixion. Paulinism in this sense certainly did not come into existence until after the downfall of the Jewish state in 70 C.E., and—if we consider its kinship with Gnosticism, and various other features which it shows—surely not before the end of the first, or the beginning of the second, century.

On the other side, we may venture to say, not later than the middle of the second century. Clement of Alexandria, Tertullian, Irenaeus, use the book towards the end of that century, and we may be sure did not hold it for a recent composition. So also Theophilus (*ad Autolycum*, 3,14), who about 180 C.E. cited Rom 13:7f. as "divine word" (*theios logos*). Basilides (125), and Marcion, who made his appearance at Rome in 138, knew the epistle as an authoritative work of "the apostle." Aristides (125-126), James (130), 1 Peter (130-140) in like manner show acquaintance with the epistle. Various circumstances combined justify the supposition that it was written probably about 120 A.D., whilst some portions of it in their original form may be regarded as somewhat earlier (cf. *Paulus*, 2, 296-303; 3, 312-315).

## 24. Value of the Writing

If, in conclusion, we are met by the question, "What is the value of the writing when one can no longer regard it as an epistle of Paul to the Romans?" it must never be forgotten that the incisiveness of its dialectic, the arresting character of certain of its passages, the singular power especially of some of its briefer utterances and outpourings of the heart, the edifying nature of much of the contents, remain as they were before. The religious and ethical value, greater at all times than the aesthetic, is not diminished. The historical value, on the other hand, is considerably enhanced.

True, we no longer find in it what we were formerly supposed to find: the interesting (though in large measure not well understood) writing of the apostle, written in the days of his activity among the Gentiles, to a church which was personally unknown to him. But what have we in its place? A book of great significance for our knowledge of the ancient Christianity that almost immediately succeeded the apostolic (the Christianity of the disciples of Jesus in the years that followed his death). There is no work from Christian antiquity that contributes more largely to our knowledge of Paulinism (whether in its first form—which it has not reached us in any deliberate writing—or in its subsequent development) in its strength as an inspiring directory for conduct, and in the richness and depth of its religious thought and experience.

## 25. Defenders of Genuineness

No serious efforts to defend the genuineness of the epistle have as yet ever been attempted. Those offered casually and in passing, as it were, rely on the so-called external evidence (e,g., Weiss, *Kommentar*, 33-34; S. Davidson, *Introduction*, 117-119, 150-152). That is to say, its defenders rely on what is excellent proof of the existence of the epistle at the time when it was cited, or what clearly presupposes an acquaintance with it, but is of no significance whatever when the question is whether the work was in reality written by the individual who from the first was named as its author.

This the Tübingen school has long perceived; Baur also did not rely on such arguments. Instead of doing so, he thus expressed himself (*Paulus* 1, 1866, 276): "Against these four epistles (Romans, 1 and 2 Corinthians, Galatians,) not only has even the slightest suspicion of spuriousness never been raised, but in fact they bear on their face the mark of Pauline originality so uncontestably that it is impossible to imagine by what right any critical doubt could ever possibly assert itself regarding them."

This utterance, however, it will be observed, wholly ignores Evanson (1792) and of course also Bruno Bauer, who did not publish his criticism till 1851; but it also ignores the view taken by so many, including F. C. von Baur himself, who have vied with one another in the disintegration of the epistle, as also the possibility that yet others at a later date might perceive what Baur himself had not observed; nor yet does it take account of the unsatisfactory nature of any assertion (however plausible it may sound) as to the "originality" of Paul, whom after all we know only by means of the picture that has been constructed with the aid of those very epistles with regard to which we wish to inquire whether they really were written by him. Nothing therefore is added to the argument when a countless host of others since Baur are never weary of repeating that "even the Tübingen school" has raised no doubts as to the genuineness. The observation is correct, it is true. Only they forget to add: nor yet have they offered proofs that it is genuine.

Weiss, Davidson, and others remain equally sparing of their arguments even after the criticism of a later date has made its voice heard. They put it aside with a single word. Weiss, with a reference to a "Parody," by C. Hesedamm, *Der Römerbrief beurtheilt u. Gevierheilt* (1891). Davidson, with the observation that the genuineness, apart from the conclusive testimony of witnesses, is fully guaranteed by internal evidence: "The internal character of the epistle and its historical allusions coincide with the external evidence in proving it an authentic production of the apostle. It bears the marks of his vigorous mind; the language and style being remarkably characteristic." He omits, however, to tell us how he knows that anything is a "production," not to say an "authentic production of the apostle;" nor yet how he has obtained his knowledge of the mind of Paul; nor yet why it is impossible for a pseudonymous author to have any characteristic language and style.

Harnack (*ACL* ii. 1 [1897], vii) considers himself absolved from going into the investigation until the representatives of the newer criticism "shall have rigorously carried out the task incumbent on them of working out everything pertaining to the subject afresh."

Jülicher (*Einleitung*, 1894, p. 17; 1901, p. 19) once and again resorted to a severe attack on "hypercriticism" and "pseudocriticism," and subsequently proceeded, in dealing with the Epistle to the Romans, as if nobody had ever at any time argued against its genuineness.

Sanday and Headlam (*Romans*, 1895, 85-98) discuss exhaustively the integrity of the epistle, especially as regards chs. 15-16, but say little about the history of the question of genuineness. They cursorily dismiss some of the objections without showing that they have really grasped their proper significance. Counter-arguments are practically not heard. So also in other commentaries whose authors had heard anything about the newer criticism referred to. Holsten ("Prot. Kirkenzeitung," 1889), Pfleiderer (*Paulinismus*, 1890), Holtzmann (*Einleitung*, 1892), Lipsius (*HC*, 1892), and others, made some general observations in favour of the genuineness that had been called in question. But these discussions were little more than insignificant "affairs of outposts;" no real battle was delivered nor even any serious attack prepared.

Then came Zahn (*Einleitung*, 1900) with his censure on his comrades in arms against the Tübingen school for their error in having defended indeed the genuineness of the epistles "rejected" by Baur, but not that of the "principal epistles," "although Baur and his disciples had never so much as even attempted any proof for the positive part of their results." Forthwith he addressed himself to the long postponed task. He gave some half-dozen general observations (pp. 112-116) not differing in substance from those which had already been made; referred to the various particular investigations to be made in a later part of the work, including the detailed treatment of the Epistle to the Romans (pp. 251-310) where 31 full pages are devoted to the subject of the integrity and not a single word to the question of genuineness.

Baljon (*Geschichte*, 1901) perceived that something more than this was necessary to put the newer criticism to silence, if it was wrong. But what he wrote with this end in view was neither (as might have been expected) a confutation of the objections urged, nor yet an argument for the genuineness at least as solid and good as (in intention at all events) that made on behalf of Philippians, but simply a couple of pages (pp. 97-100) devoted to the history of the newer criticism and a few observations upon the objections urged by van Manen.

So far as appears, no one has as yet addressed himself to the task of an orderly scientific discussion of the arguments on the other side, or to an effective setting forth of the arguments on behalf of the genuineness.

## Basic Works Referred to in Discussion

Baur, F. C. *Paulus, der Apostel Jesu Christi. Sein Leben und Wirken, seine Briefe und seine Lehre* Second edition: Leipzig: Fues, 1886-87; E. Zeller, ed., 2 Vols.; First edition: Stuttgart: Becher und Müller, 1845; ET of first edition = *Paul the Apostle of Jesus Christ, His Life and Work, His Epistles and His Doctrine*, 2 Vols., London: Williams & Norgate, 1875.

——. *Kritik der paulinischen Briefe*, 3 vols., 1850/1851/1852.

——. *Christus und die Cäsaren. Der Hervorgang des Christentums aus dem römischen Griechentum*, 1877.

Eichhorn, J. G. *Einleitung in das Neue Testament*, 5. vols. Leipzig, 1804-1827.

Evanson, Edward. *The Dissonance of the four generally received Evangelists*, 1792.

Harnack, Adolf von. *Geschichte der altchristlichen Literatur bis Eusebius*, Leipzig, 1897.

Holtzmann, Heinrich. *Einleitung in das Neue Testament*, Freiburg, 1892.

Jülicher, Adolf. *Einleitung in das Neuen Testament,* [1]1894; [2]1901.

Loman, A.D. "*Quaestiones Paulinae,*" *Th.T.*, 1882, 1883, 1886.

Pierson, A., and S. A. Naber. *Verisimilia. Laceram conditionem Novi Testamenti exemplis illustrarunt et ab origine repetierunt,* 1886.

Sanday, William, and A. C. Headlam. *The Epistle to the Romans,* Edinburgh: T. & T. Clark, 1895.

Spitta, Friedrich. "Untersuchung über der paulinischen Hauptbriefe," in indem, *Zur Geschichte und Literatur des Urchristentums,* vol. 2, 1901.

Steck, Rudolf. *Der Galaterbrief–nach seiner Echtheit untersucht, nebst kritischen Bermerkingen zu den paulinischen Hauptbriefe,* Berlin, 1988.

*Th.T. = Theologisch Tijdschrift*

Van Manen, W. C. *Paulus, I, De Handelingen der Apostelen,* 1890.

——. *Paulus, II. De brief aan de Romeinen* 1891.

——. "Paul: Later Criticism," in *Encyclopaedia Biblica* (New York: Macmillan, 4 vols., 1899-1903), vol. 4, 3620-3638.

——. "Old-Christian Literature, III. Epistles," in *Encyclopaedia Biblica* (New York: Macmillan, 4 vols., 1899-1903), vol. 4, 3480-3491.

Völter, Daniel. *Die Composition der paulinischen Hauptbriefe, I, Der Römer- und Galaterbrief,* 1890.

Weiss, B. *Der Brief an die Römer,* KEK4, 1899.

Zahn, Theodor. *Einleitung in das Neue Testament*, Leipzig, [1]1900; ET = *Introduction to the New Testament*, 2. vols., Edinburgh: Clark, 1909.

# The Church of Rome

*How are we to explain the fact that nowhere in history has there remained any trace of the existence of an important Pauline community in Rome, after the apostle's epistle had been sent thither?*

Not founded by Peter and Paul (1-2).

Not by Peter alone (3).

Not by Paul (4-7).

Origin among Jews in Rome (8-9).

Age (10-12).

Character (13-16).

Constitution and government (17-18).

Influence and importance (19-20).

Bibliography (21).

## 1. Peter-Paul Tradition

The earliest period of the Christian community in Rome is wrapped in impenetrable obscurity. Tradition attributes its founding to the joint labours of the apostles Peter and Paul. This tradition, however, is unworthy of our confidence. It is comparatively recent. The oldest traces of its existence do not go back farther than to the close of the second century.

According to a notice in Eusebius (*HE* 2:25:8), Dionysius of Corinth, about the year 170 A.D., or somewhat later, wrote to the Romans as follows: "So also by this so weighty admonition [of yours]—the allusion is to the Epistle of the Romans to the Corinthians (=1 Clement)—ye have brought together [anew] that planting [aforetime] made by Peter and Paul, of the [churches of the] Romans and of the Corinthians. For, indeed, these two both planted us in our Corinth and likewise taught us; in like manner also after having taught together in Italy they suffered martyrdom about the same time."[21]

Here the "planting" or founding of the churches, alike of Rome and of Corinth, is clearly recognised to have been the work of the apostles Peter and Paul. It is of no avail to say with Sanday and Headlam (*Comm.* p. 29) that the "planting" referred to (*phuteuein*; cp 1 Cor. 3:6+, 9:7) is not to be taken "in the sense of first foundation." We are not responsible for what Dionysius says; but we are under obligation to understand it in the sense in which he meant it.

The same remark holds good with reference to Irenaeus when he speaks of the church at Rome as having been "founded and constituted by the two very glorious apostles Peter and Paul" (*a gloriosissimis duobus apostolis Petro et Paulo Romae fundata et constituta*, 3:3:1). These two, subsequently spoken of as "the blessed apostles," the same authority (about 180 A.D.) goes on to state, after having founded and built up the church, handed over the government to Linus, 3:3:2; Eus. *HE* 5:6:1). In Eus. *HE* 5:8:2 he tells us that Matthew wrote a gospel for the Hebrews in their own tongue "whilst Peter and Paul were preaching the gospel at Rome and founding the church."

## 2. Not Trustworthy

These clear testimonies, however, to the founding of the church of Rome by Peter and Paul—however unhesitatingly they may have been accepted and built upon in later times—are one and all quite unworthy of credence. Not only are they relatively recent and obviously framed in accordance with a settled policy of glorifying the unity of the church as having been

---

21. Not necessarily, of course, at the same hour, or on the same day, the same month, or even the same year.

manifest even in its oldest communities; what is more to the point, they are at variance with older representations, whether we receive these with absolute confidence or not, of the course of events connected with the founding of a Christian community in Rome.

"Ignatius," in his epistle to the Romans (4:3), written about the middle of the second century, indeed mentions "Peter and Paul" as known and influential teachers of the church he is addressing, but says nothing as to their having founded it. The church of Rome itself speaks by the mouth of "Clement" in the First Epistle to the Corinthians, dating from about the year 140 A.D., of Peter and Paul as known witnesses to the truth (1 Clem. 5:3-7), but not as founders of the church. Acts is not aware of any labours of Peter and Paul carried out in common at Rome. From 28:17-28 it might seem to be a possible inference that Paul was the first to speak about Christianity to the leading Jews there; but of Peter there is no word in this connection.

Just as little is Peter mentioned in the canonical Epistle to the Romans, even in conjunction with "Paul" when this apostle is speaking of his desire to become acquainted with the Christians of the metropolis, whose faith is everywhere spoken of, and whom he hopes ere long to be able to meet (1:3-15, 15:22-24, 15:28-29, 16:19). Indeed, the arrangements between Paul on the one hand, and James, Cephas, and John on the other, according to Galatians 2:9, "we to the Gentiles and they to the circumcision," do not lead us to expect to find in epistles of Paul any word of co-operation between Peter and Paul in the founding of individual churches. What is related as to this at a later date with regard to Rome cannot hold good in presence of the assurance given us by the Epistle to the Romans, whether by Paul himself or by an anonymous author using his name, that at Rome there was a considerable Christian community before Paul could possibly have been able to speak a single word there.

## 3. So Also Peter-tradition

Matters do not stand much better with the belief—held absolutely for many centuries, called in question at the Reformation, and again at a later period maintained by many Protestants also—according to which the church of Rome was founded by Peter alone. This tradition also deserves no credence, whether in the form which represents Peter as having been bishop of Rome for twenty-five years after the founding of the church, or in the simpler form which merely conjectures that the apostle may have contributed something to the formation and extension of the church, or at least in later years may have visited it for a shorter or longer period.

The founding of the church by Peter is excluded by the silence of Ignatius and Clement on the subject, and still more by the evidence of Acts, Galatians, and Romans. Not only do they say nothing positive to this effect; they make it perfectly clear that from the point of view of their respective authors such a thing is not to be thought of. Acts closes its account of Peter in 12:17 with the words, "and he departed, and went to another place," and in the rest of the book Peter's name is only once again mentioned, and in a different connection (15:6-20), where he is represented as again in Jerusalem.

In view of this passage 12:17 cannot be understood as referring to a journey to Rome for any lengthened period, not to speak of a period of five and twenty years. Neither, however, can we understand a visit to Rome of shorter duration, such as Harnack (*ACL* 2:1 [1897], 2:240-244, 2:704-710) still, with many, regards as probable, not even with the aid of the assumption that the contents of Acts 15 were taken from another source than that from which "Luke" derived his other statements regarding Peter in Acts 1-12. The words quoted do not "of course" say that we are to think of a mere visit whether to Rome or to any other place. They are quite clearly intended merely to indicate that the author does not propose to follow the fortunes of Peter further: "and going his way, he journeyed to another place."

To understand Rome as intended here becomes possible only after one has learned otherwhere, rightly or wrongly, to speak of a sojourn of the apostle in the metropolis. Acts says nothing of this, and plainly presupposes rather the exact opposite, since chap. 15 alludes to Peter as again in Jerusalem, and 28:17-28, speaking of Paul's meeting with Jews at Rome, leaves no room for the supposition that Peter had preceded him there as a preacher of Christianity. Galatians knows no residence of Peter other than Antioch (2:11-21)—apart from Jerusalem where, according to 1:18, 2:1-10, he seems to have his home, an agreement that he is to address himself "to the circumcision" being expressly mentioned.

Romans knows of Christians in Rome; refers to their conversion from Judaism and heathendom, their fidelity to the Pauline type of doctrine once received (6:17), and the spiritual bond subsisting between them, or many of them, and Paul; but has not a word to say about any connection, whether of long or short duration, between them and the Apostle Peter, and does not even so much as mention his name. The writer, whoever he may have been, it has been rightly remarked, has no acquaintance with any tradition which represented Peter as having been the founder of the Roman church. His declaration made in 15:20-21 that he, "Paul," would not build upon another man's foundation, however inconsistent with the desire expressed in 1:8-15 and 15:22-24, 15:29, wholly excludes it. Especially so as soon as by the word "another" we understand, as is usually the case, an apostle—in this instance Peter.

It is, in fact, improbable that Peter ever set foot in Rome. The later traditions regarding this, including those handed down by Eusebius, have no claim to our acceptance, as has often been convincingly shown by many scholars (and recently by C. Clemen, *Preuss. Jahrb.*, 1901, pp. 404-417, and C. Erbes,

*Ztschr. f. Kirchengesch.*, 1901, pp. 1-47, 161-231). They possess no higher value than those relating to Thomas's preaching to the Parthians, Andrew's to the Scythians, John's in Asia Minor.

When Eusebius, immediately afterwards (3:3:2, cp 2:25:5), gives expression to the conjecture that Peter preached to the Jews of the Dispersion in Pontus, Galatia, Bithynia, Cappadocia, and Asia, before his crucifixion (head downwards) at Rome, he attributes to him, obviously with his eye on 1 Peter 1:1, a career which he himself could not possibly reconcile with the details that he gives elsewhere. According to 3:36:2, Peter was for some time bishop of Antioch before Ignatius; according to 2:25:8 he was, along with Paul, founder of the churches of Corinth and Rome; according to 2:14:6, the powerful opponent of Simon Magus at Rome in the reign of Claudius (41-54 A.D.); according to 6:25:8, the rock upon which the church of Christ is built, and the author of two epistles.

A reference to 1 Peter 1:1, though often made in conjunction with 5:13, is of no avail to support the view that Peter at some time or other had indeed made a stay, longer or shorter, in Rome. There need, indeed, be no hesitation, not even in presence of the objections of Erbes, to see in "she that is in Babylon, elect together with [you]," 1 Pet. 5:13) an allusion to the church in Rome. In 1 Peter, however, it is not Peter himself who is speaking, but an unknown author writing in the first half of the second century, 130-140 A.D. He is the exponent of a tradition, not met with elsewhere, regarding Peter as apostle in a portion of the countries of Asia Minor where Paul also had laboured, and at the same time of the other widely spread tradition that Peter had his home in Rome. Acts, Galatians, and Romans, so far as we can see, are not yet acquainted with this latest tradition.

Even 1 Clement, written professedly by the church of Rome, and probably, in point of fact, originating there, says nothing of a sojourn of Peter in Rome. The writer assuredly would not have passed it over in silence when speaking of Peter's glorious past in chap. 5, or treating of the life-work of the "apostles" in chaps. 42 and 44, if he had known anything of it. Hermas and Justin, both of them witnesses belonging to the Roman circle, are similarly silent as to aught that Peter may be supposed to have done, said, or endured there.

There are, then, as regards Peter's going to Rome, and as regards his journeyings as a whole, traditions which, in part, are mutually exclusive and in no case admit of being combined together into one consistent whole. The older ones do not imply the supposed fact of the church of Rome having been founded by Peter; they have no knowledge of it, or even bear witness against it by making statements which cannot be harmonised with it. Acts, Galatians, Romans, 1Clement, undoubtedly come chiefly into consideration here. On the same side there fall to be grouped other NT testimonies to the martyrdom of Peter, and, more precisely, his crucifixion, drawn from very old, if not the oldest, traditions relating to the careers of the apostles, though without mention of the place where this violent death occurred.

See John. 21:18-22 (cp 13:36) Matthew 10:5-6, 10:16-18, 10:22-33, 23:34, 23:39, 24:9, 24:14, Mark 13:9-13, Luke 24:47, Acts 18. Within the circle of these ancient witnesses we can safely say—apart, if you will, from 1 Peter 1:1, 5:13—of all those in the NT, to which also may be added that of the Apostolic Fathers, that not a single word or even the remotest hint is found in them as to a sojourn, whether of long or of short duration, of Peter in Rome, whilst, in fact, more than one of them, by implicit or explicit declaration, are irreconcilably at variance with any such supposition. Rather does everything plead for the view that Peter never visited Rome, but worked continuously in Palestine—occasionally, perhaps, outside its limits, but never very far off—and that there, it may well have been in Jerusalem, somewhere about 64 A.D. under Sabinus, 1 or, at all events, some years before the destruction of the temple and city in 70 A.D., he died a martyr's death.

What remains of the late tradition as to the founding of the church of Rome by Peter and Paul conjointly does not need any careful scrutiny after the name of Peter has been eliminated. We are not in that event shut up to the alternative: if not by Peter and Paul together, then probably by Paul alone. This is nowhere said in any tradition so far as known to us. Tradition seems rather to have followed this course: since it is impossible that Paul can have founded the church along with Peter, his name must not be thought of in connection with the founding at all. Acts and Pauline Epistles, writings frequently read in a large circle, indicated this.

## 4. In Acts

Acts knows of no Christian church at Rome at a date prior to a possible foundation by Paul after he had proclaimed the glad tidings to the Jews assembled at his lodging (28:17-31). In 28:15, indeed, we read of the "brethren" who came from Rome to Appii Forum and the Three Taverns to meet Paul, and it is no doubt usual to regard these as having been Christians, but on no adequate grounds. They are, to judge from vv. 17-28, Jews, just as Roman Jews (v. 21) call their kinsmen in Judaea "the brethren." They are amazed at Paul's plans, and declare as distinctly as possible in v. 22 that up to that hour they had heard nothing of "this sect"—i.e., of the Christians—beyond the mere name.

All this is in perfect agreement with the current representation in Acts, according to which Paul in his journeyings invariably first addressed himself to the Jews and thereafter to the Gentiles with a view to proceeding to the setting up of a Christian community, whether composed entirely of converted Gentiles, or partly also of former Jews (cp 13:46 and 13-28 passim). The view that by the "brethren" of Rome, alluded to in

28:15, as also by those of Puteoli in v. 14, we are to understand Christians, rests solely upon the representation in Romans, according to which Christians are found in Rome long before Paul has ever visited that city.

At the same time it must be remembered that the opposite representation in Acts has no historical authoritativeness, being inextricably bound up with the tendency of that book which has been already referred to. Moreover, in Acts 28:30-31 the founding of a Christian church at Rome by Paul is rather tacitly assumed than asserted in so many words. It is possible that in the "Acts of Paul" (which were worked over by the writer of our canonical Acts, and also made use of in the composition of the Pauline Epistles, and which themselves in turn had their origin in a redaction and expansion of the recognised We-source) the original journey record may have given a somewhat different account of the conditions which Paul found at Rome and elsewhere in Italy. It may be that, according to that representation, there were already in more than one place at Rome Christians, "brethren" in another and higher sense than that of mere kinship, and that their figurative designation is adopted by Acts so that the "brethren" in Puteoli and Rome, according to Acts 28:14-15 to be understood as Jews who were friendly disposed towards Paul, were at the same time the original Christians of these places.

## 5. In Romans

However that may be, Acts nowhere contains any express statement as to the founding of a Christian church at Rome by Paul; and as little does the Epistle to the Romans. What Romans implies is, clearly, rather this—that the church had already been long in existence when Paul was cherishing the hope that he might have an opportunity of personally visiting it. This view is wont to be accepted on all hands as just: by the majority, because they hold it to come from the Apostle Paul; by others, the friends of advanced criticism, because, however

fully convinced of the pseudepigraphical character of the
epistle, they have no reason for doubting it.

## 6. Romans versus Acts

These have this advantage over the others that they are not,
like them, sorely perplexed by Acts which betrays no
acquaintance with the epistle held to have been addressed to
the church of Rome by Paul at least two years before he himself
undertook the journey thither only to become aware on his
arrival in the metropolis that no one there had ever heard
anything about him or even about Christianity at all otherwise
than by report merely. They set down the divergent
representations in "Luke" and "Paul" simply to the account of
the separate writers, and as regards a supposed founding of the
church at Rome, can only say that according to "Luke" it was
perhaps the work of Paul, but according to "Paul," certainly
not. According to Luke, perhaps it was, since we must interpret
in accordance with the general tendency of his "historical"
work; according to "Paul," because everyone thought so in
those days nor yet had anyone any knowledge of a founding of
the church in Rome by Peter and Paul, or by Peter alone.

## 7. Other Epistles

In other Pauline epistles also there is no trace of acquaintance
with any tradition which sought to represent that founding as
having been brought about by Paul. In Romans there is no hint,
of the kind we meet with in 1 Corinthians 4:14, 2 Corinthians
6:13, 12:14, Galatians 4:19, that "Paul" can regard those whom
he addresses as his "children."

There is no suggestion of such a relation of Paul to Rome even
in Philippians, Philemon, or 1 Clement 5:5-7, where there was
such ample opportunity to call to mind the founding of the
Roman church by Paul had the writer been minded to refer to
it. The Pauline literature says nothing at all about it, nor yet do

the kindred writings, 1 Peter, 1 Clement, Hermas, Ignatius. Rather must we say that in all of them the undisputed and indisputable presupposition is that Rome was won for the gospel without the intervention of Paul, either by his epistles or by his later personal intercourse.

## 8. Founders Unknown Jews

Whom then are we to name as founder of the Roman church? "Not any of the apostles," as long ago Ambrosiaster in the so-called commentary of Ambrosius in the fourth century rightly answers (cp Sanday and Headlam, pp. 25, 101). We could almost venture to guess: one or more of those who probably at a quite early date spread the glad tidings of salvation from Jerusalem westward. There was abundant opportunity in the constant intercourse between Rome and the East, even before the middle of the first century, for travellers from Palestine to return, or come for the first time, to the banks of the Tiber and there to discourse, as they had done in the various other ports and cities they touched on their route, of the "things concerning Jesus;" (Acts 18:25, 28:23, 28:31), "the kingdom of God" (Acts 14:22, 19:8, 20:25, 28:23, 28:31), "the preaching of the gospel" (Acts 13:32, 14:7, 14:15, 14:21, 15:35, 16:10).

It is not necessary to have recourse to the hardly historical account of the first appearance of the apostles at Jerusalem in Acts 2, where, as we read in vv. 10-11, Romans, Jews as well as proselytes, were sojourning. Such Jews living in Rome, as well as Gentiles who had attached themselves to them and professed their religion, may well have visited Jerusalem on other occasions and become messengers, possibly very capable ones, of what they had seen and heard there to their brethren in the metropolis.

## 9. Jewish Settlement at Rome

We shall best picture to ourselves the subsequent course of events if we suppose that the preaching of the gospel and the establishment of the new religion made its way amongst Jews and proselytes in Rome. Whoever wishes to picture to himself the nature of the field in which, now here, now there, the good seed was scattered by unknown sowers, must try to form some conception of the Jewish settlements in Rome as they then were.

Very many they were, ordinarily confined within certain precisely defined limits, but within these moving with social freedom bound only in so far as they themselves chose to be so by the customs and practices received from their fathers, the law and what it was held to enjoin on the faithful children of Abraham by descent, or on the proselytes who had joined them. Alternately receiving the favours of the great and bowed down under the heavy burden laid upon them by authorities of a less friendly disposition; constantly exposed to risks of persecution, scorn, and derision, and seldom allowed to pass altogether without notice; engaged in the pursuit of trade and dependent on this for their daily bread, now envied for their wealth and now plunged into the depths of poverty or reduced to the ranks of professional beggars.

Such, just before and during the opening decades of the first century, was the manner of life of the Jews in Rome: a great brotherhood, we may call it, broken up into a number of smaller communities; a band of aliens who knew how to maintain their old manners and customs, their nationality, and their religion, in spite of many divergencies and divisions among themselves, in the midst of the surrounding Gentiles amongst whom their progenitors had settled.

At first they had come to pay a visit there because commerce and political reasons had brought them to the world-city; so it had been already in the days of the Maccabees. Others again had been brought to Rome from their native country as slaves, but on closer acquaintance were hardly found suitable and often received their freedom or even were invested with the privileges of Roman citizens. So, in particular, shortly after the capture of Jerusalem by Pompey in 63 B.C. by Caesar and others they were shown great favour. Under Tiberius they were expelled from Rome in the year 19 A.D. and partly employed in the war against the pirates of Sardinia. Under Claudius about 49 A.D. they were again banished. Under Nero it would seem they enjoyed no small power and influence. (For details see Schürer, GJV (3), 1898, 3:28-36 and specially the literature referred to there on p. 28, n. 70).

## 10. Age

On this Jewish soil the earliest Roman Christianity, we may safely affirm, had already come into being before the middle of the first century. The oldest distinct trace of its beginnings is found in Suetonius (Claud. 25), where he says of the emperor Claudius that he expelled the Jews from Rome on account of their persistent turbulence under the instigation of Chrestus [sic] (*Judaeos impulsore Chresto assidue tumultuantes Roma expulit*). The banishment of the Jews (Acts 18:2 and Dio Cassius 60:6), although probably in the event not judged expedient or perhaps even possible, and in any case not carried out on any large scale, had its occasion in troubles and disturbances which had arisen among the Jews *"impulsore Chresto"*—i.e., at the instance or with the help of Chrestus. This Chrestus was, to judge by the manner of speech of those days, no other than (Jesus) Christ; his person and work, the views and expectations connected with him, and his cause were what led Claudius to seek to remove the Jews who had thus become troublesome.

Now, though the exact year in which this resolution was come to by the emperor is uncertain, if we remember that at the beginning of his reign (41-54 A.D.) he was, according to

Josephus (*Ant.* 19:5:2-3), favourably inclined to the Jews, we are led to think of a somewhat later date—let us say with Schürer (32-33) and others, the year 49 A.D. In that case the movement we are supposing, and its procuring cause, the first systematic preaching of Christianity in Rome, can have begun some months or years previously. We must leave open the question as to whether at a still earlier date some converts, in the course of pilgrimages to Jerusalem or through the agency of third parties in their adopted country, may not have been won for the new confession and the expectations connected with it. Rome had already for a long time been a favourite and much frequented harbour for new ideas in the sphere of religion.

## 11. Theory of Acts and Romans

With the date thus arrived at for the founding of the Christian church in Rome it agrees tolerably well that a writer many years later, in Acts 28:17-28, could still speak as if the new sect were known only by name in the world capital when Paul first proclaimed the tidings of salvation to the Jews there, and that another writer—the author of Romans—did not hesitate to assume throughout his work that at that very time there had already been for a long time in Rome believers belonging to various schools of Christian thought and practice.

When these books were written the days of the first founding of a church in Rome were already so far removed that in different circles divergent representations were given regarding it, though there was some danger of misrepresentation. "Luke" is wrong because he does not take account of the existence of any Christian church at Rome before the apostle Paul had made his voice heard there. The Pauline writer, on the other hand, represents the Apostle of the Gentiles as knowing that before his arrival among them the faith of the Roman Christians was already "proclaimed throughout the whole world" (Rom. 1:8), and in 6:17 it is the Pauline form of doctrine whereunto they have been delivered. Both the one view and the other may well be questioned as strict history.

Both writers make it manifest that they no longer know the true position of matters so far as details are concerned. At the same time they confirm, each in his own way, the correctness of the date we have arrived at; at the beginning of the second century, the founding of the church at Rome belonged to a considerably remote past and at that distance of time could, speaking broadly, be connected with a delineation of the period when Paul was setting out for, or had arrived at, the metropolis of the empire.

## 12. Further Data

The nearer determination of the date is to be sought in such data as

> (1) the tradition regarding Paul's plans with reference to a journey to Spain, by way of Rome where a Christian church no longer needed to be founded (Rom. 15:28-29, cp 1 Clem. 5:5-7);
>
> (2) the tradition of Paul's death at Rome, whether, as the ordinary reckoning has it, in 64, as Erbes thinks, on 23rd Feb. 63, or as yet others judge, at some date that cannot be more exactly determined, shortly before or in connection with the persecution of the Christians in the summer of 64;
>
> (3) all that relates to the fact of the persecution of the Christians at Rome by Nero;
>
> (4) the appearance of the "church of Rome" as the writer of Clement's first epistle to the Corinthians;
>
> (5) the activity of Marcion and Valentinus among the Christians at Rome;

(6) all that tradition tells us of the establishment of a bishop's see at Rome by the apostles Peter and Paul;

A very large series of testimonies continuously assuring us, each in its own way, that the founding of a Christian church at Rome goes back to the middle of the first century of our era.

## 13. Character of Church

The character of this church was, to begin with, no other than was to be expected from its origin within the sphere of "Jews and proselytes" (4). Ambrosiaster in speaking of Jews alone as fathers of the Christian community at Rome has here again truly said that those who believed confessed Christ and held fast by the law (*"ex quibus [Judaeis] hi qui crecliderant, tradiderunt Romanis ut Christum profitentes legem servarent"*). In this there is no "exaggeration" as Sanday and Headlam (p. 25, n. 3) have thought. They indeed could hardly have thought otherwise as long as they were dominated by belief in the genuineness of the Epistle to the Romans.

Whoever deems himself bound to maintain that belief must inevitably assume that already, before Romans was written by Paul—on the ordinary reckoning, that is to say, before 59 A.D.— there were to be met with in Rome two divergent types of Christian faith and profession, the Jewish-Christian and the Pauline. Such an one cannot avoid facing the question: What was the church of Rome at that time? Jewish-Christian? Pauline? Mixed? Yet all the while he is well aware—or the discovery is ever anew forced upon him—that no satisfactory answer to the question can be given.

Some texts speak very clearly for the view that the church in question consisted of former Gentiles, whilst others say the exact opposite—that it was composed of former Jews (see van Manen, *Paulus*, 2:23-25, 16:6-7). Yet we cannot hold with Sanday-Headlam (p. 26) and others the theory that it was a "mixed" church. To such a theory can be applied to the full what these scholars remark in another connection: "there is no hint of such a state of things," which moreover would compel us, contrary to the manifest intention of the writer, to think of "two distinct churches in Rome, one Jewish-Christian, the other Gentile-Christian, and that St. Paul wrote only to the latter."

Anyone who, on the other hand, has been able to free himself from the axiom of the genuineness and has satisfied himself of the pseudepigraphical character of this writing of a later time no longer feels his hands tied by the various impossible attempts that have been made to answer the questions proposed.

He is no longer perplexed by that other troublesome question: How are we to explain the fact that nowhere in history has there remained any trace of the existence of an important Pauline community in Rome, after the apostle's epistle had been sent thither? He takes no notice of all ideas of this sort, the pictures suggested in the epistle of the outward appearance and inward semblance of the Christian church in Rome in the days before Paul could possibly have preached there—as being not renderings of historical actuality but pictures of a past that never had been real, attempts to represent the old-Christian period after many decades had passed. Such a student holds fast by the seemingly insignificant phrase, which yet tells us so much, of the instigating "Chrestus" by whom the Jews in Rome, according to Suetonius, in the days of Claudius (ob. 49 A.D.) were troubled; and holds by the pretty generally accepted conception as to a Christian church at Rome which had arisen out of the faith and life, the active exertions, of "Jews and proselytes" who had been converted to Christ; by what Ambrosiaster has said, with equal sobriety and justice—that Jews living in Rome in the days of the apostles had taught their brethren to confess Christ and to hold fast by the law.

## 14. Jewish-Christian

In other words, the church in Rome was originally Jewish-Christian, and probably long remained so. Gradually more liberal ideas crept in, thanks perhaps to the influence of more advanced preachers from abroad who had wholly or partially outgrown their Judaism, but thanks still more to the ease with which in every sphere of thought new ideas made way in Rome.

Whether Paul may have had any active share in this work we are not now in a position to say. Acts leaves us in doubt. Romans testifies to good intentions but not to any work actually done. The "epistle," in spite of the seeming abundance of the light it sheds on the events of the years immediately preceding 59 A.D. in Rome, really draws over them all an almost impenetrable veil. It gives surprising glimpses into the history of the development of the church in the direction of greater freedom, the emancipation of Christianity from the dominion of the law, but all from a remote distance in space, probably from the East—Antioch or somewhere else in Syria, it may be, or perchance Asia Minor—at all events, a long way off and in a distinctly later time.

## 15. Struggle of Paulinism

In reality, in the more trustworthy tradition there is no trace of all this, but on the contrary, unmistakable proof that Paulinism at Rome though

> (i.) it struggled for a time for the victory in the days of Marcion (ob. 140 A.D.)
>
> (ii.) never really took permanent root there, and never was other than an exotic.

i. That Paulinism flourished in some degree at Rome is very certain, as we may safely infer:

(a) from the way in which it is throughout presupposed in Romans (written probably about 120 A.D.) that, before his first visit to the capital, Paul already had there a large circle of friends and followers, of whom a whole series is mentioned by name in 16:3-15, and who already for a long time had been instructed in his distinctive type of doctrine (6:17);

(b) from the support as well as the opposition, which Marcion met with in Rome, in various capacities, and not least of all as advocate of his "Apostle," the Paul of the epistles;

(c) from the friendly relation between Peter and Paul presupposed in "1 Peter," probably written at Rome, in evidence of which relation we point not only to the Pauline form of the writing and to the mention, at the end, of Silvanus and of Mark (cp 2 Peter 3:15-16), but also and chiefly to the strongly Pauline character of the contents;

(d) from the liberal spirit of the Gospel according to Mark, probably also written at Rome, along with which perhaps that according to Luke may also be named;

(e) from the honour with which "Clement" as spokesman of the church at Rome writes "to the Corinthians" concerning Paul (1 Clem. 5:5-7, 47:1), and more than once declares that he is influenced by the reading of his "epistles;"

(f) from the mention of Paul along with Peter as a teacher of authority by "Ignatius" in his Epistle to the Romans ( "I do not command you as Peter and Paul did," 43);

(g) from the wide currency of the later tradition of the founding of the Christian church at Rome by "Peter and Paul."

ii. Paulinism was, however, only partially successful, as is no less clearly evident:

(a) from the way in which in Romans Paul now admonishes the Jews (chaps. 1-8, passim, and especially 2:17-29) and now shows them the greatest deference (chaps. 9-11 passim, especially 3:1-2, 9:1-5, 10:1);

(b) from the opposition met with by Marcion in Rome which ended in his expulsion from the new religious community;

(c) from the position of the name of Paul in the younger tradition—already in "Clement" and "Ignatius"—after that of Peter;

(d) from the spirit of works brought out at Rome and extensively read there, the most outstanding of which is the so-called First Epistle of Clement to the Corinthians. The spirit there breathed, notwithstanding the reverence expressed for "Paul" and the deference occasionally paid to the principles inaugurated by him, is much more of a Jewish-Christian character than one that testifies to warm sympathy with the gospel of freedom; rather one that is slowly gravitating toward the left than one that is averse to the right in principle; a conciliatory and advancing spirit, if you will, yet rather in many respects showing lingering attachment to the old than still standing with both feet upon the basis of the law, firmly rooted in Judaism, filled with the rich contents of the Old Testament; in a word, a spirit that in its inmost nature is becoming Catholic.

## 16. Gradual Change

The Christian church of Rome, in its beginnings a shoot from the Jewish stock, in the course of years took up and assimilated elements that were brought to it from other quarters: from the East, and particularly from Syria and Asia Minor. Its power of adaptation was of great use to it in regard to those elements in the new faith which were originally strange in it and were at home rather in the more developed circles of Paulinism, but in adapting itself the original power of the Pauline spiritual movement was in many respects taken away.

In the course of years—let us say, in round numbers, between 50 and 150 A.D.—the character of the church at Rome, from being Jewish-Christian with occasional deviations towards the right and towards the left, had become, we shall not say Pauline or Gentile-Christian, but Catholic. At the later date—i.e. , about the middle of the second century—it had recently been the scene of the labours of Marcion, who was excommunicated afterwards, Marcion the eager and serious advocate of "Paul" who had already probably some years before become known to it by means of the "epistles." It had at the same time come into touch with, among others, that highly gifted teacher, well nigh lost in broad and deep speculations, alternately held in reverence and covered with scorn, the gnostic Valentinus. It had learned to listen to preachers of repentance like Hermas who, eminently practical, sought to win it before all things else to the urgent duty of conversion.

But, however divergent may have been the paths by which it was so dissimilarly led by these and other leaders to clearer insight on many sides, and deeper experience of the fruits of faith as that translated itself into a genuine Christian life, the structure as carried out appeared always, in spite of the multifarious and manifold additions, to rest upon the old foundation—destined, as it would seem, never to become obsolete—that of the law and of Judaism, to which, as a new and indispensable element, confession of Jesus as the Christ, had been added.

## 17. Constitution of Jewish Community

How this Christian community at Rome was originally governed and organised can probably be best conjectured, in the absence of all positive information, by calling to mind once more what we know of the spirit of that religious fellowship of the Jews out of which it arose. Like this last it had no political aims, and consequently as yet knew nothing of those who at a later time were to be called rulers and leaders, charged with the care of the outward life of Christians as subjects of the state.

The Jewish "Church," although it can be so called in respect of the religious confession of its adherents, formed no unity placed under the leadership and government of a single council or of one head. It was made up rather of a great number of separate and independent congregations (*synagogai*), each having its own synagogue, its own council (*gerousia*), its own rulers (*archontes*), who also sometimes at least, were partly called "elders" (*presbyteroi*), and, whether for life (*dia biou*) or for a limited period, were chosen at the beginning of the Jewish civil year (in September). They were charged with the general leadership of the community, sometimes also with the task associated with the special office of chief of the synagogue (*archisynagogos*). The language employed was Greek, as indeed the whole constitution with rulers (*archontes*) and councils (*gerousiai*), so far as form was concerned, seems to have been borrowed from the civil organisation usual in Greek cities (see Schürer, *Die Gemeindeverfassung der Juden in Rom*, 1879, and GJV (3) 3,pp. 44-51 [1898]).

## 18. Of Christian Church

The Christian church also, we may safely take for granted, very soon after its members had been excommunicated, or had voluntarily withdrawn from the Jewish synagogues in Rome, had their own centres, with a government proper to themselves (modelled mainly, so far as form was concerned, on that which they had left at the call of religious principle and duty), their own places of meeting (*synagogai*), their own rulers (*archontes*), who are often called elders (*presbyteroi*).

This was what happened elsewhere throughout the cities of the Dispersion. Why not also in Rome? Acts calls the rulers "elders" (*presbyteroi*) in 11:30, 14:23, 20:17, whenever Jerusalem is spoken of, where the apostles are regarded as having lived and laboured, we read of "apostles and elders" (14:2, 15:4, 15:6, 15:23, 16:4), just as the same writer elsewhere when referring to the rulers (*archontes*) of the Jews speaks of their "elders" (2:17, 4:5, 4:8, 4:23, 6:12, 23:14, 24:1, 25:15). For the rest, in Acts we find no allusion to any government of Christian communities, just as, in fact, of the community that arose after the arrival of Paul in Rome nothing more is said than that they met in Paul's own house (28:30-31). In Romans there is no evidence as to the terms employed in this connection by the Christians at Rome, except in a single passage where allusion is made to "him that ruleth" (*o proistamenos*: 128).

One Clement, the "epistle" of the "church of God" at Rome to that of Corinth, has more to say. The church (*e ekklesia*) comes before us as a unity embracing all believers within the boundaries of a definite locality; so in the opening words and also in 44:3, 47:6 (cp 2 Clem. 2:1, 14:1, 14:2, 14:41) we are not precluded from thinking that, as in the case of the Jews, this unity was made up of various circles or congregations within the larger whole which comprehended the whole body of the faithful.

The supposition finds support when we consider the manner in which the occurrence of divergent ideas and practices with regard to the choice of officials is spoken of. Some consider themselves free in their choice; but others, including the writer, hold themselves bound to tradition and obliged to adhere to the ancient holders of spiritual offices as long as they have not disqualified themselves by misconduct (cp 1:3, 3:3, 21:6, 42, 44, 59:2).

True, this applies, so far as form is concerned, in the first instance and especially, only to the Corinthians who are being addressed, but yet also to the Romans who are speaking of themselves in the plural number (cp 7:1). The most obvious explanation is to be found in the supposition that the divergent views and practices referred to were found in the different circles or congregations (*ekklesiai*) within the bounds of the one church—*e ekklesia*—whether that of Rome or that of Corinth. However that may be, "the church" had its rulers or leaders (*egoumenoi*; 1:3) just as had the Jews (32:2), the Egyptians (51:5), and others (37:3, 55:1, 60:1). They are usually called "elders" (*presbyteroi*; 1:3, 1:33, 21:6, 44:5, 47:6, 54:2, 57:1, cp 2 Clem. 17:3, 17:5), but in one instance, though in no different sense, "overseers" (*episkopoi*) and "deacons" (*diakonoi*, 42:4-5, cp 44:1, 50:3), charged with the sacred service (*leitourgia*, 41:1, 44:2-3, 44:6). They were "ministering" (*leitourgountes*; 463) just as in their manner were the Jews (32:2, 40), Enoch (9:2), Aaron (43:4), the angels of God (34:5-6). In this service or ministry were included, or at least came under their superintendence,

> (1) the reading of scripture—the OT as we now know it and whatever other writings were at that time reckoned as belonging to it; also Christian writings such as Paul's "Epistle to the Corinthians" and other treatises, including 1 and 2 Clement, (cp 2 Clem. 19:1, 15:1, 17:5, 1 Clem. 47:1, 63:2, 7:1; Herm. *Vis.* 2:1:3, 2:4:1, Eus. *HE* 2:25:8, 3:38:5)
>
> (2) exhortation (cp 1 Clem., passim) and
>
> (3) prayer (1 Clem. 59:3-61, 2 Clem. 22).

All of these, as with the Jews, at least down to near the end of the second century, were performed in Greek.

Of a monarchical government of the church there is as yet no trace in 1 and 2 Clement. Neither is there any in the Shepherd of Hermas which, like the Epistles of Clement, knows only of elders (*Vis.* 2:4:2-3, 3:1:8) and overseers, along with "teachers" and "deacons" (*Vis.* 3:5:1, *Sim.* 9:27:2). The oldest traces of monarchical church government in Rome are met with in the seven epistles of "Ignatius" which were probably written there about the middle of the second century, and in the earliest lists of Roman bishops—little trustworthy though these are in their substance, and put together in the interests of the recognition of the episcopate, which was then coming into being, or had recently come to be important. They do not go farther back than to Anicetus, and were probably drawn up under his successor Soter, about 170 A.D. (see Harnack, *ACL* ii. 1, 1897, pp. 70-231, esp. pp. 144-202.)

## 19. Importance of Rome

If the question be asked, finally, as to the influence and importance of the Christian church at Rome, it was small and certainly for the first few decades not to be compared with that of the church at Jerusalem nor yet with that of other churches of Palestine, Syria, and Asia Minor. It was only gradually in the course of the second century that a change in this respect came about, under the influence of great historical events such as the fall of Jerusalem in 70 A.D., the rebuilding of that city as Aelia Capitolina under Hadrian, and the continual process by which the West manifested its preponderance over the East.

In all this there made itself felt the favourable situation of the Christian church at Rome in the centre of Graeco-Roman civilisation; the inborn inclination, and the corresponding aptitude, of what had been the Gentile element in the new church, to lead and soon to dominate believers who had their homes elsewhere, as well as unbelievers; and last, certainly not least, whatever that church was able to contribute from its own resources towards its internal growth and its external prestige. In this connection we may particularly specify: the accession not merely of slaves and people of the lower orders but also of rich and often influential persons, sometimes even from the immediate entourage of the emperor; the courage shown by martyrs there as elsewhere; the zeal of outstanding personalities such as Valentinus and Marcion; the activity of efficient men such as "Clement" and "Ignatius" in labouring for the establishment of the Catholic Church; the labour expended on various sides to advance far and near the cause of knowledge, of Christian practice, of edification, of consolation.

## 20. Christian Literature

Marcion laid the foundations of a recognition of a written norm of truth, of belief, one gospel and ten Pauline Epistles, which the church as it grew Catholic soon spread far and wide and accepted—along with the older tradition—as the touchstone of truth. Into this (ecclesiastical) canon Rome, according to the list discovered and published in modern times by Muratori, introduced a larger collection of Old-Christian writings differing but slightly in extent from the NT as that was finally fixed by well-nigh the whole of Christendom. Marcion also wrote an orthodoxly conceived "Epistle" and "Antitheses" or "Separation of Law and Gospel" (*Antitheses* or *Separatio legis et evangelii*); Valentinus was the author of "Epistles," "Homilies," and "Psalms."

Some unknown writer prepared the Gospel according to Mark; "Clement," two "epistles" to the Corinthians, of which the first is a "Treatise concerning Peace and Harmony," conceived, according to its own description of itself (63:2), in the interests of peace in the churches, and especially in the matter of the election of elders, and the second is an "Exhortation concerning continence" (15:1). Hermas wrote his *Shepherd* to stir up all to repentance; "Ignatius" composed his "epistles" upon love for the promotion of martyrdom and on behalf of right views in doctrine and in life. He and others contributed largely to the upbuilding of their own as well as other churches, where their epistles were diligently read.

Thus the Roman leaders exercised influence in ever-widening circles, and opened up the way, often quite unconsciously, for the spiritual predominance of their fellow-believers abroad. From the middle of the second century another element that had no small influence also was the effort after a one-man government of the church, first on the part of Rome alone, but afterwards also on that of others who afterwards associated themselves with it in this.

Polycarp of Smyrna, seeking for comfort at the hands of Anicetus of Rome in the matter of orthodox observance of Easter, still knows how to maintain his freedom of thought and action in another direction than that prescribed to him. But one of his successors in the Asia Minor controversy of the Quartodecimans, Polycrates of Ephesus, was excommunicated by Victor of Rome and cut off from the fellowship of the faithful (see Baur, *Das Christenthum u. d. Christl. Kirche der drei Ersten Jahrh.* 1853, pp. 141-157). In this manner the preponderance and authoritativeness, and ultimately the supremacy, of the church of Rome had already come to be recognised in the East before the end of the second century.

## 21. Bibliography

For the extensive literature dealing with our subject reference may be made, amongst others, to such studies on the supposed sojourn of Peter and Paul in Rome as those of A. Harnack, *ACL* ii. 1 1897, pp. 240-244, 703-710; C. Clemen, *1st Petrus in Rom gewesen?* in *Preuss. Jahrb.* 1901, pp. 404-417; C. Erbes, "Petrus nicht in Rom sondern in Jerusalem gestorben?" in Brieger's *Ztschr.f. Kirchen-gesch.* 1901, pp. 1-47, 161-231; "On the Jews in Rome" in Sanday and Headlam, *The Ep. to the Romans*, 1895, xviii-xxv; Berliner, *Gesch. der Juden in Rom*, 1893; E. Schürer, *Die Gemeindeverfassung der Jüden in Rom*, 1879 and *GJV* (3), iii. 1898, pp. 28-36 44-56. Also to the commentaries on Romans such as those of Sanday-Headlam, 1895, xviii-xliv; R. A. Lipsius in HC(2), 1892, pp. 70-78; Meyer-Weiss (9), 1890, pp. 16-22: to the NT Introductions such as those of S. Davidson (3), 1804, 1105-113; H. J. Holtzmann (3),

1892, pp. 232-236; Th. Zahn (2), 1900, pp. 299-308; J. M. S. Baljon, 1901, pp. 88-92.

# Shepherd of Hermas

*Not to be despised as a praiseworthy production in
the field of edifying literature it is still more to be
prized as a valuable contribution to our knowledge
of the Christianity that was widely spread and held
as orthodox about the middle of the second century.*

## 1. Name: Transmission of Text

Under the name of *Poimen* (*Pastor*, "Shepherd") with which
from an early date the name of Hermas came to be connected, a
book of some size, originally written in Greek, has come down
to us from Christian antiquity. At one time greatly read, and
even for a while regarded as canonical, it afterwards fell very
much into the background without, however, being wholly lost
sight of.

The Greek text, though still without the concluding portion
*Sim.* ix. 30.3.x., was first brought to tight comparatively
recently (1856). A Latin version, the Vulgate, was published as
early as 1513 by Faber Stapulensis; an Ethiopic by Anton
d'Abbadie in 1850. Ever since Cotelier's time (1672) the work
has been wont to be included in editions of the so-called
Apostolic Fathers.

We now know the Greek text of *Vis.* i.- *Mand.* iv. 3.6a from the
*Codex Sinaiticus* edited by Tischendorf in 1861; the contents
of the rest of the work (apart from the concluding portion
already spoken of, and certain lacunae) from the so-called
Athos MS of which three leaves are now in the University
Library at Leipzig (since 1856) and six still remain in the
Monastery of Gregory on Mt. Athos; that of *Sim.* 2.7-to 4.2-5
from an old papyrus now in Berlin, formerly at Fayyum,
described by U. Wilcken in 1891; that of other fragments, we

have known for a longer period from the citations of ancient writers.

Valuable help can also be obtained throughout from two Old Latin versions, the Vulgate and (since Dressel, 1857) the Palatine, as also from the Ethiopic. For the establishment of the original text, since the edition of Anger and Dindorf, 1856, who at first were led astray by Simonides (afterwards proved to be a forger) but were ultimately put upon the right track by Tischendorf as he in his turn was corrected by Lipsius, specially meritorious services have been rendered by A. Hilgenfeld, 1866(2nd ed.), 1881(3rd), 1887; O. de Gebhardt, 1877; J. Armitage Robinson, *A Collation of the Athos Codex of the Shepherd of Hermas*, 1888; F. X. Funk, *Patres Apost.*, (2nd), 1901.

## 2. Divisions

*The Shepherd*, in view of its contents, is usually divided into three parts, entitled respectively (i) Visions, (2) Commandments [= Mandates], (3) Similitudes. The printed editions, in fact, all follow each other in giving five Visions, twelve Commandments, and ten Similitudes. This division, however, is hardly accurate, and it would be better to say that the book in the form in which it has come down to us consists of Visions (*Oraseis*) or Revelations (*Apokalupseis*) of which the first (*Vis.* 1.i) can be regarded as an introduction to those immediately following (*Vis.* 1.2-4) and the last (*Vis.* 5) as an introduction to the immediately following series of Commandments and Similitudes (*ai entole kai parabolai: Mand.* 1-12, *Sim.* 1-8) to which is added an appendix called "The rest" (*ta etera; Sim.* 9) and a conclusion (*Sim.* 10).

## 3. Form and Contents

So far as the form of the book is concerned, Hermas, a former slave of a certain Rhoda in Rome to whom his father had sold him, and who had afterwards come into the service of the Christian church, now comes forward as a writer, relating certain things that have happened to him and what he has seen and heard—or, in a word, what has been revealed to him.

As he was walking outside the city "to the villages,"—*eis komas*, as the Greek text has it, for which the printed editions, after a conjecture of Dindorf, wrongly read *eis Koumas*, to Cumae—he falls asleep and there appears to him the woman whose slave he formerly had been and whom he had not been able to seek in marriage (*Vis.* 1.1). Afterwards the Church appears to him at longer or shorter intervals (a year, or less); first in the form of an old woman (*Vis.* 1.2-4; cp 3.10-11), next with a more youthful aspect (*Vis.* 2; cp 3.12); again, as quite young (*Vis.* 3.1-10; cp 13); finally, as a maiden in wedding attire (*Vis.* 4).

She reveals to him the future and expounds with regard to it the will of God. She gives instructions and shows visions which have reference to the necessity for repentance while yet the building of the tower, symbolising the Church, is still unfinished, or rather suspended for a while—in other words while yet God affords the opportunity to repent, an opportunity which ere long will cease with the coming of the last great persecution.

After these revelations (*Vis.* 1-4) Hermas relates how the angel of repentance appears to him in the form of a shepherd, as previously (*Vis.* 2.4; 3.10) in that of a young man, and bids him write down "commandments and similitudes" (*Vis.* 5). The twelve commandments which follow relate to faith in God; a life void of offence, full of compassion, love of truth; chastity; long suffering; our attendant angels, good and bad; the fear of the Lord; abstinence from all that is evil; prayer without ceasing and with unwavering confidence; two kinds of sadness; two kinds of spirit; two kinds of desire (*Mand.* 1-12).

The eight similitudes which follow teach us how here we have no continuing city; how the rich can be helped by the prayer of the poor; how the righteous and the wicked cannot at first be discriminated, but will ultimately be separated (*Sim.* 1-4): how useful fasting is; how good it is to keep far aloof from luxury and temptation; how indispensable is chastening; how many are the varieties of saint and sinner (*Sim.* 5-8). Next, by way of appendix, is set forth in new images that which the Holy Spirit that spoke with Hermas in the form of the Church had showed him. They are revelations vouchsafed to him by the Shepherd, the angel of repentance, with reference to those who are saved (*Sim.* 9). To round off the whole, yet a further earnest admonition is given by the angel who had sent the Shepherd; a last exhortation to repentance in accordance with the precepts of the now completed work (*Sim.* 10).

## 4. The Form Artificial

The form in which the whole is clothed, far from being simple or natural, is artificial in the highest degree. It sets out, apparently, with the intention of relating what has passed between two known persons, Rhoda and Hermas. The names are reminiscent of a Christian woman Rhoda, mentioned in Acts 12:13, and of a Christian slave at Rome, Hermas, mentioned in Romans 16:14. Here they become representatives, the one (Rhoda) of the Church in various successive forms, the other as one devoted to her service, and one of her followers and members. "Hermas" soon goes on to speak with poetic freedom like a Paul, a James, a John, a Barnabas, a Clement, an Ignatius, a Polycarp, in the epistles handed down to us under their names, as if he were the recognised elder and faithful witness addressing himself with words of warning and admonition to his "house," his "children."

## 5. Unity and Composition

The original unity of the work in its present form, although frequently called in question since Hase (1834), cannot be denied. Even less, however, can the existence of inconsistencies and contradictions and other marks of interpolation, adaptation, and redaction be disputed. These point to it having been a composite work made up from earlier documents, not in the sense (so Hilgenfeld, 1881; Hausleiter, 1884; Baumgärtner, 1889; Harnack, 1897) of its being a combination, effected in one way or another, of two separate works, entitled respectively "Visions" and "Commandments" and "Similitudes" by one author, or by more than one; nor yet (so Johnson, 1887; Spitta, 1896; von Soden, 1897; Völter, 1900; van Bakel, 1900) in the sense of its being the outcome of repeated redactions of an originally Jewish writing. Rather in the sense of being a second edition of the original *Shepherd*, a bundle of "Commandments and Similitudes" from the pen of but one writer who laboured on the whole independently, yet at the same time frequently borrowed from the books which he had before him. It is not possible to distinguish throughout between what he borrowed from others and what we ought to regard as his own.

## 6. Author

The writer, who comes forward as if he were an older Hermas, the contemporary of Clement (*Vis.* 1i, 3), must not be identified with him of Romans 16:14 nor yet with a younger one, brother of Pius I, bishop of Rome 140-155, who is referred to in the Muratorian fragment. The real name of the author remained unknown.

From his work it can be inferred that he was an important member, perhaps even a ruler of the Christian church, probably in Rome. A practical man. No Paulinist, nor yet a Judaiser in the Tübingen sense, but rather a professor, little interested in the dogma of the Christianity that was already in process of becoming Catholic, in the days when it was grappling with the ideas and movements that had originated with Montanus, one who attached much value to revelations and yet was very particularly in earnest about the need for quickening, for the spiritual renewing of the Church, for which reason he laid peculiar stress upon the possibility of a second conversion.

This possibility would ere long come to an end at the close of the present period; even now many were denying it as regarded those who once had received baptism, though others hoped to be able continually afresh to obtain the forgiveness of their sins. There is nothing that indicates the merchant supposed by Harnack-Hilgenfeld.

## 7. Date

In date the author is earlier than Eusebius, Athanasius, Origen, Tertullian, Clement of Alexandria, Irenaeus, but later than the apostles and their first followers, the martyrs and leaders of the church, such individuals as "Hermas" and "Clement" (*Vis.* 24 3). Later than the first great and flourishing time of the church (the history of which can already be divided into different periods, and the spiritual renovation of which, in conjunction with the revived expectation of Christ's second coming, is regarded as imperatively needful); in the days when the spiritual life of Christians was being stirred by Montanistic movements. Therefore, certainly earlier than 180 A.D.; yet not much earlier, nor yet much later, than about the middle of the second century.

Perhaps some chronological truth may underlie the tradition that "Hermas" was a "brother" of Pius I (140-155 A.D.). The work was from the first intended for reading aloud at the assemblies of the Church whether in larger or in smaller circles (*Vis.* 2.4.3).

## 8. Purpose and Value

Its value, at first placed very high from the point of view of the interests of edification, but afterwards almost wholly lost sight of in Christian circles, has in recent years in spite of the diffuseness of its contents come anew to be recognised. Not to be despised as a praiseworthy production in the field of edifying literature it is still more to be prized as a valuable contribution to our knowledge of the Christianity that was widely spread and held as orthodox about the middle of the second century.

## 9. Literature

A. Editions: F. X, Funk, *Patres Apostolici*, (2nd) with prolegomena and notes, (1), 1901; also (in shorter form) *Apost. Väter*, 1901; O. de Gebhardt and A. Harnack,. *Hermae Pastor* (*Patr. Apost. Opera*, iii.), 1877, with introduction and notes; also in smaller edition,(4) 1901.

B. Translations: English: Roberts, Donaldson, and Crombie, in *Apostolic Fathers* in Ante-Nicene Library, 1867; Lightfoot, *Apostolic Fathers*, 1891. German: J. C. Mayer, 1869. Dutch: Duker and van Manen, *Oud-Christel. Lett.: geschriften der ap. Vaders*, with introduction and notes, i. 1871.

C. Discussions: In addition to those already *referred* to, see G. Krüger, *Gesch. d. altchr. Lit.* 1895, § 12, and "Nachtrage," 1897, p. 12; Th. Zahn, *Der Hirt Hermas*, 1868; also *Einl. i. d. NT* vol. 1, (2) 900, pp. 298, 430-8, vol. 2. 104, 154; J. M. S. Baljon, *Gesch. v. d. Bb. de NVs.* 1901, p. 451; G. Uhlhorn, *s.v.* "Hermas" in *PRE* (3) 7 (1899) 714-718; C. Taylor, *The Witness of Hermas to the Four Gospels*, 1892 (cp van Manen, *Th.T.* 1893, pp. 180-194); A. Hilgenfeld, "Hermae Pastor" *Novum Testamentum extr. Can.rec.*, (2) 1881, (3) 1887; P. Baumgartner, *Die Einhheit des Hermas-Buchs*, 1889 (cp van Manen, *Th. T*, 1889, pp. 552-550); E. Spitta, *Zur Gesch. u. Litt. d. Urchristentums*, 2, 1896, pp. 241-437; A. Harnack, *Chronol.* 1897, 1 257-267, 437-8 (cp. von

Soden, *TLZ*, 1897, pp. 584-7); D. J. E. Völter, *Die Visionen des Hermas, die Sibylle u. Clemens von Rom*, 1900; H. A. van Bakel, *De Compositie van den Pastor Hermae*, 1910.

# Afterword

## By Robert M. Price

Theology is generally supposed to be based on scripture, and new versions of Christian (at least Protestant) doctrine have been occasioned by fresh scrutiny of the old texts. Theologians dissatisfied with the status quo on this or that point are ready to spot things in the Bible they had hitherto ignored. But they are looking only to make minor adjustments. Scriptural texts serve mainly as proof texts for a new version of their theology.

Unhappy with Calvinism, Arminius goes back to scripture and has no trouble discovering verses that seem to teach free will rather than predestination. Charles Parham, desperate to discover some sure token that one has indeed received the sanctifying Baptism of the Holy Spirit, suddenly notices that the Book of Acts seems to supply one: speaking in tongues. And so it goes. Theology is the locomotive, with biblical texts serving as the coal to be shoveled into the engine.

And yet the degree to which the interpreter can be truly open to an inductive scrutiny of the texts is limited by the intended use of the results. There are some exegetical results that would prove unacceptable, because they would overthrow the whole enterprise of treating the texts as fodder for theology. If, for instance, you discover that one verse (or scriptural author) contradicts another, or that the texts are all occasional, their teaching *ad hoc* and culturally determined (not just conditioned), you inevitably begin to realize that scripture neither presupposes any underlying system of theology, nor naturally lends itself to the construction of any such system.

That may seem at first like a loss. But it quickly reveals itself to be a great gain, for now we find ourselves free of blinders and open to see in the text what we never allowed ourselves to notice before. Theology, as "the Queen of the Sciences," did what rulers do—magnified itself by ruthlessly appropriating the wealth of its subjects, in this case biblical studies. But suppose the slaves rise up and depose the queen: Then they are no longer exploited serfs, alienated from the fruits of their labors. They do their own work and enjoy their own wealth.

And so, ironically, the better we understand the Bible via the Higher Criticism, the less useful biblical study becomes for theology. The more the student of the Bible is obedient to an inherited theology, the less he can *understand* the Bible, for his vision will be clouded by a vested interest in having what he reads there say one thing and not another.

W.C. van Manen was able to make his breakthroughs in early Christian literature, especially Paulinism, because he had ejected theology (with all its nagging) from the study. After he got some peace and intellectual privacy in this manner, he understood many things for the first time. What he understood, and the method he used to understand it, made traditional theology impossible.

Martin Luther promised that scripture was "perspicacious," easy enough to understand where it counted. This implies he understood deep down that it really was not. He protested rather too much, subconsciously aware that mere ambiguity in the text was sufficient to render scriptural "authority" moot. Imagine the ringing tones of the preacher averring that scripture *most likely* teaches salvation by grace through faith, that the Eucharist is *very probably* the very body and blood of Christ and not a metaphor, that there is perhaps a fifty-five percent chance that God abominates homosexuality.

Such nuancing about probabilities would by itself seem to render scripture unfit, inappropriate for authoritative proclamation. But it gets worse. Despite the supposed "plenary inspiration" of scripture, it's always been apparent that there is a functional theological hierarchy within the canon: The New Testament overrules the Old; the Pauline Epistles pull rank over the gospels in that the Epistles "interpret" the gospel texts. Like the snooty pigs in Orwell's *Animal Farm*, some of the inspired books wind up being more equally inspired than others.

Without Romans and Galatians, one might get the decided impression that the gospel Jesus teaches "salvation by works," and we can't have that! So even as erudite and critical a scholar as Joachim Jeremias felt obliged to cram the works-oriented Sermon on the Mount into the Procrustean bed of Romans (as interpreted by Luther). Protestants are first and foremost Paulinists. It is Paul's calling, hence his authority, that governs their faith and practice. Even the rest of the epistles (ascribed to James, John, Peter, Jude) are but garnishes on the side of the plate.

Here we see why critical scholars are willing to surrender the historical accuracy of the gospels but stubbornly hang onto the genuine Pauline authorship of at least seven of the "Pauline" Epistles. It almost does not matter what Jesus may have said, since it is going to end up fed through the Pauline (Lutheran) meat grinder anyway. Thus the long struggle over Pauline pseudepigraphy.

Schleiermacher made enemies when he argued that Paul had not really written the so-called First Epistle to Timothy. F.C. Baur argued forcefully that the author of Romans, Galatians, and Corinthians simply could not have written any of the others. Bruno Bauer and the Dutch Radicals used the same methodology to demonstrate the pseudonymous character of all thirteen "Pauline" Epistles. F.C. Baur repudiated these conclusions, while Rudolf Bultmann would recoil even from Baur's boldness, allowing Paul to have written not only the four *Hauptbriefe* ("principal epistles") but 1 Thessalonians, Philippians, and Philemon as well.

At stake here is the undermining of the very foundation of Protestant theological authority: the Apostle Paul. For even if today's liberal Protestants feel they must reinterpret Paul as a feminist, a pro-Jewish ecumenist, a critic of Roman (American) imperialism, they take the trouble because Paul, however refurbished, remains the Protestant totem.

This is, I believe, the true agenda behind the contempt with which the Dutch Radical position (where it is even known) has always been dismissed. We are looking at a proxy war in which theological apologetics fields its troops like Vladimir Putin's soldiers invading Crimea: Unmarked by national insignia, their identity was nonetheless all too clear. The goal of criticism ought not to be fronting for any particular theology, whether orthodox or liberal, but getting beyond theologies (which may perhaps be held on other grounds) and looking as honestly as we can at the phenomena of the texts, especially the anomalous ones that have always puzzled us. Those may turn out to be the very keys we have sought to unlock a greater understanding.

www.ingramcontent.com/pod-product-compliance
Lightning Source LLC
Chambersburg PA
CBHW060013100426
42740CB00010B/1475